It's Already Tomorrow Here

Never Underestimate the Power of Running Away

A Memoir

By Lucetta Zaytoun

Valerie,
Run back
to You!
♡ Lucetta

Some names and identifying details have been changed to protect the privacy of individuals.

ISBN 13: 978-1-944260-03-3

Published by City of Oaks Publishing, Raleigh North Carolina, USA

Interior formatting by Tugboat Design
Editor: Alice Osborn
Cover Design: Myriah Zaytoun

Author's Note

My dream for this book is that many will see themselves somewhere in these life experiences, relate to the situations, and find hope.

Acknowledgments

There is an African saying:
If you want to go fast, go alone. If you want to go far, go together.

Though one sits alone in front of the computer creating words from combining keys, the creation of a book is not a solo endeavor. Many people along the way have helped me tremendously, to bring this book to life. Without them, it would not have been possible, and I will be forever grateful.

First, appreciation for my coach Kioka Dunston who coached me around all of my fears every step of the way. She also lovingly held me accountable to my self-promised deadlines. Dr. Kevin Snyder convinced me over coffee one day, that writing and publishing this book is not as difficult as I think. He taught me the ropes and stated it is a worthy goal and I should begin right away. Suzanne Miller, a screen writer, was my first beta reader and her input was a game changer for the readability of this book. Many thanks to other readers and their suggestions as well: Laura Neal, Julia Meder, Kathleen O'Grady, and Jeff Lawson. A special thanks to my daughter Myriah, for her input and even more so for designing my book cover!

I would also like to thank my editor Alice Osborn at Write From The Inside Out, and the designer who my formatted my book, Deborah Bradseth at Tugboat Design.

Dedicated to

Leah

Contents

Part One

Running Ridiculous

Life is all about how you handle plan B.
—Suzy Toronto

Chapter One

After breakfast I wave a thank you to the owner of the hostel and head out for a run. I am a little anxious as I take off by myself, a white woman, running to nowhere. Will the Africans see me as ridiculous and not know what I am doing? Will they hate me for being out for leisurely exercise as I pass by them walking many miles to school and work carrying water just to survive? Will I frustrate them enough that they harm me? To date I have only experienced a generous and loving Africa, but will it be different for me to be out alone? I put my headphones in my ears, turn my music on low enough to still hear any approaching sounds, and begin turning my head side to side to see all movement in my periphery as I run.

As my feet pound the orange dirt I begin to relax. It feels good to be in motion again, and I let my mind replay all of the experiences I've had since landing here. Along the way I give and receive smiles, waves and nods from everyone I pass. What was I worried about? Several miles go by and I turn down a road in a village, just as a young woman runs out of her shack screaming, "*Kunisaidia, Kunisaidia!* Help me, Help me!"

A few feet closer and I recognize her as Keta, one of the students I'd worked with. She notices me and runs toward me. Tears pouring down her face, she grabs my arm.

"Please come, please come—it's my sister!"

She guides me into her dark one room shack. I notice a horrid smell, a combination of feces and urine, and put my hands over my nose holding back a gag. With no windows it takes a few minutes for my eyes to adjust. I begin to discern a young woman on the floor sitting cross-legged on a tattered rug, holding a baby wrapped in an equally worn blanket. Despondent, she is rocking silently back and forth staring straight ahead.

"My sister, she sit from last night. I wake up she still like this!" Crying, Keta continues, "She won't listen, I even smack her! Please help!"

The young woman appears to me to be in shock. I squat down before her on the floor and gently touch her arm. "I am here to help you." She rocks and stares.

I look back at Keta. "What is her name and does she speak English?"

"Yes, English, she in Secondary before baby. Her name Neema."

If she's been like this all night, the stench is probably the baby in a soiled diaper.

Gently I ask Keta about her sister. "Did something happen to her?"

"I don't know, baby sick two days. Last night she hold it and today she still here."

I look back at the mother and ask softly, "Neema, may I take your child to change the diaper?"

I peel the baby from her arms and for a second I'm wondering if I am being taken for a scam to get me into their shack to rob me, because the baby feels like a doll, hard and stiff. I quickly unwrap it to see, as Neema keeps rocking.

Oh. My. God.

It is a real baby.

A baby boy, dead, his body rigid and his eyes open.

A familiar shock wave courses through my veins, every nerve stands on end. My heart is pounding; my breath short and even though I am sitting, I begin to feel dizzy. My mind wanders in awe and horror as I reflect at how I have come to this very space in time in a circular trip that has taken almost three decades, and a journey to the other side of the world. This is a moment to be reckoned with, from which I cannot run. My heart is caught in a trap and the first thought that comes to mind is: I don't think I can go through this. Again.

* * *

As I come into our house one evening, after a meeting for work, the lights are off and a dark figure lunges out from around the corner and throws me down on the couch. His body crushes me as his hands press down on my throat choking off my air. My head is dangling over the edge of the cushion causing a searing pain down my spine. My eyes go wide from the pressure and from the fear. It is not until I hear his voice that I realize it is my husband.

"You see! You see, bitch! This is what can happen to you if you stay out after dark. It's a mean world out there. It's not safe and don't you ever stay out late again!"

I hadn't been there earlier to make his dinner and I'm sure that infuriated him. I manage to wrangle myself out from under him because I've been lifting weights to get strong enough to fight back one day. The combination of this outrageous nonsensical behavior, my getting stronger, and getting fed up with being his punching bag culminates in a surge of courage as I explode, "The only place I am in danger is right here in my own home!"

That bold comment led to more bruises and an evening filled with terror.

I'd met my "Prince Charming" when I was twenty years old, waiting tables at a restaurant by the university I was attending. He was handsome, brilliant and had a successful business franchised across the U.S. He was in town to open a new location. While there he treated me like a queen, and charmed the pants off me, such that when he offered to have me move across the country to live with him, I accepted.

We had a fine life, yet over time I discovered he had a bit of a temper, but to me that translated as, he was a passionate person with strong feelings about what he believed in. His temper was never directed at me. That is until I signed on the dotted line of the marriage certificate.

For years after I was taught that I was an awful wife, a shameful terrible person, and that's why he always got mad. If I were a better person he wouldn't get so mad. I took his every word as law. A forced amnesia, I forgot who I was and tried to become whom he wanted me to be. I wrecked myself trying to be perfect. I lived every minute of the day trying to please him. I knew he wanted his shoes by the front door before he did. My being perfect was literally a survival tactic. It took me years to figure out that it didn't matter what I did or didn't do—he would still blow up.

One morning came the breaking point for me. I cooked his eggs wrong and he became so outraged he turned the dining room table over smashing dishes and food everywhere. He jumped on top of me pounding and pounding.

Our four-year-old son, Ford, jumped on top of him trying to choke him, screaming, "Don't you hurt my mom! Don't you hurt my mom!"

I looked over to see our two-year-old daughter, standing by with a look of terror in her tear filled eyes. That was it for me. I knew then and there I had to leave because my son would grow up thinking "that's how you treat a woman," and little Myriah would think, "this is what love is."

No more. I hid a trash bag of toys and a bag of clothes in the back of a closet. My heart was pounding out of my chest, remembering he'd always said the only way I would ever leave him would be on a stretcher. Just stay strong for the children, stay strong for them. With every nerve ending standing at full alert, when the time was right, we made our escape.

We worked our way back across the country to my parents' house in Winston-Salem, North Carolina. They took us in with open arms. I was a shell of a person, weighing 90 pounds and looking like death. I was afraid of everything and felt like I didn't deserve to take up space in the world or even oxygen in the air. I didn't want to leave the house.

Finally, after a few months, my mother convinced me to help her with a Mother's Morning Out program, and it took everything I had in me to stay focused and work three mornings a week.

Time passed and I began to get emotionally stronger. I wanted to provide for my children and move out, letting my parents have their life back, so I took a position selling business telephone systems. As the company grew I was asked to train a new salesman they had hired. For two weeks I devoted my time to his training, which meant I wasn't selling, thus no commission. Our manager usually handed us our paychecks in an envelope, but at the end of this two weeks, he was out of town and the duty was given to another manager. On Friday he called us into his office and handed us both our checks face up. I'm sure he was clueless. With a glance, disbelief flew all over me. This man, whom I had just trained, was making twice the amount I was!

I was furious! I left the office, went to my car and burst into tears. They were paying me less because they knew I was a single mom and had to take the job. He was a man, so they paid him more for the same job. It was so unfair, and I knew I could not stay one minute longer. Over the weekend I began to try to figure out what I wanted to do next. I couldn't work for anyone else and allow this to ever happen again.

When I was with my husband, I'd been an entrepreneur and learned how to run a business. So what kind of business would I want to run now? I always loved to bake as a kid, and several times had baked for friends and companies at their request.

"I'll start a bakery, that's what I'll do."

On Monday morning I turned in my resignation.

* * *

A woman walked into my bakery and we became fast friends. At lunch one day as we got to know one another, she asked about my children.

"I'm divorced and only have two now, but I came from a large family and I've always wanted lots of kids around my table. It's a dream of mine."

"Oh," she lit up. "You should meet my brother, he's a widower and he's got four."

I added that up in my head and laughed. "Uhm that might be too many."

The seed had been planted in her mind and when the time was right she put us together. It took me about one minute to fall in love with him and his endearing children. After a year and a half of dating, I shut down my bakery, and we moved to his city, just in time to tie the knot. I was so excited and bursting with love that I wanted to run down the aisle. My children and I moved into his home with his children. Where there were two broken families of sadness, we were now a whole. And this is where the beautiful chaos began.

Chapter Two

After one night of a honeymoon to ourselves, my new husband and I walk in the back door to be swarmed by all six of our combined elementary-aged children talking simultaneously.

"Daddy, when are we leaving for Florida?"

"Mommy we're packed for our family honeymoon."

"We want to leave now, please!"

I lean down to their level. "I'm so glad you're excited."

My husband chimes in, "Me too, but first your mom and I need to shower and then we'll load up the van and go."

They go silent for a moment with perplexed looks on their faces, until someone blurts out, "Together?!"

"Eww, my dad is going to shower with your mom!"

Giggles take over the room, "Gross, my mom is going to shower with your dad."

We laugh and my husband intervenes, "Hello, people, we're married now. Run along and we'll be ready to go soon."

As we step into the shower, we hear them still giggling and listening outside the door.

* * *

"Are you freakin' crazy! You already have six kids and now you want to take on another? An African child at that!" My girlfriend Sharon couldn't contain her astonishment.

"But he needs help to acclimate to this country. He's been living in the bush in Liberia while their country is in the midst of civil war, and has witnessed awful atrocities in his young life. And it's really okay, what's one more kid when you already have six?" I laugh. "Plus, David is adorable and the kids love him."

"But that means one more child to take to the doctor, the dentist, to feed, and help with homework. Really? Don't you have enough on your plate?"

I appreciated her genuine concern for my well-being. I place my hand gently on her arm. "I love this. I really do."

Our church got involved in a program that helped airlift the Liberians out of a refugee camp in the early nineties during the war. David and his mom arrived and I knew I wanted to help. Soon his mother, Hawa, took a job. She would rise at 4:00 a.m. and walk to the local university where she would do housekeeping all day. Then late in the afternoon she would take an acclimation class to help her learn to live here, and go to a naturalization class after that to become a citizen. Such a strong woman, she was determined to make a life for her and David. She'd then walk home, wake up at 4:00 a.m. and start all over again.

When I heard this, I offered to have David stay with us during the week. I would take him home on the weekends to stay with his mom when she wasn't working. Even though he was ten years old, the school system put him in the third grade to help him catch up. He was in such culture shock and traumatized that when he arrived he couldn't speak. He understood English, but was rendered mute. For several years I communicated with him by asking yes and no questions, and he would nod or shake his head. After about a year, I knew he was going to be okay because he started laughing at my lame jokes, while my other children rolled their eyes.

Time went by and he became a member of the family. He would do chores and homework just like the others. Over time he started talking and the children eventually started calling him "brother." As he grew to high school age, he became good friends with another family from the church too and would often stay with them. We would laugh and say we had shared custody.

David thrived in his new world and won the hearts of everyone. In high school he became an outstanding member of the wrestling team. Then became a wrestling coach for the Boys and Girls Club. He went on to become an EMT in an ambulance giving medical care, comfort, and at times, saving lives.

He said, "I'm staying. It's my time to give back."

I wept.

Chapter Three

It's all just too much to bear. My friend Emmy calls my phone. I don't pick up. She calls again, and again, and again. I hear someone banging at the back door. I am not dragging myself downstairs in this condition. Soon I hear a tap, tap, tap on the window.

"What the hell? This is the second floor."

I crawl to the window and look down to see Emmy throwing pebbles up at my room.

"Come down and open this door right now," she yells up at me.

Damn it, I think to myself. I breathe a heavy sigh, "Okay. I'll be right there."

As I let her inside she takes a good long look at me. "When's the last time you ate something? Get your jacket; we're going for food. And how long has it been since you've even been outside?"

I wash my face, put on a coat and slowly drag myself out the door. I squint as my eyes adjust to the brightness, and I can't help but feel a little betrayed by the early spring sunshine. My world has crumbled and I am filled with fear. I've been shaken to the very core of my being. I am in a very dark and lonely place. As I try to pick up the shattered pieces of my life, each day is like scraping an open wound with the anger, rejection and humiliation. And on top of that shit sandwich, now the sun has the audacity to shine brightly over the front yard. I notice the flowers are budding and will soon bloom. Ah me.

My dark mood is my own, and outside the world keeps on moving as though nothing has happened. I realize that only the trajectory of my own life has been skewed off its axis and is spinning wildly. This feels isolating, yet oddly comforting to know the world will still be here when I do finally put myself back together. Ashamed and humiliated, I do what anyone experiencing an earth-shattering heartbreak might do; I curl up in the fetal position and stay there for six months. My grown children stop by to check on me, but all I do is cry, so it's hard for them to stay.

Later, with a little nourishment in my stomach, I climb back into bed. Sometimes the sadness brings me comfort. Sometimes I like to wallow in it because I can feel sorry for myself and have such pity that it allows me a small amount of soothing. I can't stay here for long or this will turn into self-loathing and bitterness.

The nights are the longest and I lay down on my bed knowing I won't be able to sleep. I'm sick to my stomach and my head spins. What will I do with my life? I don't have a plan B. I never imagined I would need a plan B. Raising six kids and launching them out into the world was my life's work and I loved it. I volunteered and sat on boards, but I didn't earn one single penny in all those years. I don't have a career built that will support me, and now suddenly, I need one.

After eighteen years my marriage collapsed in a second. How did I not see this coming? I feel like a housewife from the 1950s, when women didn't work. I stay home with the kids, and when they leave, my reward is that he falls in love with someone else. I believe I've heard this story a thousand times. I feel like I just got laid off. How stupid of me not to plan ahead, or at least build something for myself along the way. And now what am I left with? My entire life, my future and my dreams, vanished right before my eyes.

What will I do? What kind of life will I make for myself now that the decision is mine alone? And I can't believe I'm even thinking this, but I can't stay in this house any longer, no matter how awesome, it is nothing but four walls. The love and life have been drawn out of it, leaving it dead space.

So where will I live now, in a house or an apartment? WAIT A MINUTE WAIT... my eyes grow wide as I have a sudden realization. An aha hits me right in the chest. I sit upright in bed. I don't have to stay here. I don't have to stay! My children live on their own now. I don't even have to stay in Raleigh. Everywhere I go I see someone I know, which drags it all back up again. My heart is too raw and I know I can't heal here. In this town I will always be "his wife" or "their mother." I cannot be simply me, whoever that is. So I will go. I will stand alone in tomorrow and allow myself to mend.

I feel myself beginning to calm as my energy shifts from sitting as a victim to becoming a creator of my new life. If I don't stay here, then where will I go? A small smile breaks across my face at the possibilities, but instantly it fades as doubt creeps in. I don't even know where to begin in making that decision. The first time I married I was still in college and barely out of my parents' home. As I think about this, I come to understand; in my entire adult life I've never made a single decision just for myself. Every choice has always been for the good of the marriage, the family, or the children. I don't even know how to make a decision solely for myself.

I am fraught with questions, and no answers. I don't know what I will do or where I will go. I don't even know who I am outside of being a spouse or a mother; I have no identity of my own. How can I possibly figure out what to do with the rest of my life when I don't even know who I am? How can I trust my own decision-making process? What if I get it all wrong? How will I support myself? What do I have to offer this world? After having the most rewarding career of raising six beautiful children, how will I ever find something to do that is as meaningful and important as that?

* * *

My sister, Malissa, asks, "Where will you go?" Her voice can't hide her concern when I tell her I want to get out of here.

"I don't know; I just can't stay here. I can't heal in this town because I won't ever be anybody but his ex-wife."

She leans in, "Have you talked to God about this?"

"No. I have nothing to say to God. I'm not angry with Him, but I don't understand why He let this happen, and I guess I don't really trust Him right now."

"Well I pray you will find your way back to Him."

I decide the first order of business is to rediscover myself. But how do you even do that? Fumbling on where to start, I ask myself two questions. What do you love to do? And what is something you've always wanted to do? I'd led mission trips when I was a youth group leader, and have always wanted to do long-term volunteer work in a developing country. Maybe I'll start there, giving myself a little time to heal and begin to figure out who the hell I am now.

I share my plans with my brother John and he tries to find a way to wrap his brain around this. "So you're going to do one of those *Eat, Sit, Love* things like the Gilbert woman?"

I laugh, "Close enough, and yes, her book has inspired me to think outside of the box." Maybe this will give him some comfort knowing she survived a journey like the one I am dreaming up.

I call my younger sister Martha in Phoenix and she begs, "Come move in with me, and live in the desert. I have room and we'll have a blast."

"Thank you, but I believe deep down in my heart that I need to do this alone."

I decide to go away to more than one place, and for more than just a little while, to places I wouldn't normally travel to. I am desperate to change the narrative of my story. If I want to go from being the broken woman left behind, to the woman charting her own path, the shit needs to get real and gritty. I want to make it count. I need to leave my comfort zone and experience something bigger than myself. A little voice in the back of my head whispers, "Africa," I feel such a connection through David, and as soon as the seed is planted in my mind I can't shake it. I am terrified at the thought of landing on that huge continent as a blond woman traveling alone. And I can't help but wonder if that is like putting a target on my forehead that says "take advantage of me." I research volunteering there as a place to start on the continent. I love volunteering and it may help me understand their culture, and get the lay of the land.

I begin to make my plans for where I will go, how I will shut down my life here, and what must happen between now and the moment I leave American soil after my divorce is final. Day after day I wrestle with my fears, forcing myself to move forward with courage.

* * *

One day, even though we are separated, I ask my husband to meet me in a coffee shop to discuss the dismantling of our lives. The lawyers are stirring up trouble and it is beginning to tear apart the children as well. I can't abide this stepfamily falling apart when we just spent the last eighteen years putting it together. Raising and blending this family was my career and I poured my heart into all of it. I can't let this destroy the love we have built together.

After we get settled into a booth with our lattes I gather up my courage. "I have a proposal for you that I have been thinking about for a while."

"Okay, I'm listening." His brow furrows slightly, I'm sure wondering what in the world I am about to say.

"I've been thinking that if you have to pay me alimony for the next however many years, you will at some point, become angry about this and it will create problems in the family. We will live in negative conflict energy, similar to what the lawyers are doing to us now." I stop to breathe and nervously shift in my seat.

"Go on. I'm still listening."

"So I have a proposal for you and if you will, I'd like for you to hear me all the way through before you comment." He nods his head. "I was thinking, let's get the lawyers out of this, they are making things worse. What if you and I decide on one number, a lump sum, then figure out how to reach that number, and we do it all at one time. Then we don't have any ties, causing problems. I have also made the decision that my goal at the end of this is that you and I are friends. We have a lot of children, which means lots of weddings and births and occasions for us to be together. Those events are so stressful already; the last thing they need to worry about is whether we can be in the same room without creating a scene. So I have decided that I don't know how long it will take, but somehow I am just going to have to get over all of this, so we can be friends. Also, I have made up my mind that you can have the beautiful house you love so much."

I watch the blood drain from his face and his mouth drops open in disbelief, "I can have the house without a fight?"

"Yes, well I'll get half the money for the house, of course, but yes you can have it, I'm leaving town."

"What? Where are you going?"

"I'm not exactly sure yet, but I am leaving the country. You won't have to worry about you and your new love running into me, and hopefully somehow we can continue to co-parent our children. They still need us as a unified front."

"My head just exploded. Give me a minute, please." He smiles slightly, shaking his head. He sips his coffee as we sit in silence.

After a while he looks me straight in the eye. "I'll admit, this is not the conversation I thought we would be having today, but I am open to looking at things differently and seeing if we can make this work. We could do a one-day closing, with lawyers just for the documents, and do all transactions at one time. And wow, thank you."

I know him well enough to know that the thank you was for the house, saving us money on lawyers, not having to pay alimony, and for me getting past our marriage crash, "You're welcome, and thank you, as this plan will help me buy some time to heal and set up a new career." I breathe a full sigh of relief.

After six months of coffee shop meetings full of tears, anger, reminiscing, apologies, and intense negotiations, we finally decide on a number and how we will reach it. What we didn't realize at the time was this gave us an opportunity to process our grieving, our anger, and push past any resentment we had against each other. We hire lawyers for our closing day and do all of the money and paperwork exchange in just a few short hours.

And suddenly it is over.

* * *

I finally get up the nerve to tell my children the current plan for my future. I know their world has been affected by the dissolving of the family even though they are in their twenties and living out on their own. Their grieving is full blown and understandable as we all worked very hard to blend this stepfamily. His kids got a mom, my kids got a dad, and now it seemed that was all thrown away, rocking their foundation. I call each one and have a conversation about my intentions for the next step in my life. The information is met with a mixed bag of emotional responses.

Myriah is stunned and fearful, "Mom, what the hell! Africa? I mean Africa is amazing and there is definitely a huge need there, but WE need you. We need you here!"

Nothing gets straight to the soul of a mom more completely than the heartfelt pleading of their child. The tug on your heartstrings is so strong it's painful. You're being selfish, Lucetta, how can you desert them when they are so devastated. But they are grown. Still, they are your children and they need you. I always fix things for them; I'm the one that makes all things better. I should delay my trip. My own desperation wells up inside of me, and my fears of the future take over.

What comes from my mouth is surprisingly strong and must be divinely inspired. "I'd like to think I raised you well enough to handle whatever comes your way. If something happens, rely on each other, help each other, remember that you have each other."

I hear her trying to suppress her weeping. Just get strong, Lucetta, figure out how to get over this whole thing so you can just stay in the States and be here for them.

But what comes from my mouth is something I have never ever said before in my life, "Myriah, I really need to do this...for me."

"Okay, Mom," she sniffs and sighs, "I understand."

As I set down the phone I collapse, break down and cry my eyes out. I am crying for them, for their loss and that I am leaving them on their own. And I am crying for me because I just experienced a tiny glimpse of the possibility of me, through a supernatural strength from out of nowhere.

A few days later I am visiting the office of my oldest brother Donald, "I'm going on a trip in developing countries and I don't know if I am ever coming back."

"So…" He leans back in his chair, "you're running away..."

I think about this for a moment.

"Yes."

Part Two

Running From

Have you ever watched a leaf as it journeys to the ground?
It does not fall
It floats and flutters
Enjoying the journey downward.
It is not crying that it has lost hold of its branch.
It lets go and enjoys the ride.

—Laura Neal

Chapter Four

After he'd called me into the room, I walk in to find my friend Stephen standing over a world map. "My friends and I have a trip planned for a week in Belize to scuba dive."

"Nice!" I respond.

Smiling, he points to the top of the map. "This is the United States."

"Yes." I'm grinning now.

He points further down, "And this is Costa Rica."

"Okaaay," I say a little sarcastically.

He points to the middle. "And here is Belize. It's on the way, so you should go with us."

I burst out laughing at his rationale, and although I am anxious to start my new life, I think to myself, well why the hell not? I can go anywhere I want and I don't even have to clear it with anyone.

After my marriage collapsed and I picked myself up off the floor, Stephen and I met through mutual friends. He's always happy and very positive, full of compassion and lots of fun. We'd seen each other only several times, given we live almost two thousand miles apart. He knows I'm not ready for a full-on relationship, and in addition to having a full time job, he is a mountain biker and skier with little time for a relationship either, so it works out. He also knows I am leaving the country, which he supports fully, and yet, says he hopes to catch up with me along the way.

Before I can get to Africa, I've got some work to do in preparation. I'd decided my first stop would be Costa Rica. I assume that when I leave the States and begin to travel in my new life alone, I will have a meltdown, a gigantic meltdown of epic proportions. Where better to do that than in paradise? I will give myself some time to freak out and grieve, so that by the time I get to Africa I will be strong and whole enough to help and make a difference. I love Costa Rica and have always wanted to immerse in Spanish, so I sign up for Spanish school and plan to live with a Costa Rican family. While there I will also go through TEFL Certification (Teaching English as a Foreign Language), which means I'll be skilled to teach English as a second language anywhere in the world.

Spring 2010 I drive to my storage locker, which holds all of my material belongings. I open the door one last time to find my recliner still in the front section near the door where my sons had placed it, just in case I ever needed a place to sleep. Although my kids would love for me to stay with them, it's my tiny piece of real estate on the planet, and it gives me a strange sort of comfort to think of it as home. I check in with my broker and my estate-planning lawyer, in case something happens to me. I go to visit my doctor one last time and we review the list of immunizations I had gotten earlier in the spring: typhoid, Hep A, Hep B, tetanus, rabies, malaria, and the biggie that gets me into Africa, yellow fever. She writes me a prescription for CIPRO, just in case...and clears me to go. I shut down my iPhone, really painful I might add, and make plans for my car to be sold. My monthly bills will consist of 1) health insurance, 2) storage locker. That's it. I am completely untethered from trappings. It's liberating, exciting, and terrifying all at the same time.

My parents are brokenhearted about me leaving the country and terrified at the thought of me traveling alone. After much discussion they have come to understand and accept that this is what I must do.

They offer their home as my permanent address, and as they do my dad stretches his arms wide open. "Well I want to welcome you home again before you leave."

A sad realization hits me. "Pa, this is the third time in my life." I run to hug them both as tears spill down my cheeks.

Mom holds me tightly. "You always have a home here, and do you have room in that suitcase?"

A smile breaks on my face. "Yes, come with me!"

They are amazed at the items I have laid out all over the floor of their spare bedroom; a mosquito net, water purifying tablets, toilet paper, flip flops, running gear, my asthma medicines which fill half a bag, soap, shampoo, a tiny camp towel, a light jacket, five outfits and two knee-length skirts for modesty while working in Africa. My father shakes his head with fear at the thought that all I will have with me for the next two years or more can fit into two bags. One is a pack with wheels, but also has straps so I can carry it on my back when the terrain gets rough, which seems like a great combination. The other is a backpack that carries all the important things I must have in my possession at all times.

Emmy pulls into the driveway to give me a ride to the airport, "I've heard that if you wear a purse in these countries people will run by or ride by and yank them off your arm. And if you carry stuff in your pocket, they will pick-pocket you, so I brought you this. It's originally designed for runners, but I thought it would work for your trip."

She hands me a little wristband that looks like a wide bracelet made of fabric. It has a small zipper, which houses a secret pocket big enough for a debit card, license, and cash. Brilliant! No one would ever guess it protects my most valuable items while traveling.

After he retired, my father turned into a computer nerd and bought a Mac, which is uncharacteristic of someone in their late seventies. As he hugs me tightly he says, "I've heard about this thing called Skype. I'm going to figure out how to use it and if you have Internet we can actually see each other." He squeezes me tightly, "You be safe." He chokes up, "I have to walk away now, be safe."

After many tears, hugs and assurances that all will be well, I finally pull myself from my mother's loving arms and climb into Emmy's car. I turn around as we pull away. The picture of them standing in the street clinging to one another is permanently emblazoned in my mind.

More tearful hugs with Emmy at the airport and I make my way through security. I am filled with equal amounts of fear and excitement, sadness and joy. I am doing this. Whoa, I've actually made this happen. A surge of empowerment takes me to my seat on the plane. The wheels lift off the ground and I say goodbye to the United States full of every emotion. Another tear conjoins sadness and happiness, yet even in my sadness I feel strong. I am an adventurer now.

Upon landing in Belize, my friends meet me at the airport, and take me to the apartment. We laugh and play on the beach, in the pool, and cookout on the grill in the courtyard. We go to visit the Mayan ruins, a Butterfly farm, fly down a zip line, and walk down the World's Tiniest Main Street in Placentia. It is a beautiful distraction from thinking about starting a completely new life.

Three days after leaving American soil, Stephen approaches me in the kitchen with a concerned look on his face, "Your daughter Myriah has called my phone and says she wants to talk to you…"

A shock wave courses through my body, paralyzing me. What has happened? What does this mean? I'm shaking as I take the phone from his hand. He puts his arm around me to infuse some comfort.

I'm terrified but try to sound composed. "Hey, Myriah."

"Hey, Mom."

I gauge her voice, trying to get a feel for what is in store.

She continues, "I know you are on your trip and I don't want to bother you but I thought about it for a while and I feel like you would want to know what's happened since you left. Everything is under control now so you don't need to panic but I want you to know."

I let out a little of the breath I'd been holding and move to our room for privacy. "Okay, what's happened?"

"It's about Tessa, and the boyfriend of hers that never really liked her little dog, Beso."

My stepdaughter Tessa lives in New York City and has been dating a guy who is in the country temporarily.

Myriah continues, "Evidently the day you left, she went to work and left her boyfriend at her apartment with Beso. He called her at the end of her shift and said to meet him at the vet. Something happened to Beso and he'd taken him there. Tessa freaked out and when she got to the vet, her boyfriend was gone. The vet explained to her that Beso had a swollen brain and was comatose. He didn't know if Beso would survive, and said that he had either been shaken incredibly hard or thrown against a wall or onto the floor. The vet wanted her to press charges against the guy for animal abuse."

"What! He abused Beso?! The most laid back little dog on the planet?" I am stunned and can't believe it. Tessa got this puppy when she first moved out of our house as an adult. For years he has been her companion, her everything. She moved him to New York with her and even had special documentation for him to fly with her because he calmed her nerves about being in the air. He really is her baby.

"I know it's fucked up." Myriah continues, "So Tessa lost her shit and immediately called Adam in Raleigh. He comforted her the best he could, then he called me in San Francisco.

He was afraid Beso might die, and Tessa would not be able to handle it, because that dog means everything to her. He asked if I thought he should fly up there and be with her. I told him I thought that was the best idea because someone needed to be with her."

I am crying now but I hold silence as I wait to hear the rest of the story.

"So Adam canceled everything, threw some clothes in a bag and raced to the airport. He caught the next flight out to LaGuardia and was there by that evening."

Now I'm really crying at the beauty of this kind of love. "So what about Beso?"

"The next day Beso slightly came out of his coma. The vet said there may be some brain damage but it was too early to tell. Adam talked with Tessa about whether to press charges and about ending her relationship with this guy. He finally had her convinced that pressing charges would alert this guy and let him know that what he did was wrong and that he can't do this kind of thing, hopefully preventing it from happening to another animal in the future."

"I really can't believe this." I am in shock.

"While they were with Beso loving him back to life, the boyfriend evidently came by and gave the receptionist his credit card to pay the entire bill, no matter what the total, which was thousands of dollars. Tessa felt like he had learned his lesson and didn't end up pressing charges. His visa was running out and he would be leaving the country anyway. She said she didn't have the energy to deal with the legal side of this. It was enough for her to keep it together for her baby Beso."

My mind is racing like crazy, shaming myself for not being there for my daughter. Stunned at this entire story, all I can say is, "So what's happening now?"

"The vet says Beso can come home tomorrow. It looks like, so far, he's going to survive, and only time will determine if there is permanent damage. Adam is flying home tomorrow now that Beso's coming home."

I collapse on the floor. "Myriah, I can't tell you how amazing it was that Adam went up there. With that sister and that dog, it was totally the right thing to do and the only way to support her fully. I love Adam even more for taking care of his little sister like this. I feel very guilty and selfish for leaving."

"Mom, I almost didn't call you for that very reason. I knew you would beat yourself up, but I decided to call because I knew you would want to touch base with Tessa. Don't feel bad for leaving. You need to do this for you, and we handled it. It's okay. Really."

Now I am swept up with emotion and love for my children and their insightful maturity around handling the situation, "I am so thankful for the love between you guys. I love you so much."

"I love you too, Mom, enjoy your trip, kick some healing ass, and I hope all goes well for you."

I am on the floor sobbing as I say goodbye. Stephen gently opens the door concerned for me and for what has happened with my kids. He sits down beside me and spoons me in his arms as I bawl.

"I was gone one day, ONE DAY and tragedy hit. I am so mixed up right now. I left them and wasn't there, yet they did it, they relied on each other, they helped each other. They did it across the country, in different states and they took care of the situation. I am crying for sadness and yet I'm thankful. I am so messed up right now, but I want to call Tessa."

"Okay, I'll be out there if you need me."

I blow my nose and try to compose myself. Tessa is very happy to hear from me and says that Adam saved her life. I tell her I feel awful for not being there for her.

"Cettie, I feel better because I can bring Beso home and I have friends in the city who will help me get over this. You go do what you need to do. I'll be okay. I love you."

"I love you too, so much! Please give Beso a hug from me."

Stephen walks back into the room and gently takes his phone from me, "They will be fine, you have strong kids."

At the end of the week, I say goodbye to my friends. They ask one more time if I am steadfast about all of this, and beg me to come home with them. I assure them I am ready, and I will make this trip happen. They head back to the U.S. and I officially begin my solo journey by flying to San Jose, Costa Rica.

When I land there, I will live in a new country, in a small town, in the home of strangers where I will be the daughter, not the mother, in a place where I barely speak the language. That is a lot of change. I am filled with appreciation that I had this transition time with my friends, and had the opportunity to learn that my children can thrive. I board my flight full of every single human emotion.

I look around the airplane and realize it is full of couples and families. I am the only single person. I glance at the couple sitting in the row with me, and notice they are holding hands. Quickly my emotions roll down from their high to a lonely low. Tears fall and I can't stop them. I try to cover up the fact that I am in dismay, but soon the woman reaches over, "Are you okay?"

"No. No, I'm not." I briefly tell her my story and that I am now traveling by myself. "Who goes to paradise by themselves?"

She puts her hand on top of mine. "Who has the courage to go to paradise by themselves?"

I looked up at her as a tiny hint of a smile breaks on my lips. "Thank you. Thank you for turning that around." This encouragement lifts me just enough to make the rest of the trip bearable.

Chapter Five

Funny how life takes its twists and turns and sometimes you end up right where you started. I am standing outside the school in Manuel Antonio after my first day of Spanish class, waiting for my "mother" to pick me up. I have my books, my homework assignment, and two backpacks. It feels like I am in the first grade again with the excitement of the first day of class, and the anticipation of what life after school means, now that everything is different. Like a six-year-old, my mother will pick me up and I will do what she says. I have no control over my day, or any knowledge at all of what the afternoon will hold for me. I am completely at the mercy of my new Costa Rican family.

Earlier that morning I awakened alone in Manuel Antonio, Costa Rica. At 8:00 a.m. I wait anxiously for a taxi. Already it is so hot that my clothes are soaked. A little red taxi finally arrives and as he tosses my two bags in the trunk, I say, "*La Academia de Español D'Amore, por favor*."

The owner of the Spanish school, Alex, greets me warmly, recognizing the generally frightened look on my face. I have no idea what I am getting into. I will study Spanish for the next three weeks and even though I am fifty years old, my plan is that I'll stay with a host family to get immersed in the language and culture of Costa Rica. This is my only plan for now. My bags are whisked away by the caretaker of the school, and I am escorted up to class.

My classroom is open air, with a porch on the front that overlooks view of the ocean and the mountains. I take a deep eel myself beginning to calm. Ah, this is okay. It doesn't ow old you are; this will be okay. My professor and one other dent are seated at a table, and already well into the lesson. I sit down, and for the next four hours I desperately try to recall my ninth and tenth grade Spanish. At the end of class, Alex finds me and we go into his office for an orientation to tell me about living with my new family.

"They live in Quepos, which is the next town over. They are a very nice family that has been hosting students for many years, and they don't speak English. The mother will talk your ear off in rapid fire Spanish, and the father won't say very much. They will provide you two meals a day, and laundry once a week. You are free to come and go as you please, but if you will not be there for a meal, please just let them know ahead of time so they don't prepare it for you. Each day you will walk from their house to the center of Quepos to the bus station, and take the 8:00 a.m. bus. This will get you to school on time."

I nod with a deer-in-the-headlights look on my face.

"Oh, here comes your new mother now. That's her pulling into the school."

And this is where the crazy in my life begins…

She greets me with a hug and a kiss on the cheek. "*Me llamo Bileida y mi esposo es Anibal.*" My name is Bileida and my husband is Anibal.

This is as far as she can contain herself in slow, careful Spanish. She proceeds to talk to me quickly in her native tongue the entire six kilometers down the hillside to her town of Quepos. I don't understand much at all, but smile and try to look as though I do.

I begin to pick up bits and pieces as she gives me a tour of her small town. She shows me where the bus station is, the bank, and her best friend's gift store, which I should patronize. Evidently those are the important things for me to know.

As we leave the lower part of the town she smiles, "*Recorde el puente y el muro verde.*"

She is pointing, so I use my brilliant mind and deduce that she means, "remember the bridge and the big green wall." At home, she shows me where the bathroom is, leads me upstairs to my tiny bedroom with a slatted door that almost closes, and then gives me a set of keys to the house. I drop my bags and she beckons me back downstairs.

My mother asks if I would like some food, as she proudly shows me she has red meat from her daughter's birthday party the night before. It is delicious. As I begin to eat, her husband comes home, nods in my direction and sits down at the table to eat as well. I jump up and run upstairs to get my gift for them as is customary when you stay with a family. I present them with chocolates from America. They smile, thank me and she immediately takes them to put them in the freezer.

She is nodding as if to ask if that is okay, and what I want to say is, "No! Don't put chocolate in the freezer! I used to own a bakery. It breaks down the chocolate, separates it, and it turns white. I've carried these chocolates, protected in my bag for four weeks now, through three countries to bring them to you. No, don't put them in the freezer!" But I say the only thing I know to say, "*Si.*"

Her husband leaves without a word and I go upstairs to get my homework. I work at the kitchen table and watch as steady streams of people come in and out of the house for various reasons. There is much hugging and kissing and laughter. I can't understand anything they are saying, but it is beautiful to watch.

The owner of the Spanish school also teaches yoga at a spa in the evenings, and I tell my mother that I plan to take his class at 5:00 p.m. this evening and will be back at 7:30 p.m. I have been traveling for three days hauling bags, and yoga would be the perfect cure for travel stress. She is going to church, so I plan to walk to yoga.

She shakes her head, "No, *un taxi.*" The driver is Danilo (someone's brother), and he will know where to go. She calls and orders a ride for me. All of this is communicated with gestures and simple Spanish words I can minimally understand.

When we arrive at the spa, Danilo pulls out a piece of paper and writes down his phone number for me to call him when I am done. The class is held in a beautiful room with walls made completely of mango wood and huge opened doors, which face the jungle. The sounds of the rainforest are fascinating and it is almost enough to help me forget how incredibly hot it is.

At the end of yoga I go out to the spa to borrow a phone, but the spa is closed. Uh oh, it is already dark outside and raining. Damn, I forgot that the sun goes down here at 6:00 p.m. every single night of the year because we are close to the equator. What should I do? I walk down the driveway toward the street and fortunately there is a guardhouse. They let me borrow a phone and I call Danilo.

I say, "Lucetta, Raindrop Spa."

He responds, "*Bueno*."

A few minutes later a taxi arrives, but it is not Danilo. I jump in the back seat and the driver asks, "*Donde*?" Where?

Uhm, uh...oh shit! I don't know where! Shit. Uhm. "Quepos."

I desperately search for information in my brain. What area do they live in? What are their names? Where is their street? Do I have any information in my tiny purse? No, nothing, I didn't bring it because I was only going to yoga and back. My first day in a foreign country and I am lost with only a few American dollars, no identification, no way of getting back to the few belongings I own, in the pouring rain with a man who doesn't speak English. Nice one, Lucetta. Way to go.

As we drive toward Quepos I peer through the dark looking for something I recognize.

I shrug and say, "*No se*." I don't know.

My driver just looks at me and after a while begins to laugh a big, deep belly laugh. He keeps it up as I sit back and begin to giggle with him. It is ridiculous to be a grown adult and not even know where you are going. I suddenly remember about the bridge. I don't yet know the Spanish words for right or left, or turn around, but I see a bridge and point in that direction. We ride across and drive down several streets, but nothing looks familiar. We drive for quite a while and finally I motion for him to turn around. As we cross back over the bridge I start pointing furiously at the bridge itself.

He laughs again and nods. "*Bueno.*" Good.

He takes me to another part of the town that has a bridge. It is MY bridge, and there is the big green wall. I am home.

The house is completely dark, and empty as we pull up. Security here in Quepos is a big concern so I use my three keys to get into Fort Knox, a wrought-iron porch, and the front door. I am actually relieved because I need a few minutes to regroup from being so rattled. The peace I'd found at yoga has vanished and I really, really want to take a shower. Locking everything behind me, I head upstairs and grab the things I need for my shower. I haven't washed my hair in days and I have been sweating since I landed.

The bathroom opens to the living room, and I flip the light switch right outside the door. Nothing happens. Maybe the light is inside? The bathroom is completely tiled in black tile, so it is pitch dark in there. I feel all around the walls in the usual places you'd find a light switch, but nothing. What? Surely they have a light in the bathroom.

Aha! My headlamp. Earlier in the spring I'd had coffee with my friend, Shelly, who lived in Africa for two years. She said to buy a headlamp for my trip, and keep it with me at all times because it would become my best friend. One never knows how crucial light is until you don't have it available. I climb up the steep little staircase, find my new compadre and strap it on my head.

Back in the bathroom I scour every inch of every wall. No light switch. Damn it, I am taking a shower. Another cuss word, this is clearly turning into an entire evening when no other word will do. I set the headlamp on the edge of the shower pointing upwards in a beam of light. I feel for the faucets and turn them on high. I'm waiting and waiting for it to warm up even just a little when the truth of the situation dawns on me. No hot water.

I'm drying off after the fastest shower possible given that I really did need to scrub, when I hear someone out in the living room. I am a little startled, as I know I locked the doors behind me, but I figure it must be someone with all of the keys. I gather my belongings and open the door to find a man lounging on the couch with a beer, watching the television. He looks at the bathroom, then at me and scans down to my headlamp.

He looks concerned. "*Problema con la luz*?" Problem with the light? I just shrug as if to say I don't know.

He jumps up, and moves to the door. He reaches up and hits the top of the right corner, outside of the back of the door jam, and a light comes on. He doubles over laughing out loud. I look up and sure enough, in the most awkward, indiscernible place outside of the bathroom, there is a small white button. We are both laughing at that point and I ask him his name.

"*Me llamo Anibal.*"

This is my "father" her husband! So who in the world did I have lunch with today? And to whom did I present my chocolates that are at this very moment deteriorating in the refrigerator?

I thank him and go upstairs, unpack my bags and settle into my new room. My mother comes home and asks if I am hungry. I haven't eaten since lunch and I'm famished but I don't want her to have to make my dinner at this late hour, so I motion that I am not hungry. Around 10:00 p.m. I finally finish my homework and am about to peel off my clothes and dive into bed when I hear the sounds of young children outside the window. Who would have children up at this hour? I hear tiny footsteps coming up the stairs and realize those children are in my house. Four little eyes peer between the slats of my door. Whew, good thing I am still dressed. My mom comes up and waves for me to come downstairs. It is her grandchildren who have come over to meet the new student.

Downstairs are eight other relatives as well, laughing and talking. I can't understand anything they say so I smile and play with the kids, trying to keep from nodding off. My first day in the country, I'd been to

Spanish class, met my family, gone to yoga, gotten lost, and showered in the dark. I desperately want to lay my head down.

Finally, the family waves goodbye and I think I will be able to gracefully make my break, but my mother jumps up and begins frantically moving furniture on the front porch. She seems to be bringing it all inside the house. Of course I get up to help bring chairs, tables, and a couch inside just in time, because the iron gate begins to open and a car pulls in. Right onto the front terrace! We all work our way around the car and squeeze between the fender and the front door to get into the house. It is their 22-year-old daughter, Milena, and her fiancé. Evidently if she left her car on the street, it would be vandalized or stolen. Milena is in nursing school at night and has just finished a very important exam.

By now it is 11:30 p.m., so after introductions I say, "*Buenos noches,*" and bolt upstairs before anyone else can come over. I dive onto my bed completely clothed, and cannot move a single muscle. I hear more laughter from downstairs and then the banging of pots. Soon the most delicious aroma makes its way up to my room, and my stomach begins to grumble. My mother is cooking for Milena.

* * *

The barking of a large pack of dogs awakens me. I don't know what has set them off into such frenzy, but there are obviously many of them. The dawn is just beginning to break and I roll over to look at the time. Only 5:00 a.m. and already the sun is coming up. I pull my pillow over my head and try to doze back off. Dogs are allowed to roam free in Quepos, so their little canine party continues for quite a while. I decide to just go ahead and rise, get ready, and see what the day will hold for me.

Bileida calls me down at 6:15 a.m. for the typical Costa Rican breakfast. Gallo Pinto, which is a mixture of rice and black beans, scrambled eggs, a flour tortilla, and some of that delicious Costa

Rican coffee. I sit up at the bar in the kitchen with she and Anibal, and we attempt to communicate as we eat. She asks me if I know how to dance the salsa and merengue. I shake my head, no. She jumps up and motions me into the kitchen. She grabs my arms and begins to dance with me. Anibal claps his hands with delight and begins to hum so we will have music. We laugh as we swirl around the floor. When she is satisfied I have grasped the basic steps, we return to our breakfast.

Afterwards she picks up her keys and leads me to the front door. She is telling me that they will be leaving early and she wants to show me how to lock the door properly because Milena will still be sleeping upstairs. We walk out the front door and she locks it, pushing it back and forth to make sure it is secure. I nod as though to say I will do it the same way. She turns the key to open the door and pushes, but nothing happens. She tries again and pushes on the door, but nothing. She is perplexed and mumbling something in Spanish. We are locked out. We look at each other and she tries once more, this time hurling her body against the door. As the door finally swings open wide it reveals Anibal being flung onto his back on the couch with a thud. In a fit of laughter, he gets back up. He had been standing inside holding the door closed the entire time. He seems very proud of himself and a giggling Bileida just waves him off as though his antics are nothing new.

They both get into the car and back it out of the front terrace. I place my homework and things I will need for the day in my pack. I lock the house properly and head to the bus. Whew, what a day. I've eaten breakfast, learned to dance, had a prank pulled on me, and it is only 7:15 in the morning.

I walk toward the center of town to find the bus station. I scan the buses and find one that says, "Quepos/Manuel Antonio." It is empty with no driver so I sit down to wait among the others, on one of the many benches. I get out my wallet and count out 240 colones, which equals about 48 cents.

I stand out of the crowd, just a little bit, with my paleness and blond hair as I sit among the beautifully brown ticos with their flawless skin.

A tico is someone who is born in Costa Rica and all other people, no matter where you come from, are gringos. This is not disparaging in any way, it is merely a distinction, which I might add comes in handy at times. I will take the bus up the hill about six kilometers to Manuel Antonio, where hotels, restaurants, nightclubs, and my school are located. On the other side of Manuel, down another hill, lay the beach and the beautiful National Park.

Sitting at the station I observe these amazing people. They greet one another with a kiss, talk, play and laugh as though they haven't seen each other in years. They stand to let elderly women sit down, they play with the children, they fan one another in the heat, and share bits of food they have brought for their breakfast. I am falling in love with these people.

The driver shows up and we all file onto the bus. It is crowded. Rush hour. I manage to get a seat, but the aisles are completely full of people standing. As we head up the mountain I realize I don't know exactly at which stop I should get off the bus. I began to look for something familiar near the school. I ride and ride but do not see anything I recognize on my side of the street.

When one is ready to leave the bus, you push a button on the handrail and this lets the driver know he needs to stop at the next bus stop. After a while I begin to get anxious. Where is my school? Finally, someone pushes the button and at the next stop all of the people file out of the aisle and off the bus.

I look over to the other side only to see the beach! The beach? How did I get down here? Oh no, what do I do? I guess that means I should get off at the next stop, hike back up that hill, and look for the Academia. I will miss most of my school day by then. As I am weighing my options and beginning to panic, the bus turns around at the bottom near the Park. A loop. The bus is on a loop! I breathe a sigh of relief, as we head back up the hill. I am the only person left on the bus, so I move to the front and ask the driver to show me where to get off for school.

I walk through the front door of the school 30 minutes late.

The receptionist smiles and wags her finger at me. "*Usted llega tarde. Estuvimos preocupado.*" You are late. We were worried. I apologize and quickly replay my bus mishap.

She jumps up, runs into the other room and tells her co-worker, in perfect English, "Lucetta tried to skip class and go to the beach. Hahahaha."

They come into the room, revert back to Spanish, tell me that my tardiness is excused for today, and I should run off to class.

That evening, after dinner back at my house, more relatives stop by. One is my mother's niece, Lyneth, who announces we are going out to a fiesta that evening. I think I understand the words, "*iglesia*" and "*baile.*" Church and dancing. Anibal lies on the couch watching TV with an Imperial Beer. He's wearing shorts; a T-shirt with the sleeves cut out, and flip-flops. He watches as the women prepare to go out for the event.

Bileida comes into the room and Anibal lets out a long slow whistle. Her hair is up in a twist, she has on makeup, jewelry and a smokin' hot little black dress. I run upstairs and put on something I think might be appropriate; a black tank and a skirt. As we head out the door, Bileida tops off her look when she slips on a pair of shiny black, patent leather, pointed stilettos. We walk out to the carport and Lineth jumps in the back seat, so I sit up front with Bileida. As we pull out, Anibal comes to close the big gate behind us. All of a sudden the back door opens and Anibal jumps in. He is going with us.

My Spanish interpretation was mistaken, and my eyes go wide as we do not pull into a church, but instead, a local club called Bambu Jam. A live band plays salsa and merengue in the corner as people gather around the dance floor. We all sit at the bar and Lineth orders us Guaro Cecique and tonic to drink. Guaro is a Costa Rican liquor that evidently kicks hard when it kicks in. Lineth claims that when you drink it with tonic you won't have a hangover the next day. I don't want to test that theory and I limit myself to only one because I am out with my "parents." After a few sips from his Imperial, Anibal stands and takes a deep bow in front of Bileida asking her onto the dance floor. I begin to giggle at the thought of my couch dad out there with his dolled up wife. How will this work?

I should have known, and should not have been surprised when he suddenly emerges with all the grace and smoothness of Fred Astaire. He holds her tightly as they swirl around the dance floor in perfect unison. Then he pushes her away and expertly twirls her around and around and back again. I am suddenly watching a final episode of *Dancing with the Stars*. It is mesmerizing. I am convinced ticos are born knowing how to dance. Really. They possess an innate ability to move.

Soon, more people began to join them on the dance floor and as the crowd thickens, it causes people to bump into one another. About three dances in, I hear a loud yelp and look over to find Anibal almost down on his knees on the floor. His flip-flop is across the room and he is holding his foot grimacing in pain. Bileida has speared him with her stiletto! I retrieve his shoe as he hobbles off the dance floor and onto a barstool. He rocks back and forth writhing in pain, so Lineth does the only thing she can do to help; she immediately orders him a double Guaro. Bileida strokes his arm and apologizes profusely. Although his dancing career is over for the night, he begins to feel better and they both seem to enjoy watching the ticos teach us clumsy gringos how to dance.

We arrive back at the house around 11:30 p.m., just in time for Milena and her fiancé to come home again from her nursing classes. I excuse myself and go up to bed. Again, the aroma of steamed rice and chicken rises and as I lay in my bed I find it impossible to sleep. This time it is not from hunger, but because downstairs, for a solid 45 minutes, they laugh hysterically as they reenact the stiletto debacle over and over. What a lovely family, laughing and loving all the time. A deep sense of joy washes over me. I am exactly where I am supposed to be right now.

* * *

The fourth morning in my house, I am awakened yet again, at dawn by the barking pack of dogs. As I come downstairs to breakfast feeling a little grumpy about it, I am greeted with big hugs and kisses from Bileida and Anibal.

Together they burst into song, singing, "*Feliz cumpleanos a ti.*" Happy Birthday to you.

I'd forgotten it's my birthday. Anibal continues to hum the birthday song as he eats his sandwich. Yes, I said sandwich, and yes, we are still at the breakfast part of this story. Each morning at 6:15 a.m., Anibal goes to the market and picks up two loaves of hot, freshly baked bread. He sticks one loaf into the fence, which separates us from the house of his sister-in-law next door, and brings the other inside. She comes out around 6:30, pulls the loaf out of the fence, and yells loudly, "*Gracias*!" Today the loaf is filled with ham, lettuce, tomatoes, and mayonnaise, lots and lots of mayonnaise. I love this because I have never had a ham sandwich for breakfast, on my birthday.

At school I try as best I can to communicate with my professor and the other students in my class. I am not one of those people to whom a foreign language comes easily. I can write a good sentence on paper if I have a minute to think about it, but speaking on the fly is difficult for me. I often find myself rehearsing a pertinent sentence in my head, only to find they have moved on to another topic by the time I get it down pat. And today I am a year older. Geez, I don't think this is going to get any easier.

My professor, Charlie, makes an announcement, "*Terminamos la clase temprano para tomar Lucetta para almorzar.*" I snap back into focus as I hear my own name. Huh? We are ending class early to take Lucetta to lunch. Wow. I sit back and tears well up in my eyes. My mind snaps back to many birthdays when my first husband completely forgot and it was never even acknowledged. These people barely know me, and yet they are celebrating my birthday.

We walk up the street to a tiny establishment owned by a tico named Jose. He is also the chef. My professor says the food is fantastic and he wants to support Jose's small business. I order Casado, the typical Costa Rican meal consisting of chicken, black beans, rice and salad. It is delicious. We spend the meal getting to know each other better, in English thank goodness.

Charlie stands, "Let's go back by the school, I forgot something."

As we walk through the door, a crowd yells out, "Surprise!"

Alex, the owner, had gathered up all of the other students in the school while we were gone and they are giving me a surprise party! I am humbled and awestruck, my heart filled to the brim with gratitude for being acknowledged on a solo journey. They even provide their own version of *queque y helado*. Cake and ice cream. They don't have candles, so they have me blow out a match after singing their birthday song.

Alex then tells the group, "It is a Costa Rican custom that everyone gives the birthday person 100 colones." (The equivalent of 20 cents American.)

All of the students dig into their pockets and pull out a gold coin for me. At the end of the party I ask Alex where this custom came from and how it had originated.

He grins. "Oh, I just made that up, hahaha."

Is everyone here a prankster? I don't mind though, because I just got four bus rides out of the deal.

* * *

One of my new friends in class is an American named Pamela. Ticos, for some reason, have a really hard time saying Pamela, so her name while in Spanish class, is PamEla. It's pronounced P-ah-MAY-la. This makes me laugh and I plan to call her this even if we are back in the United States. She has been to Manuel Antonio many times before on vacation, so she becomes my mentor and sets out to show me the ropes of navigating this foreign land.

After the surprise party, our first stop on the PamEla tour is a restaurant called Agua Azul. Blue Water. It is perched on the crest of a hill with an expansive view of the ocean. She orders two Imperials for us and as we wait, we begin to hear a chopping sound coming from the distance. We finally narrow down the area where the noise is coming from, and one more chop brings down a tree limb to reveal an amazing sight. There is a barefoot tico, 30 feet up in the air, in the top of the tree, with a machete. No ropes or repelling gear, no OSHA requirements, no lawyers waiting at the bottom... just him. For the next hour he methodically takes down limb after limb holding himself in the tree. He expertly makes every single cut count and when the final top of the tree severs, it opens up our view exposing a most beautiful island in the ocean beyond.

PamEla clinks my beer and cheers. "You see, Lucetta, all of Costa Rica celebrates you today."

Our next stop is a place that most tourists want to visit when they come here. It is a place called El Avion. The Airplane. Evidently, back in the '80s this C-123 cargo plane was a part of the Iran Contra scandal. The owners disassembled it, brought it up to the top of Manuel Antonio and put it back together again. It is now the home to a restaurant and bar with sunset views. Why? How? And who thought to put an airplane on the top of a hill? I have no idea, but it is fascinating nonetheless, and they make a mean Margarita. It is still my birthday after all. The last place on our party trip is a restaurant named Gato Negro. Black cat. After a delicious steak dinner that does not include beans and rice, PamEla hails me a cab and sends me back to Quepos. Needless to say, I did not do my *tarea*. Homework.

It is Friday morning and at the bus station I whip out my workbook and Spanish/English dictionary; racing the clock. The bus arrives and as I search for a seat I see a woman with blond hair and the most unbelievably vibrant blue eyes. Aha, an American. I sit beside her and ask if she wouldn't mind helping a fellow citizen with her homework.

She laughs. "Of course."

I put the finishing touches on my conjugations as my new friend, Colleen, hops off at her stop to go to a different Spanish school.

At the beginning of class each day, we have Spanish conversation to practice creating sentences and learn to communicate effectively. We talk about what we did the day before, our host families, or things about our life in general. Charlie, my teacher, is an American and says that he has been living in Costa Rica, for the most part, for the last twenty years. He lives in a small village 30 minutes south of Quepos called Matapalo.

There, he once owned five buildings on the beach, which comprised a small resort called The Jungle House. Tourism was good and this provided him an ample income. He poured his heart, soul, and resources into the community. In his resort he employed young ticos and taught them about strong work ethics. He began a lifeguard-training program to create jobs for the young men in the town, and made designs for a community center that would teach valid trade skills as well. He adopted two tico boys that came from troubled homes to give them a better chance, and wrote a monthly column called, "Making A Difference" in the local paper.

A year or so ago, the government changed the maritime laws on the beach and said that three of his five buildings were in violation as they were too close to the beach. They would have to be torn down. I know that Costa Rica is good about protecting the environment and the sea turtles, but have they never heard about "grandfathering" in a building until it falls on its own? It seemed so unfair. Charlie's buildings came down about the same time the economy fell and tourism died. It was a crushing blow. Having to generate a new income is how Charlie came to be my Spanish teacher.

When he talked about the Jungle House his eyes lit up. "Oh, I just wish you could see it. It's so beautiful there."

PamEla and I are totally engrossed in this real time history lesson on living in Costa Rica and we agree we wish we could see it too.

"Well, why don't we go there this weekend? I have my truck and I can take you."

PamEla and I look at each other and you can see our American brains kick into action reasoning why we can't possibly just pick up at the last minute and go away for the weekend. This would have to be planned out and things rearranged. But the truth is we are in Costa Rica and there is not one other thing we have to do except enjoy the beauty of this experience. Charlie helps me write a note in Spanish to leave with my host family, telling them I will be away for the weekend. I go home, pack my bag and leave my note because I am immediately headed to Matapalo.

My field trip begins two hours later as Charlie picks us up at PamEla's hotel and we drive through the countryside to Matapalo. I am happy to see more of Costa Rica. We pass mile after mile of palm trees and I ask Charlie about them. He explains that back in the 1940s these were all banana fields owned by the United Fruit Company, or as we know them, Chiquita. There was a banana blight that came in from Panama and destroyed all of the bananas. Chiquita decided to try the African Palm to save its business, and it worked out wonderfully. The oil from the tree is the basis for lotions, cosmetics, soaps, candles, and is also used as cooking oil. By the time the banana blight had passed, the palm industry was firmly established and profitable.

We arrive with enough daylight that we are able to tour the Jungle House property and walk across the dirt road to the beach. It takes my breath away. It is truly the most beautiful beach I have ever seen in my life. I feel like I have arrived at the end of the earth. It is long and wide with dark sand created by volcanoes. There is not one single person on the expanse of the entire beach. I want to cry at the beauty and simplicity of it. PamEla and I walk in silence, rendered speechless, both of us being consumed by an immense stirring in our souls. It is one of those unforgettable, life-altering moments that hopefully we all experience at one point or another in our lives, jolting us out of our numbness, if only for a short while, opening our hearts to something bigger. We leave when the very last glow of daylight falls below the horizon, as we are afraid we might not find our way back to Jungle House in the dark.

That evening, Charlie piles as many people as he can from his communal house into his truck and we drive to the next town. We all want pizza and there is a great little restaurant that serves it in Dominical, a surfer's beach, located about 16 kilometers south of Matapalo.

Over dinner we get to know Charlie's funny friends, through a combination of Spanish and English. They mock him from time to time about being our professor.

I come to Charlie's defense. Grinning, I say, "He has taught us many useful things in class. He taught us how to say, *Echo un pedo*." He is letting out farts, and "*Echar un pedo*." He farted.

I cannot, for the life of me, remember how this phrase even came up in class, but they fell out of their chairs laughing hysterically, pointing at "*un profesor*"

I look at Charlie and ask, "*Como se dice en Español,* how do you say in Spanish, 'don't flap the sheets'?"

Charlie and PamEla burst out laughing. Ignacio, who speaks very good English, asks what I mean by that question. Evidently he doesn't have any brothers or sisters or he would understand. I explain that when someone passes gas in the bed and they want to pull a prank, they "flap the sheets" and the smell goes everywhere torturing the poor person next to them.

He immediately relays this in Spanish to everyone else. They laugh and laugh. They had never heard of such a thing. Is this only an American custom? What can I say; I am doing what I can to be an ambassador of goodwill for the U.S.

Charlie gives us a riding tour of the surfing town of Dominical after dinner, and on the way home we see police standing in the road with guns. My heart leaps into my throat even though I am with locals.

We are stopped at a police checkpoint. Several officers lean into the window and ask many questions in Spanish that I do not understand. From the back seat, Ignacio pulls out his ID and hands it to the officer. The policeman seems satisfied and hands it back. He then asks Charlie's friend Romero for his. Romero does not have his papers with him. In Costa Rica, it is required that everyone carry their ID card on them at all times, gringos included. They ask Romero to step out of the car and take him back to the guardhouse.

Ignacio whispers to me, "They think he is Nicaraguan and therefore an illegal."

We grow quiet in the car as we wait for them to return Romero to the car. If he can't prove he is Costa Rican, he will be arrested and taken away. Twenty minutes pass and we grow more anxious as we wonder if they might keep him.

Finally, they return to the truck and Romero climbs in the back with us. He says that he had memorized his ID number, and over time he was able to convince them to check that number against their records. After a while, headquarters responded back that he was indeed Romero and he was, in fact, a tico.

We ride in silence holding the gravity of the situation, understanding that his life could have been severely changed at that moment. Several miles down the road we pass what must be a wastewater treatment plant because our nostrils flare at the stench. Ignacio breaks the silence as he yells out, "Who flapa da sheets?!"

* * *

Back in Quepos it is business as usual in my neighborhood of Boca Vieja, which translates into Old Mouth. Okay, I have no idea how they came up with that. Really. As Charlie pulls onto my street to drop me off, I watch the children play, the dog's roam, and a strange feeling washes over me. It is a feeling of being "home." But then, I am home, aren't I? I don't have another home.

My family, all fifteen of them that are in the small house at the moment, welcome me with hugs, kisses, and a thousand questions all at once about my weekend. Bileida immediately goes into the kitchen and whips up a huge plate of food for me. Gallo Pinto, a salad, and the most amazing piece of delicate fish I have ever eaten. She said she bought it at the market because it had been caught that very day in a nearby fishing village.

Anibal laughs at me because I only drink one inch of Coca-Cola every night. When they offer me something I always accept because I don't want to seem ungrateful, but I have never been one to drink soda at all. I didn't realize he was watching so closely. I am learning, though, that everyone is watching. Watching very closely. I have always lived in cities, and I am an urban dweller by nature. Part of the attraction, beyond the energy and excitement that a city provides, has been that I can wander around in an anonymous fashion if I so choose. Here though, I am learning, I'm in a very small town and although I think I am just going about living my new life incognito, people are taking note.

One day PamEla asks me to walk with her down to the beach after school because she has to buy something for her son before she leaves. He is a surfer and wants her to bring him a hemp necklace from the local beachside market. We trek down the main road to the beach and stop at the first booth we find. It is draped with dresses, jewelry, towels and T-shirts for sale. A beautiful Tico woman greets us and assists PamEla.

I ask the woman her name. "*Como se llama*?"

She answers, "PamEla."

I laugh with delight, "*Mi amiga es PamEla, tambien.*" My friend is PamEla too.

She kisses my friend on the cheek and we all laugh at the odds. Then I tell her that my name is Lucetta.

She looks at me and shakes her head. "*Oh, sé lo que eres.*" Oh I know who you are. What?

I step back as she wags her finger at me, "*Usted es la chica mala que estaba haciendo su tarea en el autobús la semana pasada.*" You are the bad girl who was doing her homework on the bus last week.

My hands fly up to cover my face in shock and shame. Oh my gosh, she's right!

"No, no, you don't understand!" I explain in breathless English, "It was my birthday the night before. I don't leave it until the last minute every time!"

She bursts out laughing and responds in perfect English, "Sure, sure, sure. Next time just ask ME for help. Very nice to meet you, *mi amiga* Lucetta." She gives me a hug as we wave goodbye.

* * *

Several years ago, I took up running. I was getting older and I wanted to stay healthy for as long as possible. My feet hadn't hit the pavement since I'd left the U.S., but I decide I need to start back up again because my tico mother feeds me into oblivion. I check the tide chart for the beach. If the tide is low, I can run on the beach and jump over the small rivers that drain into the ocean, without getting my running shoes wet. Nothing ever dries out here. If the tide is high, the rivers are too wide and I will have to remove my shoes to wade through them, making running impossible.

I get up several times that week at the crack of dawn, according to the charts of low tide, and run down to the beach. It is a steep run down a gravel road. I pass several beautiful homes on the way down, waving and exchanging hellos in Spanish with the caretakers of the houses as they work in the yards.

On the weekend I sleep in and walk to the beach with a friend visiting from the States. As we head down the gravel road we notice there is a man firmly planted in the middle of the road staring at us, his hands on his hips. Startled, we slow our pace. My friend begins to get a little anxious. As we near, the man reaches his hands out as if to stop us. My heart starts pounding.

My friend grabs my hand. "What's going on?"

"I don't know."

We continue walking slowly. As we get closer he takes one hand and taps it on the top of his other wrist where a watch would be.

Suddenly a grin breaks out on his face and in English he says, "You're late."

The ticos are unbelievably polite and respectful to everyone. As I've mentioned before they stand to let the elderly sit, they say hello to every single person they see, they kiss on the cheek as a greeting, they stop traffic to talk to one another, they laugh, they play with children, and so on. They are also so nice that when you go out to a restaurant and have a meal, they will not bring you the check in the end. You could sit there for hours and they will not bring you the check until you ask for it, because to them, if they bring it without a request it would be like asking you to leave which would not be polite at all. Also, in some Spanish-speaking countries when you say "thank you" you get the response, "*de nada*" which means, "it's nothing." To the Costa Ricans it would be a negative to say it was nothing. It would discount the act that was being thanked. Instead they say, "*Mucho gusto.*" It is my pleasure. Or, "*Con mucho gusto.*" It is with much pleasure, that I do this for you. And if they really want to make their point they will say, "*El gusto es mio.*" The pleasure is mine. To me, these are just added reasons to love the Costa Ricans. It would be nice if more people in the U. S. would adopt this "*much gusto*" custom. Who created the trend of everyone saying "no problem" after we say "thank you"?

Ticos are happy for you to learn their language too and they will help you if you ask, but they are far too polite to correct you. At times, this can be a problem because many words are similar, and we gringos get mixed up. The ticos will just try to figure out what you are saying and respond.

Sometimes though, their playful spirit gets the best of them. I am at a restaurant one evening and at the end of the meal I wave to the waiter, "*La cuenta por favor.*" The check please. Some gringos at the next table overhear me, so one of the men waves to his waiter and says, "*Lo cuento por favor.*" The waiter stops, turns and says, "*Muy bien.*" Very well. He takes a deep bow, puts his pencil behind his ear, his check pad in his pocket and somberly says, "*Un día un hombre entró en un bar.*" One day a man walked into a bar. My table bursts into laughter. The gringo, instead of asking for the check, had asked for a story. We laugh with the men from Texas as we explain the difference between *la cuenta* and *lo cuento*.

Sometimes though, the faux pas can be a little more convoluted…

At the Academia we are going to learn about cooking terms and all types of foods in Spanish. Our professor decided we should each bring ingredients with us the next day and we would prepare a meal for the entire school as a fun way to learn the words.

We show up for class with our assigned ingredients in hand. Our class goes down to the kitchen and preps for an hour as we practice terms for utensils, foods, spices, and recipes. When all is ready, we call the other students to the dining area to enjoy a meal with us. As Alex, the owner of our school, approaches I motion him to the front of the line.

"No, why should I go first?" he humbly asks.

I summon up all of my Spanish speaking courage and practice a new word I had learned.

"*Porque disgraciado.*" I say.

Alex's eyes go wide and his mouth falls open, "What?! What did you just say? Who is your professor?!"

The room falls into a stunned silence. I back pedal, not knowing what went wrong.

"What?" I say in English, "Because we are grateful."

The other teachers then double over in laughter speaking Spanish amongst themselves rapidly while pointing at me and trying to catch their breath. Instead of saying, "*agradecido*," which means grateful, I had said, "*disgraciado*" which means disgrace, and even worse, it is a slang term in Costa Rica. I had unwittingly told my headmaster he should go to the front of the line because "he was a son of a bitch." My face goes beet red as I apologize profusely. Alex laughs and laughs as I beg him not to fire Charlie, my teacher.

* * *

A few weeks pass and my friend, Stephen, is coming to visit from the States for the weekend. There is no extra space in my tico house for visitors so I take a room at La Mariposa, The Butterfly, which is up the mountain from Quepos in Manuel Antonio. Ah…air conditioning, hot water, and an amazing view, it is luxurious. He arrives tomorrow so I am fortunate to have some quiet and calm all to myself tonight for the first time in a month.

I am a little anxious, though, as I anticipate the collision of my old life with the new one. I teeter on feeling not ready to brush up against it yet. It hasn't been long enough for me to be on my own, especially since my life has been consumed with my tico family. I haven't really had a moment to process everything and I don't even know if I've grown. But it's Fourth of July and he has the time off from work. I say yes, knowing he has always wanted to come to Costa Rica.

I walk out onto the terrace and sit enjoying the stunning view of Manuel Antonio National Park and the beach. As the sun is going down I notice there is another side to my terrace. I walk over to see what the view might be in that direction. There is a large potted plant around the corner, and stretched from there to the wall is one of the largest and most amazing spiderwebs I have ever seen. I want to take down the web and see around the corner, but I just don't have the heart. It's getting late, and some spider spent a lot of time weaving this web for tonight. I'll just pass on the view. I snuggle in the bed early, excited to know I will not be awakened at the crack of dawn by dogs and roosters. I quickly fall asleep in the quiet.

I may not be in Quepos, but I'm still in Costa Rica. At the first sign of daylight, a repetitive banging on my roof awakens me. Really? What in the world is going on up there, and why is the universe against me getting some shut-eye? I climb out of bed when I realize it isn't going to stop. Is the hotel working on my roof at this time in the morning? The sun breaks the horizon at five each morning and by 5:30 or 6:00 everyone here is up and going about their day. I may have to call the front desk and ask them to please stop.

I squint against the sun as I move out onto the terrace to see what is going on. I look up to find, not workers, but a group of White Faced monkeys jumping up and down on my tin roof like a trampoline! They are having the time of their lives as they jump and roll and play. I suddenly forget I am grumpy as I watch them mesmerized, from only a few feet away.

They move off the roof and down onto my terrace to play with an iguana. He does not seem at all amused by their antics, and fights back, but he takes a few hits that stun him. He rallies and scampers off when they became distracted by discovering the ledge and began playing there.

One monkey works his way around the corner where the big spider web is located. He stops in his tracks. The largest spider I've ever seen is there, right in the center of her web. The monkey works his way closer until his face is one inch from the web. He balances on the rail as he looks and studies, cocking his head curiously from side to side. Suddenly, CHOMP! He eats my spider right out of the web.

I jump back a foot at the shock of it and shout, "Hey, what was that?"

I am actually angry at the monkey for a few minutes as I feel the loss of my friend I'd protected the night before. Slowly I realize this is the cycle of life, this is the world of survival in nature, and I am merely an observer. Sometimes things just are what they are. I pick up a stick, take down the web and wander around the corner to enjoy the morning from a different point of view.

* * *

My Spanish classes are ending and so is my term with Bileida and Anibal. It is time for me to leave the nest and look for my own place to live. I make appointments and look at several places that would suffice, but I'm just not finding the right place and time is running short. At school during break, Alex inquires about how the search is going.

"Exactly what is it you are looking for?" He asks.

"Well, the vision I had in my head when I imagined this trip was a place with a view of the beach, and a hammock, but I can't seem to find it."

He is a sage, and in his usual wise manner says, "Don't settle. Why shouldn't you have your dream? You should. And so should others, but I am afraid they usually give up too easily."

"Thank you for the encouragement. I'll keep looking."

In class Charlie announces that we will read the local magazine that has just come out, and discuss it in Spanish. He flips open the latest issue of the *Quepolandia*, and it lands on a full-page ad about a villa for rent in Manuel Antonio.

Charlie shouts, "Lucetta, look. It has a view and a hammock!"

"Wow, this looks really nice, I'll call about it this afternoon."

"I think you should call right now before it's gone."

PamEla offers up her phone, and I'm thrilled they allow me a few minutes of class time to follow this lead. I announce, "I have an appointment to see it this very afternoon."

The small villa is beautiful, affordable, and the view is stunning. The place is set up on a hillside overlooking Manuel Antonio National Park. It is fully furnished, and when I tour the tiny bedroom I go to the closet to check it out, and there, where my clothes would have hung, is a washer and a dryer!

"Hot water too?" I ask.

When she nods her head I yell, "I'll take it! I'll take it today and pay you whatever you need for deposit."

Lineth, my new landlord, laughs. "Why don't you move instead in two days? I have a lady coming to clean up the remodeling dust."

"*Si, claro, gracias*." Of course, thank you.

Two days later I stop by the farmers' market in Quepos on the way home. I buy an orchid and some fresh pastries as a gift for Bileida and Anibal. I pack my two bags and say goodbye to my tiny room with the slatted door. I am sad that this phase of my journey is coming to an end, but excited to have my own space.

I go downstairs with my gifts to find that a large group of extended family has gathered to say their farewells, even though I am only moving a few miles away. Bileida and I both have tears in our eyes as we hug. This has truly been a special experience for me. Anibal hugs me, and laughs as always. I work my way around the room with kisses on the cheek for everyone. The last ones in line are my tico brother Michael, and his wife.

Michael hugs me, takes a step back and places both hands on my shoulders. "My parents want me to tell you they adore you. They say you have been a wonderful guest and you must come back to their home for dinner very often." He grins.

Stunned, all I can say is, "You speak English. VERY. GOOD. ENGLISH."

Chapter Six

This villa is the vision I had in mind as a place to restore my soul. I plop myself down in my hammock for two hours, realizing I haven't slowed down long enough for restoration to even become possible. My emotions play with me as I am simultaneously overcome with deep sadness and elated joy. My heart breaks at the loss of our family and the plans we had for the future, the dreams now unrealized. I must grieve the loss of the life I once knew and learn to love a new life as it unfolds. Moments later I have a minute of possibility that expands my heart. I'm here, this happened. I am in Costa Rica this is crazy. Who would have ever imagined? And look at this view. Maybe I *can* live on my own, maybe I can survive this devastation and create something new for myself. Maybe it really is possible.

It takes me all of 10 minutes to unpack and move into my small villa on the hill. After all, the sum total of my material belongings consists of one bag and a backpack. Here I am. No phone, no Internet, no way to connect with the outside world. Tears of gratitude for the peace and quiet spill over. My little villa is so much more than I could have ever hoped for.

Back in my hammock for two more glorious hours, I soak in the view. The warm sun and the quiet are healing. My villa is so high on the hill that I am overlooking the jungle below and beyond that, the ocean. I am literally on the top of the world. The scenery changes as clouds float across the sky changing the color of the day, while jungle animals wander below me across the top of the canopy. Monkeys play in the tops of the trees and sloths delight me as they do their thing, which is nothing.

Even in paradise though, one must eat. So I drag myself out of my cocoon and make a grocery list of the things I will need. I walk two kilometers to the market not realizing I can only purchase half of the items I want because then I will have to lug them all home. I decide to reduce the list to essentials: eggs, bread, cheese, peanut butter and Imperials. Back at home I step outside to eat on my terrace. Out here I have a table for six, which I will fill up with new friends, laughter and food. This is where I will spend my days.

I pick up my certificate from Alex for completing my Spanish classes, and in the evening host a goodbye party at my new villa for everyone in the Academia D'Amore Spanish school. They come early enough to enjoy the view. We laugh, eat, drink and then we cry at the thought of never seeing each other again.

* * *

And now it is time to play. There are so many cool things to do in Costa Rica. I could live here for a very long time and never get through the list. There are tours available for excursions to river raft, kayak, zip line, and rappel. You can go to see the active volcano, hot springs, a cloud forest, surf, and more. One of my favorites is the simplest. Running on the beach in the solitude of dawn creates an explosion of joy in my heart, and I look forward to this several times a week.

My favorite play day in Manuel Antonio is the day some of my new friends and I hike to a waterfall. It is a rugged hike about 45 minutes into the rainforest. It follows a stream, and much of the time we are hiking in the stream itself. This is not a tourist destination and the only reason we get to go is that a tico friend is taking us. This is the Costa Ricans' own beautiful secret. There are little pieces of cloth tied to the trees, which a previous hiker must have placed to find their way out. This is quintessential jungle and I am in love with it all. The waterfall was about 25 to 30 feet high, and once you are there you can jump off into the pool that swirls below. I am terrified, but can't back down in my new life. We keep our shoes on as we jump because we then have to climb back up the rocks to do it again. We stay for four hours since we have paradise all to ourselves.

Another day I go white water rafting with some different friends. We laugh and scream as we try to stay in the boat careening down the rapids. We stop for a lunch break and one of the ticos asks if I like peanuts.

"Sure."

He grabs my hand, "Come with me then."

We head into the jungle. He's examining trees, searching for something.

"Yes, here they are." He directs me over.

"What? What is this?" There is a tan line going up the middle of the tree.

"Termites," he says with a grin.

On closer inspection I see the brown line is moving, a trail of hundreds of tiny creatures heading up and down the bark, "Oh that's cool. I've never seen them like this before."

He reaches over and picks several of them off the tree. I back up a little, thinking that's sort of weird. Then he puts them in his mouth and eats them. Gross!

He looks at my horrified face and laughs. "Peanuts. They taste like peanuts. Try one."

Everything in my head screams no. I want to run. My heart, though, begins to rustle up something different, a very strong desire for courage and bravery. I'm on this journey to expand myself; I'll never have this chance again, and he ate one and is still alive. My hand shakes as I reach over to the tree and pinch several of the creatures between my fingers. Will they crawl around in my mouth? Ugh, I pinch harder hoping to squash the life out of them as I pop them into my mouth... Peanuts. Who knew?

We head back to the boat and I am filled with an adrenaline shot of boldness. It felt good to push past scary and try something new. The feeling of expansion stays with me all day and I decide from now on, my new mantra is: yes.

* * *

"Are you okay, Momma?" she asks within minutes of our reunion.

"Yes, I seem to be just fine. I thought I would have a meltdown but it hasn't happened."

My stepdaughter Liza comes to visit for a few days over the weekend. It is wonderful to see her and we cry as we hug, repeating over and over how much we've missed each other. One of the beautiful things that came from the marriage collapse is that Liza has fully claimed me as her mother and now calls me Mom. Their mother died when they were young, so if they called me Mom I knew it completely discounted that fact that they had another mother who lived, and birthed them. I get this. So I have always understood why they wanted to say stepmom and never took it personally, and yet, after twenty years my heart explodes every time I hear her say Mom.

We play on the beach, swim, surf, hike the National Park, and then book an amazing adventure with a professional guide where we climb up the middle of a 90-foot waterfall and repel down. It is frightening and exhilarating all at the same time! I am deathly afraid of heights, but this is my time to get strong so I must conquer all of my fears.

Liza and I have a very quick, but spectacular time together. We have girl talks and I acknowledge how wonderfully she is moving forward in her own life. She catches me up on the news of all the siblings. The fact that she came down here, and hung out like nothing ever happened in our family, is like a breath of fresh air to me. It tells me that I'm still her person, her mom. We kiss, cry and say goodbye at the airport as I ask her to carry the message back home that I am fine.

* * *

He took my hands and wrapped them around his waist as his full body pressed me up against the railing of the deck. Inches from my face he looked longingly into my eyes. "You stood me up on the beach that day."

"I know, I'm sorry, something came up." I lied.

"I waited for you. You owe me a date."

I'd met Greivin several weeks earlier at a bar while out with my new pack of friends listening to live music. He had a fantastic smile and approached me in the usual charming tico manner. He spoke very good English. He said I was beautiful, and asked if he could buy me a drink. I agreed, thinking he was just being cordial.

He stayed by my side all evening, begging me to go to dinner with him sometime. I explained numerous times, in numerous ways, that I was not looking for a relationship, as that was not my purpose while in Costa Rica.

He persisted all evening, not taking no for an answer. I thought he must be drunk. I didn't take him seriously because he was much younger than me, and I couldn't figure out why he was so tenacious about this. I pointed out all of the beautiful women in the bar who were his age, but he was not interested. He said they were young and silly. He liked older women. He finally wore me down, and by the end of the night, in my predictable people-pleasing way; I agreed to meet him at the beach to go surfing the next day.

The next morning I woke with a knot in my chest. I said yes, when I meant no. I didn't want to crank up a relationship while here, and I didn't want to lead him on. My time in CR was for me to figure out who I was now, but damn, my compliant personality said yes again. I was angry with myself for not standing firm. I knew I would get up and go to the beach because I said I would.

The knot tightened, choking my concession. Wait. I don't know this man, and I don't want to go. This is my life now, and I don't have to do things I don't want to do. I decided I would not go. I had no way to contact him, yet it stepped all over my integrity to leave him hanging. After a while though, I pushed through the guilt and began to feel better that I'd actually stood up for myself.

Now, here he is again. Maybe it isn't actually a lie. Something did come up; me, honoring my own feelings is what came up, and it's finally time for me to take care of myself. Time for saying yes to me.

As he leans in closer, I can smell his cologne and it ignites something inside of me. He presses his lips against mine in a most passionate kiss that weakens my knees and knocks down my defenses. After a moment, I reciprocate.

All evening he stays on me trying to persuade me, "You must let me see you again. You are on holiday, why not have some fun?"

Determined to stick to my guns this time, I reply, "No, this has been fun, but we won't hang out again."

"Just let me walk you home, so I know you are safe."

"Thanks, but I can get home on my own."

"You must let me know you are safe, you at least owe me something for standing me up."

Damn, that hurt. I know he wants to walk me home to find out where I live. Fortunately, my villa is behind a locked gate, so I relent. "Okay, I live right across the street."

He walks me to the gate and we say goodbye. I go in feeling relieved that the entire situation is now over. And yet, moments after getting in my hammock to look out at the ocean, I begin to think about that kiss…

* * *

Now that Spanish school is over, I would love to spend the rest of my time in Costa Rica doing nothing other than playing, but I have another goal to accomplish. Part of my plan while here is to become

TEFL certified which will be helpful when I get to Africa. This new skill in my tool belt will allow me to travel freely, as I will always be able to earn an income.

I am sitting on my terrace with my laptop overlooking the ocean, filling out the application for certification. I laugh as I realize I studied Spanish while living in Quepos, commuting every day up to Manuel Antonio, now I live in Manuel Antonio and will commute to Quepos every day for TEFL. I'd always heard this four-week program was very intense with lots of homework, lesson planning, and very little sleep. There is actually a place in the application where we have to assure them that we are of sound body and mind, and all of our domestic affairs are in order, so we will be able to complete the course. Yikes, this could be scarier than a 90-foot repel drop.

I sit with my finger on the send button. Hmmm...this means I will be giving up four full weeks; one complete month of my time in paradise. I won't be enjoying my view, my hammock, or my peace and quiet. I only have a short time here. Do I really want to give it up to sit in a classroom? Can I give up my early morning runs on the beach, and watching the monkeys come home every night?

Now, I do realize that no one is crying for me right now. I know this sounds ridiculous, but still, this is **my** time—for the very first time ever. No. I must go forward. TEFL is the plan, and it is a good plan, a worthy goal and part of a bigger dream. Paradise will still be here, but this opportunity for me may not. I take my hand and quickly smack the send button before I can change my mind.

I show up in my TEFL class to discover it consists of ten American students, and one Australian. For the next four weeks we will eat, sleep and breathe the power of the English language. Heidi, the head of our school, is not only pretty but a brilliant educator. We discover she is obsessed with grammar and it is her favorite thing to teach, which informs us we will be doing it a lot. A few groans are heard throughout the room.

Toward the end of class she pairs us up in order to work together on the Communicative Activity. This is the part of the lesson where the students combine everything they have learned into one activity that promotes self-generated conversation between the students. Heidi pairs me with Mark. All I know about him so far is that he is a really tall guy, and a stand-up comedian from Chicago.

Heidi gives each set of partners a sheet of paper with a small apartment drawn on it. Then she gives us miniature cutout pictures of objects one would find in an apartment. The goal is for us to discuss and agree on where we should place these things.

For example, she says, "I'll put the flowers ON the table." To check our true understanding of the words she says with a thumbs up, "Is that okay?"

We reply, "Yes."

Then she says, "I'll put the television IN the refrigerator. Is that okay?"

"No!" We giggle like new learners.

"Now it's time for you partners to set up your own apartments."

I look over at Mark. "You know, we haven't known each other very long. Don't you think it's too soon to move in together?"

Mark laughs. "Baby I knew the minute I met you that you were the one for me."

I bat my eyelashes. "Aww, Marky, you always say the right thing."

Heidi stops by our desk to check our progress. She grins yet implores, "Stop trying to solve your moral issues and move in together. NOW."

Five minutes into the activity she asks for volunteers to demonstrate, and Mark raises his hand. We move to the front of the class and begin placing the tiny pictures on the board.

The first one is a floor lamp and Mark tells me, "Put the lamp BEHIND the chair."

I point to the kitchen, "Put these dishes IN the sink."

The next picture is a baby grand piano.

Stunned, I cry out, "Mark, you brought the piano?!? You never even play it!"

"But, honey, you know I've had it since I was a kid."

I yell, "Put that ON Craigslist, there's no room here!"

Heidi jumps up and intervenes, "You two clowns sit your butts IN your chairs."

Under her breath we hear her mumbling something about it being a very long four weeks.

* * *

We all plan to go out for drinks after class to get to know one another and bond. We decide on when and where to meet, and as soon as I walk up the stairs at the bar, someone grabs my hand. It is Greivin. He looks particularly hot tonight and there is that damn cologne again, doing what it does.

He spends the evening telling me how wonderful I am and how he can't get me off his mind. He says I'm fascinating, brave, and beautiful. I am flattered as he says all the things a heartbroken woman would love to hear. But I am not even bonding with my classmates. Once again he asks me to go out with him and even though my resolve is weakening, I stand firm, as now I have a legitimate response with the time-consuming TEFL class.

He takes me to the deck out back. "I will win you over."

He leaves me with one of those velvet kisses.

* * *

Several days into class our heads began to spin. They cram so much valuable information into the curriculum we are afraid our minds may literally explode.

The very first time I teach classes on my own, I am given the upper intermediate class two days in a row. What?! The lessons are complicated and the grammar for both days is advanced, calling for close study and concentration. I have my class plans laid out, and have practiced numerous times. I'm nervous, but excited because the ticos are so eager to learn.

During the second day, I look up to see Greivin siting in class! I am so flustered that in the middle of the lesson, I somehow switch back to the grammar from the day before. The students are so confused. They finally figure out what I am trying to teach them, and they are very gracious about it, but I made it ten times harder for them. I feel horrible and inadequate.

During my assessment with my teacher Drew, I walk in and tell him what he already knows. "I had a grammar bomb go off in my class today." He consoles me and gives me tips on how to avoid it in the future.

I am shaken at how Greivin is showing up everywhere now, even in stores and restaurants. And because he is in classes and hanging out at TEFL, he hears if we are planning to go for beers after work and he shows up there as well. It feels like borderline stalking to me. I am not really happy about this, even though I'm aware that I may be sending him mixed messages. Now that he is a student, I feel I must honor TEFL and not bring my personal life into this, by saying something to the staff and asking them to make him leave.

We are in class all day long, teach in the evenings, go home and create new lesson plans into the wee hours of the morning. We wake up the next day and do it all over again. It's brutal, but we all want the end goal, which is to be skilled at teaching English to someone who needs this language. We tough it out, commiserating yet encouraging one another to not quit. In order to make it through the rigorous curriculum, we decide as a class we are going to make it fun.

One day Heidi emphasizes that to reach a second language learner, one should always consider using meaningful dialogue that is relevant to each particular class in our lesson planning. We should be teaching vocabulary with topics and language they can go out and practice using immediately such as playing a sport, interviewing for a job, dating, etc. If our lesson plans are meaningful to their lives then their interest level, motivation to learn, and retention will be higher.

During the morning break, several of my classmates tried their hand at meaningful, relevant dialogue:

SHUT UP
Shut (the fuck) up
Shut (yo ass) up
Shut (the hell) up

* * *

One Saturday we finally have some time off and several of us decide to go white water river rafting. Greivin hears about this and asks if he can go with us. He has been so adorable in class and such an eager learner, that he pulls at my heartstrings once again, and in a weak moment I say yes.

We have a blast careening down the white water, and after the river trip, our guide takes us to a place for food and dancing. I am not much of a beer drinker, but in the heat of the day, combined with the unencumbered-no-responsibility fun, I am several beers in before I know it. Greivin has been a gentleman all day long, and very charming to be with. The guide takes us back to his tour shop and Greivin flags a taxi to take us home. Not really knowing the territory, I am surprised when we pull up to a house, which it turns out, is Greivin's.

"Please, let me pour you a glass of wine, then I will call you a taxi."

"Oh, okay."

Once we are in his house, he pulls out all of the stops. I capitulate and soon find myself in his bed. Our time together is equal parts tender and rough. I am confused and so messed up. I jump up as soon as we are finished, and begin to put my clothes back on.

"No, I want you to wear my clothes."

"What? No. I'll put my clothes on."

"No, I want you to wear my clothes and be comfortable to lounge."

Maybe this is how things are done here. I'm not sure I want to stick around for long, but I concede as the good girl always does, and I put on his boxers and a T-shirt. We go out into the living room, and in just a few short moments, his roommate comes home with one of my TEFL colleagues.

What the hell!? He knew they were coming over, and now it was clear to them that we'd had sex because I am sitting there in his clothes. His plan worked and now he is all puffed up with pride. I am angry at his manipulation, embarrassed, and upset with myself for falling for his prowess. I immediately change my clothes, politely say goodbye to everyone and walk out to the main road to flag down a taxi. I must seem like one of those crazy drama bitches, and maybe at this point, I am.

* * *

On the last day of class I go to TEFL early to make 45 copies of small pictures as part of my materials for my lesson that night. As I stand at the copier with my first set of copies ready to go, the power in the building suddenly goes out. In fact the power is out in ALL of Quepos for the entire day. Not a single copier was in operation anywhere.

I evaluate the situation for my class plan. It had taken me four hours to formulate the lesson, an hour of assessment for approval, another hour for revisions and second approval, and the rest of the materials were already made, which took many hours as well. There is no way I can alter this lesson plan. I have no choice but to draw, by hand, all 45 of the pictures. Thank goodness I have come in early. (Of course my hope was to get my copies made and go to the beach for the morning.)

My lesson theme is all about relationships such as dating, engagement, and marriage. Consequently, I spend the next five hours drawing stick people in love. None of us brought our own lunch because we planned to call and have lunch delivered on our last day. With no power, we have no phone lines to call and no time to walk to town, which means no food. Hungry and grumpy at the end of the day, I vow to take an art class when I settle back into the U.S., so I'll never have to draw another stick figure again.

At 4:15 p.m. we start setting out small candles all over the room because it will be dark half way through class. At 4:30 my students arrive and class begins. At 4:35 the power turns on! My class is a success with no grammar bombs at all. A few of my fellow teachers were suspiciously amazed that the power had been out during our exact work hours that day. They lightheartedly accuse the TEFL staff of pulling the switch so we would learn to make materials the old fashioned way, and be able to teach in developing countries with no resources. Heidi and Drew laugh and say one day we just might be grateful for the experience.

So after numerous hours of lesson planning with no sleep, teaching, evaluating, creating a final exam, and bouts with the copy machine, we graduate.

TEFL throws a beautiful pool party and dinner for all of the graduates and our students. With tears in our eyes we say our goodbyes. We wish our students well in their continued quest to master the language with the next round of student teachers. Then we wish each other well as we will soon be spread out all over the world, teaching the power of the English language.

* * *

Greivin asks me to join him on a picnic one day. He says this place is the most beautiful, romantic place in all of Quepos. By now I am more clearly identifying red flags for a controlling relationship. I feel ridiculous that I didn't see this sooner, given that I sat on the board of InterAct, our domestic violence agency in Raleigh.

I replay several of his communications, such as:

"I looked at your profile on Facebook and if you were my girlfriend, I'd take you to a salon and change your hair." Ouch.

And, "Are you wearing that top to attract attention? Because I am the only one for you."

"You *will* give yourself to me, no matter what you want."

Even during the rough sex, he said, "You know you love it."

And, "No one will ever love you the way I do."

Finally, "My last relationship was with an older woman and she took me to Europe for six months, why aren't you taking me to Cuba for a vacation?"

Oh, that's what this is really about. I'm his ticket out of this country. One minute I believe that's the truth, and the next he is convincing me of something beautiful and loving. I know there is a phrase in domestic violence called "crazy-making," and I feel like that's what he is doing to me.

I tell him I will not go on the picnic with him. He is relentless and after a thirty-minute conversation he finally wears me down enough to agree to meet him instead at a restaurant in Quepos. This is my opportunity to end this for good.

He shows up at the cafe with provisions for a romantic picnic, discounting that I said no and assuming he will convince me to go. He pulls his chair up so we are sitting nose to nose. I tell him no again. He gives me numerous logical reasons why I should, how he wants to spend loving quality time with me, and how I owe this to him because I've been so busy with TEFL. I keep shaking my head no. I am trying to gently let him go and telling him it is over, but he is not listening.

Things began to ramp up, as he takes his knees and spreads them around mine, literally cornering me against the wall such that I cannot move. This goes on for quite a while. I keep shaking my head no; hoping someone in the restaurant will see me, intervene and rescue me.

Suddenly he grabs my wrists tightly, pinning them down to my knees, so I can't move. My hands began to go numb, as he has cut off the circulation. I'm trying not to make a scene in the restaurant and I suddenly have an idea that if I cry he will have to let go so I can wipe my nose and my eyes. I bring up a cry and in that very moment a miracle happens. A taxicab pulls up outside. The second that he lets go of my hands, I dash out the door and run to the cab screaming, "*Vamanos, vamanos!*" Let's go! Let's go!

Greivin runs after me and is pounding on the window, running beside us while we pull away. I can't look. "*Vamanos, vamanos!*"

As we begin to make our way up the hill to Manuel Antonio, I am wiping real tears this time. Tears of shame, for taking the coward's way out and bolting, while at the same time, tears of pride for getting myself out, in whatever way that had to happen.

Riding up the mountain I am trying to figure out how I allowed myself to get into this situation again. I am upset that my need for validation after being rejected in such a devastating way is so strong that it overtook my reasoning and my intuition. I am angry at myself that I fell for control again. Thirty years later, here I am right back where I was before. Was it luck that I fell in love with my second husband and lived in safety, not falling back into that trap? I just don't understand. We pull up to my villa and I hand extra colones to the driver with a heart-felt thank you. Still shaking, I dart to refuge behind my locked iron gate.

* * *

It is time for me to leave my beloved Costa Rica as my visa is up. Sad. Sad. Sad. The voice in my head is refusing to be ignored. Why are you voluntarily leaving this paradise? No one is making you leave. There is not one reason you have to leave. You are just now really getting a handle on the language, you're settling into your community, you could teach English here. Even your salsa dancing has improved. You love the sun, the food, the people, the jungle, the surf, the animals, even the rain. You love this place with every fiber of your being. Everything about it suits you. You are leaving to go live in a village in Africa? WHAT ARE YOU DOING?!? Shhhhh. Just shhhhh.

I don't have an answer. There really is no explanation other than I have been called in my heart to Africa. All I know is that if I don't go now, I will never go.

Part Three

Running Uncertain

A bird sitting on a tree is never afraid of the branch breaking because its trust is not on the branch, but on its own wings.

-Unknown

Chapter Seven

I stop back over in the United States on my way to Africa, to say goodbye to family and friends, knowing I might be gone for several years. It is a whirlwind tour on the continent, couch surfing along the way, enjoying time with my loved ones, and eating everything in sight.

My biggest concern at the moment is how to survive the 16-hour leg of my flight from Dulles airport to Addis Ababa, Ethiopia. Armed with reading material and a fully charged iPod loaded with new music, I enter the airport and head straight to the first store I find to buy one of those circular neck pillows.

As I find my seat on the plane I discover Ethiopian Airlines has a packet of goodies for me. It is full of thoughtful, necessary items; a blanket, earplugs, an eye cover, a pair of long socks, and a disposable toothbrush. I feel cared for and acknowledged.

I am headed to Africa! Africa is the birthplace and cradle of mankind, the land of exotic animals, and the home of beautiful Africans. As I gaze out the window my mind wanders back to the first time a special love for African Americans was planted in my heart.

It was 1971 and the year of the first school desegregation movement where students would be cross-bused to all corners of the county to mix and mingle the races. This news drew a great deal of public attention across the nation. The entire state was riddled with anxiety and protests broke out regularly. Society was teaching us to fear and hate black people. (Which is what they were called back then.) White parents were outraged at the thought of their children sitting side by side with folks they saw as lesser human beings. All this while the Vietnam War was emotionally ripping us in two, creating its own conflict. It was cultural mayhem.

I was entering the seventh grade and a completely new school assignment plan was about to be announced on the local news. My parents called a meeting of all five of us kids to discuss what was happening. We gathered in their bedroom with my older brothers and sister sprawled on the bed and my little sister and me on the floor, wide-eyed waiting to hear our fate.

Our parents sat together holding hands and after a deep breath said, "We have thought long and hard about this, and here is what we would like to say to you. Some of you may be uncomfortable with this situation and that's okay. It's understandable because this won't be easy. Just remember what we've always taught you; no matter what color their skin, they are people. Human beings just like us, no different, and God loves them the same as He loves us. We have a choice to offer each of you, and a decision for you to make. Given that there are five of you, we can afford to either send you to private school now and you must pay for college, working your own way through OR you go to public school now, and we can pay for your college. It's your choice."

We all sat in perfect silence staring at one another, weighing the odds. I was more afraid of having to pay for my own college than going to school with black people.

I raised my hand, "I choose public school."

My brothers and sisters made the same decision, so we moved as a family into the living room and nervously gathered around the television to see about our new school assignments. The system they revealed to us was mind-boggling. A student would spend grades 1- 4 at their home school, then starting in 5th grade you were bussed to a new school every two years! This meant that all five us were assigned to different schools, and our commutes were 45 minutes to an hour each way on the bus. Big yellow buses filled with either black kids or white kids crisscrossed their way back and forth throughout the county every day.

The next few years were chaotic. There were riots in the schools, daily fights, stabbings, and lots of drugs. There was a white girl in my school who had the most beautiful long, straight blond hair down past her waist. In the bathroom, three black girls with scissors dragged her into a stall and cut the hair up to her ears. She was horrified and so were we. Two white guys took a black boy out behind the school, beat him unconscious and left him there to be found by a cafeteria worker. We were stunned and couldn't believe white guys our age had that kind of anger in them.

In the mornings we weren't allowed in the building until the school bell rang; I'm guessing to prevent trouble. A white kid overdosed on the front stoop one morning while waiting to get into the building and an ambulance was called to move him so we could enter for class. And this was middle school! We were all messed up. There was a police car or two parked out front almost every day. It was crazy and very difficult to stay on task.

The tax base for the black schools had been so poor they'd had no resources and as such, very little education, which is why it was so crucial to do this integration. Many of the kids in my class couldn't even count sequentially, so if the teacher said "turn to page 247" they had no idea how to even begin. This made me really sad so I spent most of my class time helping them learn how to find the page.

There was one bright spot in all of this for me. Around this time the radio started blowing up with the music of a phenomenal group called the Jackson Five. Michael Jackson was twelve years old, the same age as I was and when I heard him swoon, "I'll Be There" and "Never Can Say Goodbye," my little pre-teen heart melted. I bought the 45 RPM records and played them over and over again to the perturbation of my family.

One day before class, my friend Gina was sharing that the Jackson Five was coming to Winston-Salem to play at the coliseum! Her father had agreed to take her to the concert, which I thought was brave, but she couldn't find any friends to go with her. They were too afraid and none of their parents would allow their child to potentially be the only white person in a crowd of 10,000 blacks.

I jumped at the chance to see Michael's Afro bounce back and forth as he sang the song, "ABC." "I'll ask my parents, Gina, maybe they'll let me go."

I brought it up at dinner that evening which caused much discussion around the table. My older sister was nervous and pointed out the dangers. Knowing how much I loved listening to their music, my parents did not say no immediately. I begged and begged and repeatedly mentioned that her father would be with us. I even offered to do extra chores to pay for the ticket.

Finally my dad relented. "Get me her father's phone number tomorrow and I'll call him, then I'll let you know the answer."

My heart leapt with joy at the possibility of going to my first ever, real live concert. Gina gave me her number, my dad called her father, and a decision was confirmed. I was going to see Michael Jackson!

I hugged my dad. "Right on! That is far out and groovy! I'm going to boogie down all night!" I screamed as I threw my arms in the air and shook my hips.

My father looked to my mom. "What did she just say?"

Gina and I both got a lot of flak at school. Some of our white friends actually quit speaking to us for a while, and the blacks said we had no right to infiltrate their music scene. I'll admit it was all a little scary, but our excitement far outweighed our fears.

The night of the concert finally arrived and we made our way to our seats through a sea of brown skin. Most people just stared at us, and a few actually gave us a thumbs up.

One man leaned down in my face with a threatening glare, "Why are you here?"

In my innocence I retorted, "Because I love Michael!"

"Well, all right then." He smiled and gave me a peace sign.

The rest of the evening went without incident. We watched Michael and his brothers dance and sing their hearts out all night. Gina and I sang along at the top of our lungs. I will forever be grateful to her father for taking us. It was a fantastic moment for me, never to be forgotten.

* * *

In the ninth grade I was bussed to yet another inner city school, a one-hour bus ride away. In the hall on the first day, I bumped into the largest black girl I'd ever laid eyes on. She was over 6 feet tall, thick and pure muscle.

"Oh, I'm sorry." I said. She shoved me off to the side, hurling me into the lockers.

My girlfriend grabbed me and whispered, "Don't talk to her, she'll stab you!"

Everyone was afraid of this big girl, even the guys, and it was like the parting of waters as she walked down the hall. I watched her from afar for a while and soon began to see her in a new way. I noticed she didn't have any friends. None. Even the black kids didn't talk to her. We were in gym class together and she always sat alone. I began to feel sorry for her, thinking she must be incredibly lonely. It tugged at my heart and I couldn't shake my feelings. Finally I decided I was going to do something about it.

The next day in the locker room we dressed out for gym class, putting on our shorts and shirts issued by the school. We headed up to the gym and waited for our teacher to come up. There sat the big girl, up against the wall on the other side of the basketball court. My heart began to race as I thought, this is it, the time is now, do it now, don't chicken out. I stood and as I began to walk away from my friends, they asked where I was going.

I walked across the court and could hear them talking, "What the hell is she doing?"

Slowly I walked straight toward her wanting to turn around with every step. My heart was in my throat. As I got close she looked up at me with a scowl on her face. By now, everyone was watching.

I reached into my pocket, held out my shaking hand and breathlessly asked, "Want a stick of gum?"

She stood suddenly and smacked my hand away with such a fierceness that the gum went flying across the court.

She yelled, "Girl, wha you doin! I'll cut you, I'll cut you!"

I back-pedaled across the gym, tears stinging my eyes for the embarrassment of it all and the fact that my hand hurt like hell. My girlfriends reamed me out for being stupid, and I wiped my tears with the back of my good hand. The teacher arrived and soon it was business as usual. But I was rattled to the core.

That night I lay in bed and cried out to God, Why would you put that in my heart only to embarrass me and create such a disaster? It didn't help her at all. Why God? I just don't understand.

Two days later it was gym class again, and as usual the whites were sitting against the wall on one side of the gym and the blacks on the other. We were laughing and playing around as we waited for the teacher to come up from the locker room. Suddenly my friend grabbed my arm.

"Oh shit!" she said as she turned my head toward the court.

The big black girl was coming across the floor headed straight toward me, walking with a dogged determination. My friends backed away and time stood still for me as my world suddenly went into slow motion. A sweat broke out on my brow. I'm going to die today. I felt myself pressing back into the wall bringing myself to a stand, wanting to become invisible. My heart was pounding out of my chest.

As she reached me, she grabbed my arm, yanked it out toward her and slapped my hand so hard I thought it was going to fall off. She turned and went back across the gym without saying a word. I shook my head trying to make sense of what had just happened and I pulled my stinging hand to my face to access the damage. There was something inside my palm. Huh? I opened my hand to find a dirty, gnarled wrapper with a peppermint inside.

I looked across the floor where she sat staring back at me. She gave me a barely discernible nod, and my knees buckled under me. I slid down the wall holding my mint, tears of joy and gratitude pouring down my face. Thank you, God. I reached her, I did.

Over the next few months we acknowledged each other with a nod or a look. I finally convinced a friend (only one would agree) to sit on the other side of the gym with me beside her. She didn't talk much, but didn't run us off or stab us either. We did get a few snarls from both whites and blacks about sitting together but I didn't care. And no one was about to give us a hard time as long as we were near her.

Down in the locker room, as we showered after class one day, the big girl stood and there was blood all over her towel and the bench. She had started her period.

I touched her arm. "You're bleeding."

"Shit, dat happen before but I couldn't find the cut."

"It's not a cut, it's your period."

"My what?"

Thinking she didn't hear me I said, "Your period, you know, your monthly."

"Wha you talkin' bout?"

Tears pooled in my eyes as I realized she didn't know what was happening to her body. It felt like this was a pretty big deal so I took her to the gym teacher's office by the locker room and explained the situation.

The teacher looked a little stunned and sad as well. "Thank you for bringing her to me, I'll take care of her."

Two days later back in gym class, the teacher called me into her office and said she'd discovered some things about our tall friend. Her mother died when she was a toddler and her father, who was an alcoholic, was basically raising her on the streets. My heart broke open with sadness and compassion. Well that explains a lot.

That spring I was in the school play and stayed after school for rehearsal. I went outside to wait for my dad to pick me up on his way home from work. As I stood by the side of the school two black men came around the corner and stopped suddenly.

They noticed me standing by myself and approached me talking to each other loud enough for me to hear, "You ever had a white one?"

"No, I never touched that milky skin, but I surely would like to."

"I think this just might be our chance."

The hair stood up on the back of my neck. I had nowhere to turn. Think, think, do something! They grabbed me, pulling at my top. From the corner of my eye I saw another dark movement. Oh no, three!

The third one jumped into the fray with a shiny glint of steel. A knife! Oh shit!

But that one screamed in a familiar voice, "Get off her! Back off or I will slice your face in two, you son a bitches!"

She gave one a right hook in the chin, which threw him to the ground. He got up and took off running. The other backed away and she chased after him with her knife yelling, "I'll cut your balls off, you bastard!"

I stood frozen, not believing what had just happened. Slowly I came to my senses and readjusted my clothing. My dad eventually pulled up and I dove into his car trying to hold it together. I was not about to tell him of the incident. He'd never let me stay after for rehearsal again.

To this day, I do not know where my big black friend came from. I don't know how she happened to be right there when I needed her the most. I'll never know, but I will be forever grateful and I will never ever forget her for taking care of me.

I would have thought time would have cured the racial ills, but even as I carried my extra son, David, to doctor's appointments and such, in the nineties, I got plenty of curious stares. Some people were even bold enough to ask with distain in their voice, why I had an African American boy with me.

I would smile and say, "Actually, he's African, and I have him with me because he's a member of our family."

Chapter Eight

The flight attendant snaps me back to the present as she sits my dinner on the tray in front of me, "You like wine with dinner?"

"How much does that cost?"

"Oooooh is free, you pay soooo much for flight."

I am delightfully surprised, "Then yes, thank you, I'll have some red, please."

After a scrumptious three course meal and many hours in flight we land in Rome. It is a fuel stop on the end of the runway and we cannot leave the plane, but we are allowed to move freely about the cabin while we wait. I meet all kinds of wonderful people of every nationality, traveling for many different reasons. I am approached by one of only three other white people on the plane.

The man looks around, blatantly noticing that I am alone. He holds out his hand to shake mine, "Hello, where are you headed to?"

"I'm going to Tanzania."

"What takes you there?"

I gave him a condensed version of my story, and how I ended up on this plane.

"That takes a lot of courage. Good for you." He smiles.

I laugh. "Part of me thinks it's good and part of me thinks it's crazy. How about you? Where are you headed?"

He grins. "Oh, me and my two buddies are going on a cruise."

"Oh wow, where to?"

"Off the east coast of Africa."

"That sounds like cool trip, how long is your cruise?"

"Three days."

"No way," I grin. "Where are you really going?"

"Really, we are going to be on a ship."

I'm laughing now. "No one in their right mind flies sixteen plus hours for a three-day cruise. What are you really doing?"

He lowers his voice. "Okay, you've got me there, but please keep this to yourself. We are ex-military and now we provide security and rescue. A major company has hired us to take out the pirates on a ship off the coast of Somalia and bring back the hostages."

I am shocked at his revelation, and I am not laughing anymore. "Do you mean you are going to smuggle yourselves onto that ship and take them out?"

"Yes, that is our plan."

A thousand movie scenes play out in my head as I imagine the danger they will place themselves in to get these hostages to safety. I ask him about this lifestyle and how they all feel about the risks.

He shrugs. "It's what we know."

I put my hand on his arm. "Oh wow. Well thank you for what you do."

He smiles and puts his hand on top of mine. "And by the way, if you encounter any danger whatsoever while in Africa, here is my card. I won't be in Tanzania, but I have connections. If you have any trouble at all contact me, I know people here who can protect you."

I am taken aback by his offer of assistance. It frightens me a little as I have not thought of being in that type of drastic situation on my trip. And yet, I also feel a little comfort that if something does happen I now have a lifeline. I admire the fact that they do this for people, even putting their own lives at stake. I take his card and give him a heartfelt thank you as the flight attendants call us back to our seats.

I am flying to Africa! With all the many preparations finally behind me, I settle in comfortably, preparing to sleep the rest of the night, breathing a sigh of relief that I am finally on my long awaited journey.

Soon the gravity of my situation rises up in my mind, and I begin to feel anxious. When I was in Costa Rica, my purpose was to decompress, have a meltdown and attain certain goals. In Africa I am looking for an entirely new purpose in life. Before now, my main focus in life was to be a good wife and mother, and I feel somewhat accomplished in those areas, yet both of those are over. So who am I now? If I strip it all away, what will I find? For all of my adult life my decisions have always included the welfare of my children and my husband. What will determine that now? What will my voice sound like when it is my own? A sudden lack of self-confidence, and by that I mean panic, wells up in my heart. Twelve hours later I land in Tanzania, Africa.

Africa was in my heart for several reasons, but when I decided to come here, my first thoughts were that of a little bit of excitement and a large dose of fear. How would I even begin to know where to start? I saw all the same news clips and media about Africa that everyone else saw, and I had the same limited and scary visions of what it might be like. I decided it would be best for me to go in initially with an organization, rather than show up on the huge continent traveling alone, as a woman. I would start with the NGO (non-governmental organization) Cross Cultural Solutions, to help me get acclimated to the culture, learn the language, and begin to see where I could be of service.

I stay at a nice resort area near the airport and have my own hut to sleep in. I wander the property in awe of the fact that I am here. How can life take such crazy turns? If you had told me two years ago, "your husband is going to fall in love with someone else, your marriage will end and you will go live in Africa." I would have said you were out of your mind, yet here I am.

In the morning a man named Ibra picks me up in an older, but clean, 15-passenger van which has seen its fair share of use, and drives me to Moshi. He is on the staff at Cross Cultural Solutions, and was sent to bring me to base camp, which will be my home for several months. He honks the horn as we pull up to the gate, and from inside a security guard opens the doors. As we drive through I catch my first sight of the compound. It is meticulously groomed with hedges and green grass. I discover they keep it this way with machetes. Yes, that's also how they "mow" the lawn. The power here is human, not motorized.

CCS houses thirty people at a time. They feed us, shelter us, and will send us out into the community to work for other organizations every day. Our placements range from orphanages, to schools, hospitals, women's groups, centers for street children, HIV testing clinics and so on. They also educate us about African culture, the traditions of the Kilimanjaro Region, give us Kiswahili lessons, and completely immerse us in Africa. The cross culturing part is that we learn from them and they learn from us. The first two days are orientation about how to live in CCS and Moshi, our job assignments, and how we can all live together in harmony as we navigate our way through volunteerism in some very difficult areas. Each of us has a different story of how we got here and why, and all are fascinating.

Our days start in the open-air dining area, where our cook prepares delicious meals of rice, meat, spinach, and the sweetest fresh fruits. After breakfast we take our malaria pills, wash our dishes, and when we start our jobs, will jump in the van and go to work. In the afternoons CCS brings guest speakers in to educate us on things such as gender roles, education in Africa, traditional healers, the HIV/AIDS epidemic here, and Kiswahili lessons.

They will also take us on trips to different villages and areas. At times, we'll go into town to run errands and spend time getting to know people in our community. Then in the few spare moments we have left, there are the details of life to attend to, such as laundry. We wash it by hand in a bucket, hang it out on the line, and then iron every item. Yes, every single article, which includes, our underwear. No, it's not because Africans have a weird ironing obsession. While drying on the line a certain bug attaches itself and lays eggs in the clothing. Ironing kills the eggs, so every article must be pressed with the heat. And maybe this is too much information, but have you ever tried to iron a bra? Not to mention that your personal items are out on the line for everyone to see. It is a little uncomfortable at first, but living in such close quarters with so many people, we get over having any personal or private space very quickly.

In the evenings you might find us across the street. CCS has a very strict policy against having any alcohol on the premises, and this is a good rule. Fortunately though, a very resourceful and clever African woman named Grace lives across the street, and has turned her side yard into the Mzungu Bar. Mzungu technically means "foreigner," but really it means, "white people." She provides local beer, brewed in Tanzania because she's brilliantly figured out that she has a captive audience of 30 people who may need a place to debrief and share experiences from the day.

After a full day we find ourselves back in our rooms. We pray that the electricity stays on so our fan will run throughout the night. It usually doesn't. It's not enough that we climb into short bunk beds, in the stifling heat, but then we basically wrap ourselves in plastic with our mosquito nets. We are usually awakened around 4:00 a.m. by roosters, and loud prayers being chanted at the Muslim mosque nearby. We eventually climb out of bed, decide we wouldn't want to be anywhere else, and start all over again. Orientation is over and now the real fun begins.

My alarm goes off and I find myself tangled in sheets and a mosquito net. The bottom sheet, for some mysterious reason, does not go all the way to the end of the bed. It's not fitted; rather, it is a small flat sheet which is tucked in on the sides, and it doesn't reach but to my shins. Consequently, the sheets bunch up all night and I mostly sleep on a plastic mattress. I somehow manage to untangle myself from the web and try to get a handle on the butterflies in my stomach. It is my first day on the job, and I have no idea what that might entail except that I will give to Africa by working until noon each day. I know that my placement is at a Women's Empowerment Center. They work with women, helping them to start village community banks where they can take out micro loans, and start a business. I also know they run a small vocational school for teenagers who wouldn't otherwise be able to attend school. CCS is very good about matching volunteer skills with each placement, and this seems like the perfect fit for my resume.

The van pulls out of CCS at 7:30 a.m. with Abby and I on board. Abby has already been working there for several months, and on the way she fills me in.

"Mama Adia is one of the founders and is also the director. She's determined, driven, and downright intimidating, but I love her because she also has a quick wit and a funny sense of humor. She's African, but had the good fortune to complete her studies in Canada and Germany, and then returned to use her knowledge to make a difference in her beloved Tanzania. Wait until you see what she's accomplished."

"She's scary, huh?" It is all I latched onto because everything in my world seems scary these days.

"Yes, very." She laughs.

We bang on a huge metal door, and a young woman in a school uniform, opens it from the other side. "*Karibuni*" You are both welcomed. We enter a courtyard, which is being swept with a tree branch, by another student. We are led to a small sitting area off to the side and told to please wait. We watch as students all over the compound clean and scrub, mopping the floors by hand with a rag while bent over in half. From around the building I hear a soft voice say, "Good morning, Mama Adia."

A large voice booms back, "What's so good about this morning?! Tell me!"

The young girl jumps back just a bit, and I am alarmed, but I can see as Mama comes around the corner that she has a huge grin on her face.

"Well," the girl stammers. "Kilimanjaro has poked her face out to say hello, and maybe the rains will come this afternoon and we will be blessed." She stands with her hands clasped nervously behind her back.

"Well then, I guess it is a good day. Very good English." Her congratulatory slap on the back sends the girl's frail body into the wall, which goes largely unnoticed because Mama has already turned to me. She wears a dress rather than an African kanga and her tall stature moves with a stride of authority.

"And what do we have here? A new volunteer?"

Abby chimes in, "Yes, Mama, this is Lucetta from America." She shakes my hand, and holds it.

"Well, you are most welcome here. Thank you for coming."

At that moment, three ladies emerge from around the corner, and a four-wheel drive pulls into the courtyard. Mama Adia glances up.

"Ah, I see we are ready. Abby, you stay here to teach the girls English. Oh, and Abby teach computers too because we have electricity today. Tell CCS that Lucetta from America won't be back until dinner."

She points at me. "You. Do you have water?"

Wide eyed I answer, "Yes, ma'am."

I have no idea what is happening and where I will be all day long until dinner, but I have no choice. She is my boss and I have signed up to do this job.

She waves me on, "*Twende*." Let's go.

* * *

As Americans, we are generally in control of our own lives at all times. Certainly there are things we have to do like work, pay bills, abide by the laws of the land, but even in those things, we choose how, when, or where they may happen. We may have to reap the consequences if we pay a bill late or don't pay our taxes, but still we are in control. This makes us comfortable. We don't like it when we don't know what happens next. What I have learned from my journey to this point is that control is an illusion. We don't ever really have a handle on everything like we think we do. I have been learning not to be afraid of giving up control because sometimes the world has so much more to offer if we just take the chance.

With trepidation, I climb into the four-wheel drive with my new boss, and the three women. Mama Adia speaks in Swahili with one of the ladies for quite some time. We barrel down the road and I absorb the sights of Africa with childlike eyes. We turn off the tarmac and onto a dirt road, driving for an hour into the hills at the base of Kilimanjaro, but not covering much ground. The going is slow as we alternate between opening the windows because of the heat and closing them due to the dust.

Finally Mama Adia speaks to me. "These women are from Uganda, where they work at a women's center. Last year, the Archdiocese, funded a trip for me to go see what they do, and now they have provided the means for them to come here. Their center is having trouble with women not paying back their loans, so we will teach them our system. Today we are going to a village to see a VICOBA in action. A VICOBA is a **Vi**llage **Co**mmunity **Ba**nk. This bank provides micro loans to members so they can start small businesses."

We pull up to a small white building and suddenly singing women surround our car. They smile, wave and sing a welcome song as we make our way out of the vehicle. They are all dressed in their best kangas, the traditional fabric African women wrap around their bodies. They press against us and take my purse and water bottle from my hand. I am alarmed, but look over to see them taking belongings from the others as well, and they seemed unconcerned. They carry our load for us as they continue to sing us into the building. This is my first exposure to the generous and considerate hospitality that Tanzanians are known for.

When we enter, I see a few benches, a table in the front of the room and chairs behind it. They lead us up to the front to be seated in a plastic chair. The others file onto the benches. I feel like a dignitary. A meeting commences.

From literally out of nowhere a metal box appears with three locks around the sides. Mama Adia says something in Swahili and four women gather around the box. She speaks again and they simultaneously open the locks, while the fourth stands as a witness to the event. Upon opening the box, they withdraw small booklets, several register pads and Tanzanian shillings. I am witnessing the operations of their bank.

The brilliant system is this: a group of 30 people in a village get together. Within this group of 30 there are "magnets" of five each. These five people are close friends and have agreed to vouch for each other's loans. If someone has trouble with repayment the others help, brainstorm, or ante up. This is how they have a high rate of repayment, and in fact, some women are paying off their loans before the time limit of four months is completed. The metal box is wrapped and stored in an inconspicuous covering, and is moved to various locations frequently for security. The "Key Keepers" each have a key they hide, and they must all be present in the same place to open the box. This keeps any one person from having access. Each person has a number on a booklet, no names, and the money is recorded in the form of the stamp of an animal. That way if the box was stolen, or broken into, no one in the village would know who had how much money to then go rob them. The entire system is about accountability and security.

Joining the bank is not free. Each person must want in badly enough to save up and contribute a small amount. (Five dollars American, which can take them forever to save up) Then, seed money is added to the pot from The Empowerment Center through donors. When members take out a loan, the interest is taken out immediately and paid up front. A portion of this interest goes to new loans, a small portion to supplies for running of the group, and another two portions go into different accounts. One is for education and the other is for medical. If someone needs help with school fees for the children, or someone has a medical emergency, they can take out a loan. These loans are interest-free, as they are designed to help care for the community. At the end of one year they "Break the Circle," and all monies are divided up. The seed money always stays in the bank, and members can sign up for another year.

I find this completely fascinating as I watch women come forward to repay their debt, and take out new loans. This process takes quite a while and as it ends, I begin to smell a delicious aroma. Several women come out of a small back room with pots of cooked vegetables. A woman comes to us with a basin and a pitcher of water. She pours the water over our hands, washing them before we eat. They serve us plates piled high and give us soda (a luxury), and utensils (they eat with their hands).

Afterwards Mama turns to me, "Now we will go see the fruits of their labor."

We pile back into the car and visit several members' homes where the loans have made a huge impact on their lives. Culturally, the women stay home, cook, clean, raise children, and are not educated. They must ask their husbands for money for food, school fees or clothes and sometimes, even if they can leave the property. If there is not enough money, they must make do, and children don't have the chance to learn. If there is a small amount they will send only the boys to school. The thinking is, "Why would we spend money on the girls when they will be married young and increase their husband's household, not ours. They don't need to read to cook and clean."

These women, however, with their new businesses are now sending their girls to school, and are able to feed their children every day. They told me, through Mama's translation, that their husbands are treating them with more respect because they aren't begging for money all the time. The women's self-esteem has improved, and their husbands aren't as oppressive. The entire family has been affected.

Back at the meeting place again, Mama Adia asks me to speak. I tell them I worked with a women's center in America. I talk to them about their courage, and strength, and thank them for letting me learn from them. They are surprised to hear that foreign women wrestle with some of the same issues they do, as they sincerely thought it was only the plight of African women. They seem encouraged and a little less isolated by this news, and say that it means we were all sisters.

The women begin singing again, and motion me around the table. As they sing, they spin me around and wrap me in a kanga, which is my gift. They turn me back around to find tears pouring down my face. They have so little, yet they fed me and gave me precious fabric. An elderly woman comes forward. She wipes my tears with her rough brown hands, and gently kisses each of my cheeks.

* * *

It is after dark when they drop me back at CCS. My new friends can't believe I have been gone all day on my very first day, and they want to hear my stories right away. I give them a short version as I am exhausted and famished. I fall into bed and wrap my mosquito net around me.

As I leave for work on my second day, I am prepared for anything. I have a full bottle of water, sunscreen, snacks, toilet paper for the squatty potty or the bushes, and mosquito repellant. I continue this practice of loading up my purse because in Africa you never know what might happen in a day; a wonderful opportunity might come your way or you could experience a breakdown on the side of the road for many hours. Who knows?

Again we knock on the big metal door at the Center, and a student greets us with a big smile. This time Mama Adia and the three Ugandan women are already in the sitting area. After pleasantries are exchanged, Mama announces that we were going to a Maasai village for discussions concerning the starting of a bank. Earlier in the month, the Maasai women sent word to Mama Adia that they wanted to start a VICOBA.

This is unprecedented and groundbreaking news for several reasons. The Maasai have always been pastoral, which means they are nomadic and move their tribes according to the rains and the grazing for their cattle, goats, and donkeys. Being constantly on the move have kept the Maasai isolated from outside influences, which is how they have maintained their unusual culture and traditions until today. They subsist on milk, meat, and drink the blood of their cattle. In recent years some of the Maasai are beginning to settle, moving less often. This particular tribe has been in the Rimit area for two years now, and Mama has been teaching them to plant vegetables so their diet will be healthier. The fact that these women asked for a VICOBA inferred not only permanence, but also that they were ready to move forward in their own personal development.

Traditionally the Maasai women do not read or write. They build the small dirt and straw huts, cook and take care of the children. Their husbands have many wives, and rotate from house to house. The women have no say regarding to whom they are married, anything their husband does, issues about their home, or within the village. They are voiceless. Women are at the bottom of the Maasai tribe. They are invisible servants, and until recently, never knew there could be another way. Evidently, within the last week, the women met privately and decided they did not want to include the men in their VICOBA because then they would not be able to speak. They sent word to Mama Adia about their decision and she knew she must visit them in person to discuss this matter.

We drive again in a hired vehicle, through the town of Moshi to a rural area on the other side. We ride for a while, passing an enormous sugar plantation on the way. The plantation owner created a man-made canal for irrigation, which runs alongside the road, and for several miles, families are washing their clothes and bathing in the canal. Our driver stops at one point for me to take a picture of Kilimanjaro, who is showing her face. Even the Tanzanians stop to gaze when she peeks out from the clouds that constantly surround her high altitude. We continue driving on dirt roads for quite a while, through the middle of a low plain filled with scrub brush, when suddenly the driver stops. We wait.

Mama turns from the front seat. "They will find us because they have seen our dust."

Within a few minutes, from out of the brush comes a large group of smiling, singing Maasai women. It is the first time I have ever seen a Maasai with their beaded jewelry and long pierced earlobes. I greet them in my limited Swahili, but realize they are speaking another language. They each shake our hands, and bow as they lead us through the bush to an area with a tree. Thank goodness for the tree! Underneath, in the shade, they place several benches and a small table. Everyone settles into the compact area and the leader greets Mama and the rest of us. A few of the women speak Swahili, but mostly they speak Maasai, so time is allowed for interpretation.

Mama Adia takes the floor. She speaks to the women of how happy she is for their courage to speak up for themselves, but explains that if the women completely alienate the men, they will become suspicious, resentful, and angry. It will cause many problems for the women. This is why VICOBAs always allow men. For the most part they are filled with women, but the men are always welcome, and they know this.

An hour of debate persists until finally Mama Adia speaks to me in English, "We have discussed this issue, and I have agreed to say to the elders of the tribe that we will start with the women first and then we will make a group for the men. At the same time we will begin to form a singing choir of men, women, and children to share with the world the beautiful gift of their unbelievable voices. I think this will keep peace among the tribe, and it will go well for all."

Suddenly, water and sodas appear from out of nowhere. They are only for us, the honored guests, and it would be very impolite to refuse the gift. I feel guilty drinking in front of everyone knowing they are just as hot and thirsty as I am. Mama Adia takes over again and begins moving people into groups.

She breaks her own rule for the first time, of limiting the VICOBA to 30 people. Thirty-six women have shown up and she can't bear the thought of losing any, so she rearranges the magnet groups. I can't understand the language, so I don't really know what is going on. This movement goes on for almost an hour, as Mama patiently moves the women here and there. Finally, it is determined that the next time they meet, it will be to start the VICOBA.

As the meeting draws to a close, Mama asks me to speak again. What could I say to these Maasai? She says that as a foreign woman, whatever my words, will be valuable to them. I speak of the courage they have to live their life in a new way, and that if they are always unified and help each other, it will be easier for them. I mention the wisdom of the advice of including the men, and encourage them to bring their husbands along with them in some way, throughout the journey. I bring greetings from their sisters in America, and thank them for the honor of being included in their lives on this day. They gather, sing us back out of the bush to our vehicle and kiss us goodbye.

On the way home I am awestruck at what I have just experienced. I sit quietly in the back because there is a roaring in my soul. I have to process the impact of what I have just witnessed. Silently, I hold all of this in my heart.

As we round the corner nearing my CCS home I finally speak, "Mama, why did it take so long for you to put the women into their groups? What was that about?"

Mama Adia doubles over with laughter. She laughs and laughs. It takes her a moment to catch her breath before she can even answer. We all begin giggling just watching her laugh.

Eventually she says, "There was an elderly woman, whose sons had so many wives, that it took me forever to figure out a group where she was not the mean old mother-in-law!"

The entire van collapses in a fit of laughter.

* * *

"Where is everyone else? Are you the only one there?"

I laugh, "No, I'm not the only one here, the other volunteers are all at dinner. I left early so I could Skype with you two."

My mother's sweetness comes through the screen, "What about your dinner? You need to eat too, don't you?"

"What I need more than food is to see your faces and hear your voice. And don't worry mom, I made a plate and I'll eat when we are done. So how are you?"

"We're fine. My knee is getting better; Pa's been taking good care of me. We're missing you."

We catch up on the entire family and Pa chimes in, "I like this Skype thing. When the kids heard I was doing this with you, they said, 'If grandpa is doing this we better learn it!' I imagine they'll email you soon to set a Skype date. So how is Africa?"

"It's good."

"Well, you left with a big heartache, so what are you teaching the world there? To be mad, sad or happy?" Pa asks in his usual truth-telling straightforward way.

I smile, "I guess I'm trying to show them love, Pa. I'm working hard to keep my own junk out of this."

My mom leans in, "So how are you, really?"

"I'm doing okay, Mom. I live right at the base of Mt. Kilimanjaro and I wake up to this view every morning." I turn my laptop to show them Kili, trying to change the subject.

"You know you always have a home to come back to."

"Thank you. I love you both so much. Don't worry about me I'm all right. I have to run now for an evening meeting. Let's Skype again soon."

I see my mom reach for a tissue at the corner of the screen, "You take care, my precious one."

Tears spill over my cheeks as I shut down my computer.

* * *

One afternoon, Cross Cultural Solutions brings in a local Adventure Company called Pristine Trails and they offer a good price to take us on safari in the Serengeti. Mussa, the owner says, "There is a holiday on Monday so you won't have to work, and if you take one more day we can get there, see the animals and get back."

A moral dilemma ensues as we decide if we are willing to come all the way to Africa, pay to volunteer to help people, and then take a day off. Several of the volunteers are only here for three weeks, so this is a hard decision for them. I am here for three months so I am fully on board at not passing up this opportunity.

Those of us who sign up, pile into the massive Range Rovers specifically designed with pop-up tops to fully see and experience the animals.

Mussa gives us the rules. "It is illegal to get out of the vehicle while there and in fact you can't even dangle arms or legs outside of the truck. These are wild animals and you never know what might happen. Also, when we camp the second night, you cannot get out of your tent after dark. We will be camping in the middle of the Serengeti, and animals will roam around our tents. So be certain you go to the bathroom before bed."

Well, that sounds exciting. We barrel down the road for several hours and stop at a store for a bathroom break and provisions. We discovered it was the birthday of two of our friends on the trip. We sneak and buy several bottles of Champagne, hiding them in our packs; we head on down the road.

In the afternoon we stop in the middle of nowhere on a high plain, and visit a Massai tribe. This particular tribe is well known for their jumping skills. They can jump five feet in the air from standing still. It's crazy to watch. How do they do this? They sing to us with their beautiful voices, which they are also known for, give us a tour of their mud huts and teach us a little about their customs. I already know much of this from my work at the center, but the others are blown away at their lifestyle, especially when the tribe leader explains to us that they take their spear and poke a tiny hole in a vein of the throat of a cow and drain blood into a wooden bowl, which they then drink. The cow meanders off as though he has just given blood at a blood bank. Several of my friends panic because they are afraid we will be asked to drink blood from their cattle and they slowly back themselves out of the circle and head for the truck. Thankfully, we are spared their custom.

Back on the road we travel several more hours and finally arrive at our campsite for the night on the edge of the Serengeti. We get out of the trucks to discover the staff of Pristine had gone ahead of us to set up each of our tents and are cooking dinner in a pavilion, which has fire pits. Our tents are placed under a huge Tree of Life on top of a big hill with miles and miles of Serengeti around us. I have a moment of euphoria as I examine my life in disbelief. How in the world did I get here? This is my life now and I could have never imagined this. Tears of gratefulness pool in my eyes, as I begin to embrace the thought that maybe all of this happened for a purpose I can't yet see.

My thoughts are interrupted as Craig whispers, "Look, it's an elephant coming our way."

We have been told to stay quiet around the animals so we don't alarm them, causing them to attack or stampede. We sit quietly watching Mr. Elephant lumber through our camp smelling things along the way. I've never been this close to an elephant before and there has always been a fence between them and me. I certainly never thought of them as dangerous until now. He could crush me with one stomp of his foot. He could destroy our camp if he goes on a rampage. And yet, he strolls casually on down the hill. We let out a collective sigh of relief and grab each other, stunned as we begin to grasp the thought that each of us made our way to Africa to work, and here we are on safari. Appreciation fills the air as we are called to dinner.

At some point Jenn left the group earlier and told the cook it was Craig and Belle's birthday. After dinner, the cook comes out with two plates. Each holds a white mound with a big candle in each one. It looks like cake, but how is that possible? We sing happy birthday and crack open the Champagne. Celebration abounds and we laugh at how they will never forget this birthday the rest of their lives. Upon closer inspection we see that each cake is actually a half of a watermelon turned upside down. The outside has been shaved revealing the only the white next layer. Brilliant! We laugh as Craig serves us slices of watermelon "cake." I love the resourcefulness of Africa. It never fails to come through in some way.

We load up our trucks in the morning and move out to see the animals. An hour in, we pull up to the entrance of the park and have a potty break as our guides purchase their permits. In my mind I imagine we will sit in the trucks all day and see a few animals every now and then. I could not be more wrong. Every few moments we run across another pack or family. Zebras, lions, warthogs, cheetahs, baboons, giraffes, monkeys, dic dics, buffalo, wildebeest, elephants, flamingos, all right here, often just a few feet away from us! This is truly like no other experience. Ever.

As the day wears on, we move to a new campsite in the park. Again the staff has thought of every detail for our comfort, given we are camping. After dinner we sit around a campfire telling stories about the day. The staff sends us to our tents before they extinguish the fire because that is what has been keeping the lions at bay. Once we are safely tucked in, they will put out the fire.

We hear the lions roar all night as they wander around us padding nearby. To hear it live, rather than on a movie screen, is something to behold, and worth staying awake for. I unzip the corner of the tent and reach for my water bottle sitting just outside in the cool night. Jenn, my tent mate, suddenly awakens and pounces on top of me terrified, which scares the shit out of me.

"It's a lion!" she yells.

"Hahaha, it's okay, it was me getting my water bottle," I push her off and calm her nerves and mine.

In the morning we pack up, ramble through the park some more and then head to Ngorongoro Crater, another gorgeous place where the animals live. We stay for the better part of the day and actually get to see a rhino. They are almost extinct and a rhino sighting is a big deal in the world of safari. After lunch we caravan back toward Moshi and

CCS. Our trip is not over yet though. Oh no, Pristine Trails can't leave it there that we've just had the most amazing time of our lives. Oh no, on the way home we stop one more time, to ride a camel.

* * *

Back at home base we quickly fall into our routines. I find the African children to be so beautiful. As a mzungu (white person) in Africa, to the children, I am often the greatest source of wonder and entertainment imaginable. They stand and solemnly stare in amazement with their gorgeous eyes wide open, until I acknowledge their piercing looks with a huge grin and a wave of my hand. Startled, they suddenly burst into the biggest smile, and wave back.

I say the easiest greeting for the children, "*Mambo*?" How's it going?

To which the standard reply is, "*Poa*." It's cool.

They giggle because I know some Swahili, and always wave to me again. This process seems to happen every single time. With the tiniest of children, though, their wonder includes shyness. Some have never seen a white person and they don't know what to think, especially when the Martian is speaking directly to them. They never get the nerve to wave and smile, but simply continue staring. I *mambo* them and their little mouths automatically form the word *poa*, but no sound can be uttered from their throats. To me, this is adorable. I always wave again to let them know everything is okay. Most children just want to touch white skin to see if it feels the same as theirs.

It is rare to see a temper tantrum, or hear a baby cry in Africa. They are silent observers studying their world intently. Some of their quietness may have to do with being malnourished. I have often seen small young boys that I thought were eight years old only to find out they were sixteen or eighteen, their growth stunted by poor nutrition.

At some point around three or four years of age the children gain their voice, but it is only for their peers and teachers, for other than that they are supposed to speak only when spoken to. They grow up quickly here with real responsibilities such as looking after younger siblings, tending animals, gathering water or wood for cooking, which could be a walk of several miles. The fortunate ones can be seen at the crack of dawn, in their uniforms, walking to school, which could also be a long hike. Even young children make it by themselves back and forth, except for rainy days. When it rains the mud is a slippery mess and no one attempts to get to school. It's like a snow day in Raleigh.

Once at school, most children are excited to learn, even with meager resources, and too few teachers available. The children are given a cup of porridge, and for some this could be their only meal of the day. If they are given a pencil they break it in half to share it with a friend. They sharpen their pencils with a razor blade, which they keep in their pockets! Some volunteers take makeshift first aid kits to school because the children are always slicing themselves. We wish CCS had thought to have us bring pencil sharpeners. At the end of the day, if you collect the pencils, some children cry. It's heartbreaking, but what is a teacher to do? If the children take them home there will be no pencil for tomorrow. Swahili is taught in the primary school because the government wants to preserve the language, which is a good idea, but secondary school is taught in English. Many kids fall by the wayside in high school if they were not able to get English lessons as a child.

Despite these hardships the young children seem unbelievably happy. They play and laugh all the time. They are children, though, and sometimes they tease and are mean to each other, but for the most part they genuinely care. Somewhere along the way, the reality of their life begins to set in and the older children become pensive. The smile fades and you can see it on their faces. The boys will hopefully stay in school and scrap out a living for their families. The girls will drop out of school at a young age to marry, have babies and keep house. Marriage is their only option, as they have no other means for a roof over their heads and food, because women can't own property and most can't have a job. If they are not married by age twenty or so, then it is considered too late, and men will say, "something must be wrong with her."

Volunteers always try to talk to the young girls, and be their role model.

They say, "I stayed in school, I am twenty-four, I live by myself, I make my own money, and I didn't have to ask my father's permission to come here. Stay in school and you can do the same." They hope their influence gets through to at least a few.

Randi, a fellow volunteer, and I were discussing the wonderful, caring nature of the children we'd met in Moshi. Randi said she could sum it up in one story for me: while she was teaching at an orphanage, Randi decided to hold a spelling bee as a way for the students to practice English. The teenagers were so excited, and as the bee went on, people were eliminated. It came down to two girls. One girl got stuck trying to spell her word, and the other whispered the answer into her ear.

Randi asked the girl, "Why are you helping her, don't you want to win?"

The girl seemed a little surprised at the question and said, "But she is my friend. Why would I not want to help her?"

* * *

One of my roommates is named Sarah, but there are too many Sarahs at CCS, so we changed it to Seri. Seri's volunteer job was with AMKA School. They just recently opened a second school called AMKA STEP UP in an impoverished village, and Seri, who has a teaching degree, is to be the nursery school teacher. Oliveri, the other teacher there, teaches the primary age kids in the one-room school, and Seri's classroom is on the concrete porch. She has only a couple of students, and asks the director about it.

"Don't worry. The village has to come to know us and trust us." The director explains, "It will take time for parents to bring their children."

Seri comes in from work one day, flops down on the bed and sighs. "The porch looks a little like a prison cell. I think some paint would brighten it up for the kids."

"I love to paint, I'll help you," says Jenn, one of our other roommates.

I chime in. "Me too, I want to help."

From out in the sitting area we hear Craig's voice, "Count me in."

Within moments of the dream, Seri has a paint crew. She seems a little floored and says, "Well, okay then, how about this weekend?"

Seri clears it with the powers that be, grabs her Tshillings (Tanzanian Shillings), and we go to buy paint. By Saturday word has spread and more volunteers show up ready to work. We all agree when we see it for the first time that, although it is a great porch, it looks pretty dismal.

We laugh and cut up as we paint for several hours, putting on the first coat. The concrete soaks up the bright colors of paint. What a difference it makes in the entire feel of the porch classroom! We are thrilled and can't wait to see it with a second coat. We celebrate with a beer at Mzungu Bar.

We wait for Seri to get home from work on Monday to hear what the kids had to say about their new room. She tells us they each stopped cold at the door as it registered in their brains, then they shouted with delight and went to touch the paint. They ran their little hands all over the bright beautiful blue and green. One boy actually hugged the wall. The mood of the classroom was lifted.

The next Sunday we go back for a second coat, and decide to paint the back wall as well. While we paint, an idea comes to Jenn. Her placement is at Upendo Art School for kids where they teach art in addition to the basic subjects. She tells Seri that she knows Josie, an African teenage boy, who is an artist that volunteers at her school helping with the children.

She offers, "He's a really good artist and I'll bet he would come over and paint some animals on this wall for you."

Seri loves the idea, so Jenn calls Josie. After a consultation with Seri and Jenn, Josie is so excited that he calls Jenn every day and asks, "Is this the day I paint? Can I paint yet?"

His enthusiasm is contagious, and by the time paint day does come around he has two of his roommates who want to help as well. Josie, Nickie, and Rogie live in a ghetto in the village of Rau. Here, a ghetto means something different from what we know. It means that these boys are underage and they live on their own in a small house. For whatever reason, they no longer have parents taking care of them, so they survive by living together and pooling resources. There are five of them in this ghetto, one being a little brother who is quite young. These three are all artists who try to sell their paintings whenever they can to buy food.

The boys come and paint the most fantastic zebras and elephants all over the wall.

Every Monday when the kids come back to school there is something new, and wall hugging becomes the new normal.

"How about some numbers too?" Seri asks as she admires the boy's work.

I muse, "Seri, when word spreads about this porch, the village will know you care."

The boys show up faithfully. They paint numbers and the alphabet on the wall.

After several weekends of work, as they near the end, Josie asks Seri and Jenn if they can paint a mural of Zanzibar on the far wall, "Please give us more time and allow us to paint a beautiful mural for the children. It will take two days. You must say yes."

Seri tears up. They have already invested so many hours and aren't being paid.

Jenn looks a little concerned, "Boys, my time at CCS is up and I must return to the States. Can I trust you to finish this to completion?"

They enthusiastically agree to finish.

She smiles. "In that case, here is money for cab fare to get you back and forth. If you have time to make the hour walk, then you can use the money for food, but the cab fare is here so you will be able to finish for Seri."

She takes the boys out for a goodbye lunch to thank them, and they eat everything in sight, getting extras to take home to the others.

The new school year always starts after Christmas, which is their summer break. In the meantime, Seri volunteers at several orphanages, which don't take a break. It is fun and rewarding, but Seri is excited to get back to her own little classroom.

Even Cross Cultural Solutions could not have imagined the cross culture that happened on Seri's porch. On the first day of the new school year Seri walks down the road toward the school and notices a crowd gathered on the lawn. Why aren't they on the porch? Did something happen? As she draws near she realizes they *are* on the porch. They are spilling out onto the lawn. Seri stops with a gasp. There are 18 children and their parents waiting for her to start class.

* * *

So many different things are happening every day in Africa that I can barely process each moment. Our days are a whirlwind of startling new experiences and activities. The excitement and energy that flows through home base is electric, although tampered with great moments of sadness at distressing things we witness. It often seems that in Tanzania you can see the most beautiful thing you've ever seen and the most difficult, all in the same moment. And that could possibly be every minute. The poverty constantly sends everyone into emotional overload. Africa is very complex. It would take years to even begin to understand the complicated nature of this continent. I watch as my fellow volunteers pour their hearts into their work, trying to make even a small difference in the quality of life for these beautiful people. They love every moment of their time spent at CCS. But something very different is happening to me.

When I landed in Africa, something in me was altered, and it has continued to plague me as the weeks go on. I go through the activities and events with awe and wonder, but I am not myself at all. I can't understand what is happening inside of me. Am I depressed? I've never been depressed in my life.

I realize this has become evident to others because several of my fellow volunteers call me "the quiet one." I'm sure anyone who knows me could not ever imagine this happening, and I myself am shocked. Quiet is something I have never been called in my life, but I realize here it is true. I have been quiet, and they don't know otherwise about me. Words will not come to my feelings, and I can't figure out what is happening. I find myself deep in thought at times analyzing the moment, rather than living in it as I have always done before. I've always been passionate about life, and have been the one to dive right in one hundred percent, but instead I am numb.

I awake in the morning and my roommate Nancy asks me how I slept the night before. As I say the words, "Not very well," I slump back on the bed, a lump forms in my throat and the secret of my feelings come pouring out. She listens intently.

"Lucetta, I think you may be getting a little ahead of yourself. You've only been here for a short while."

"But the others are already bonding with the people here and with Moshi. I admire the African women and I want to fight for their plight, but I don't feel anything."

She puts her hand on mine, "First of all, most of the others only have three or six weeks here, they have to bond quickly. You have three months. Second, it's a very different experience for the rest of us. We have come here as an interlude to our lives, while you have come here as a way to begin an entirely new life."

"But, I thought I was going to come here and fall in love with a cause, a people or a group, and stay for two years or more."

"Maybe you're putting too much pressure on yourself to make this particular situation work."

"But this was my plan." I am disheartened.

"Perhaps you need a new plan. Maybe Africa is right for you, but it's somewhere else, doing something different."

A big sigh comes out of me and I feel some relief, as I realize I had not even considered thinking outside of the box. Also, I breathe deeply when I remember that back in the States Nancy is a psychiatric nurse.

"Why am I feeling this way while I am in the middle of one of the most amazing experiences ever? I don't understand. When my previous life was obliterated a year and a half ago, I went to Costa Rica to have a meltdown and to heal, so that by the time I got to Africa there would be something of me to give. These people have nothing and I have everything."

"Did you have a meltdown?"

"No. I loved Costa Rica and had a fabulous time."

She smiles, "Did you really think you could put your emotions on a schedule and rush your healing?"

It became apparent that my meltdown had come not in the form of sobs; I had done enough of that during year one, but in the form of an emotional shut down, not in Manuel Antonio, but in Moshi, Tanzania. My heart was closed up, a knot in my chest. I am afraid to fall in love with this place or these people because I will risk being hurt again, and my wounds are still so raw I can't bear another painful experience. But why now, when I want to help? I am riddled with guilt at not being on top of my game for these deserving people.

"I guess I'm not as healed as I thought I was."

"Lucetta, you put your entire life into a storage locker, and moved to Africa. Who does that? Don't be so hard on yourself, and give yourself some time. Plus, I am certain when your service is up at CCS, you'll know what your next step will be."

Tears fall down my cheeks. We hear Ibra ringing the bell signifying it is time to go to work. I take a deep breath, and realize that eventually I am going to be okay. It feels good to have it out of me, in the open. A next step, that's all I really need to have. I thank her. She gives me a long tight hug, the kind that breaks through your defenses and translates into unconditional love.

Somehow I manage a half smile. "How much do I owe you for the session today?"

* * *

There is one thing that breaks through my numbness. Orphans. The mere mention of the word tugs at heartstrings. We're talking about children who have lost the very core of who they are, their stability in a crazy world: their families. We can't seem to think about it for very long because it's too distressing, and we can't even begin to imagine life without ours, flawed as they may be. But these children have no choice. Life has dealt them a blow and they must carry on, there is no other way. The best they can hope is that they land in a place where people love them. Really love them. But how often do you run across people who will love another person's child, much less thirty of them, or a hundred?

This afternoon as a part of our cross culture, CCS is taking us to an orphanage to spend time with the children. We drive an hour up into the foothills of Kilimanjaro, and go through a huge metal gate, to find forty tiny children running down the hill toward us. The Catholic Church runs this orphanage, with nuns and volunteers as the caregivers. The facilities are large and striking by African standards with three buildings, one for the infants, one for toddlers, and the last for older children. Progress is being made on a fourth building with the goal of caring for the children until they are eighteen years old. We play at the gate, hugging and holding as many children as we can possibly fit into our arms. Eventually the nuns say it is potty time.

We herd the children up the hill to their dorm. At the building, the volunteers pull off the children's little shorts (no undies), and throw them in a pile as they go inside the door; their rubber sandals go into another pile. Lined up against the wall is a row of ten small plastic training potties. The first set of children takes a seat to do their business. From there they move onto another station where their shirts are removed and they are given a stand-up bath in plastic tub.

Afterwards, they go to sit on a table where lotion is applied to their arms and legs. A new set of clothing awaits them, which they will wear for the next several days. At the door the children slip their feet into the top two shoes on the pile, matching or not, and take off again to play. It is an amazingly efficient system they have created, and at every station, the caregivers speak lovingly to each child while they tend to them. The children go through this routine mindlessly as though they have done it a hundred times before. It seems a little like growing up in a summer camp. All of their needs are taken care of, and they are loved, but a handful of adults for 80 children means undivided attention is nearly impossible.

Children end up in the orphanages for different reasons. They may have lost both parents, due to AIDS, or to other circumstances. The AIDS epidemic alone has orphaned children at astonishing rates. Even if a child has lost only one parent he could still be orphaned. If his father dies, his mother cannot earn money and feed the children, so they go to an orphanage. If she remarries, the new husband often will not accept her children, and they are sent away. If the mother dies the father does not know how to care for a child, and must work to earn money, so the children are left on their own or sent to an orphanage. The children are screwed either way. Sometimes the children may actually have family, but the parents are too sick, destitute, or don't want to care for them. Sometimes a parent may be trying to get them out of a bad situation by sending them to the orphanage.

Many children have been abused or molested and orphanage workers must keep careful watch to make sure they don't abuse each other, because that is all they know. The ideal situation would be to keep them in their own home, with a relative, or at least in their village, but this does not always happen. The Tanzanian government doesn't fund or run orphanages because they say the relatives and villages should take care of their own. The orphans are left to the goodwill of the private sector.

Tuleeni Orphanage is also full of good will, even from the children themselves. Tuleeni has a relationship with CCS, so several of my fellow volunteers are placed there for work. They tell me that the older girls, who are teenagers, take turns doing the cooking. They will leave class early on their day, make the porridge, serve it and clean up. Everyone has specific jobs at this small, dilapidated orphanage run by a mother who began "inheriting" children. The young boys clean, and chop wood, with an axe. The girls clean, cook and do laundry. Older children look after the younger ones, and everyone takes care of each other. They sleep in small rooms with bunk beds, several children to a mattress, until they no longer fit.

We are invited over on Christmas Eve to watch a performance by the children. We pile into two vans, and stop at a grocery store on the way to buy gifts to take with us. Bags of rice, beans, oil, towels, notebooks and pencils are loaded into carts. One volunteer holds in his hands a soccer ball and bags upon bags of candy. We give him dirty looks.

"What?! They're kids. It's Christmas, for crying out loud." We concede.

The performances are adorable and afterward we play and hug. At one point Seri is looking for a particular little boy and she finds him in the bunkroom. He owns one cardboard box of possessions, and he is folding his clothes neatly and storing them in the box. Seri can't hold back her tears and comes to find me. Being with the children is a beautiful way to celebrate the holiday since we cannot be with our own families.

We get back to home base at CCS and discover they have a delicious Christmas meal prepared for us. They have pulled out all the stops because we have chosen to spend our holiday helping Africa. They put up a Christmas tree with lights in the dining pavilion. Deo keys in Christmas Carols on his phone and sets it in the tree. We have a singing Christmas tree at dinner, causing us to smile and sing along, loudly and badly.

I Skype with my children on Christmas day at two separate times, because half are grouped up on the East Coast and half on the West Coast. They are barely awake, with disheveled hair, yawning and it is hilarious to me. This is just like every other Christmas I've experienced with them and I am so thankful for electricity and Internet today.

In the afternoon we go to Tuleeni Orphanage again to play with the kids over the holiday. We play Duck-Duck-Goose, which to them is *Chui-Chui-Simba*. Leopard Leopard Lion. At one point I sit to feed baby Jonathon his porridge. A running child bumps into us, spilling some of the porridge. A young girl appears with a rag (filthy), wipes the porridge off Jonathon, off me, and off the dirt floor of the courtyard. I choke up at the thought of her wiping porridge off the dirt, and wonder what is the point? Then I realize this is her home, her only home.

I move across the courtyard where my friend is sitting on a table reading books to the kids. They are piled all over him. A small girl named Irene climbs up onto the picnic table behind my friend. She bunches her tattered sleeve into her hand, and I watch curiously wondering what she is doing. After a moment, she takes off my friend's cap, and gently wipes the sweat from his brow.

* * *

In the adult world of Africa there looms another quandary, that of the invisibility of women: My friend Faidha needed bags for her dried tealeaves and spices, to sell at the market the next day. Without the plastic bags, she had no way to distribute her goods to make money for food, and pay back her small loan.

"If I could just go into town, it wouldn't take that long. I wish my husband were here so he could take me," she said to no one.

Faidha was not allowed off the property without him or his

permission. The day wore on and her husband did not return. "I need those bags." Silence. "I'm going. I'm going to town." She gathered her Tshillings, and tucked them in her kanga before she lost her nerve. Glancing around the room she picked up a basket, and strolled nonchalantly to the edge of the property as though she were going to collect a basket full of produce from the garden. As she neared the edge of the land, she looked right and left to see if anyone had taken notice of her. No one was near. Her heart was pounding out of her chest as she dropped the basket and took off like a rocket running down the road as fast as she could, not realizing this made her much more of a spectacle. As she ran, her blood pounded like a hammer in her head. After a while she calmed slightly and began to feel...liberated.

"I'm out. I'm off the property all by myself! I'm free!"

She swallowed huge gulps of air that went all the way down to the bottom of her lungs. Euphoria came over her, and soon she was running with a light step.

"If I can do this I can do anything!"

She turned the corner, sailed into the market, and with a big smile on her face ordered the bags. She bargained down the price, just as she had watched her husband do before, wished them all a wonderful day, and skipped out of the store.

Halfway home unsettling thoughts began to come over her. Her steps slowed, and she wondered if he would be home when she got there. Fear gripped her heart as she stared at the ground before her. If he were inside the house she would get the beating of a lifetime. Would the owners of the store tell him she came in without him? What if one of his friends had seen her on the road? Why didn't she think this through? Her steps slowed to a crawl, as she was overcome with regret.

"I will pay for this now."

She arrived home ready to accept the consequences. She stood outside the door and listened. Nothing. Peering in, she realized the house was empty, and breathed a tentative sigh of relief. She was safe for now.

I have a theory on how to fix what ails Africa. It would remove the need for aid from the outside world; it would feed the children, and would end corruption in the governments, which hoard the financial resources. I am not presumptuous enough to think that I could come here and in a few short months devise a plan to correct all the problems Africa has experienced for the last five hundred years. No, this is not something I've had any part in creating, but it is happening, little by little thanks to people who care. I call it: Waking the Sleeping Giant. It is one third of the population, which has been relegated to silence and in effect, has been asleep: African women.

I've touched on this topic before, that of the oppression of African women. Their culture says this is the way it is, period. Their traditions and beliefs are so ingrained in their lifestyle that they go unquestioned. And whom would they ask for the answers anyway? They believe that the husband should have ultimate control and say in every aspect of their lives. I recently read an article in which the author had done a survey of East African women. Forty-five percent of them thought they deserved to be beaten if they burned the food.

If women don't know how to read, or have very little contact outside of their bubble, how do they gain any knowledge to know anything different? You don't know what you don't know. And can we really be angry with the men because they don't know any other way either. This is how it was in their home growing up.

If the women were happy in this lifestyle, and it was healthy, then no one should come and try to change it, or stir things up. But they are not content. It is an unnecessarily difficult life, simply because that is the way it has always been. Many Maasai and Muslim women are especially miserable because on top of it all their husbands take several wives. Rejection, resentment, jealousy, and longing, all play a part in being one of many wives. Just because it is the tradition, doesn't mean they are happy about it, or agree. No one asks a young woman's opinion when her marriage is arranged.

Despite these traditions though, the women of Tanzania are strong, hardworking, and indomitable. They carve out a life for their families from nothing. They take what life hands them with grace and humility. They are incredibly resourceful and generous. They take in children who are orphaned by AIDS though they can barely feed their own. And even though they don't have a shirt, somehow you will walk away with the one off their back. If this determination were turned toward a nation, it would be unstoppable. The continent has squandered one of its greatest resources, and if women were empowered, the face of Africa would be different.

The answer, as always, is education. Women must be shown that another possibility exists. If they understand or experience even one small glimmer of hope, they hold onto it like a precious jewel. The education of men would best come from the women themselves. They can bring them along in a compelling way and not lord over them this newfound empowerment, but say, this is better for everyone. Faidha began to earn money and express her own ideas, consequently earning respect from her husband. She no longer asks permission to leave, and her daughter, when she is married, now will not either.

If a woman knows that she can chose to have a life where she reaches her potential, a life fulfilled, she will choose it every time. If you develop a man, you change a family, for he is provider. If you develop a woman, you change the family, then the village, the town, and the country, for a woman is a teacher, and a nurturer. She will not withhold, but will share what she has learned with other women. She will teach the children and the grandchildren. She will wake up as the veil of unknowing is lifted from her eyes, and all of Africa will be changed.

She will say to them, "I will not be silent. I have something to offer the world for I am a valuable human being."

* * *

Another group has intentionally kept themselves by the wayside. As I go into work at the Empowerment Center one day, I see two men standing in the corner. One stands perfectly still for a moment.

"A child has died," claims the Maasai warrior turning to face me in the courtyard. He appears sad, yet anxious.

Mama Adia asks, "Do you want to bury the child?"

It seemed a strange question to me.

The other warrior speaks hesitantly, "We have discussed it, and the tribal ancestors have decided. Yes, we will bury the child. We have brought money for a… a…"

"Coffin." Mama gives him the word.

"Yes, for a coffin."

Mama calls to Monica, one of the older students at the school.

"Please take this money to town and bargain a good price for a small coffin. If these men go for themselves, the shopkeeper will charge them three times the price because they are Maasai."

"Yes, Mama."

It wasn't until later that I came to understand the significance of the moment I had witnessed. The Maasai tribe is set apart from the rest of African society. They are nomadic and wander from place to place, with their own traditions, speaking their own language. They have migrated over the years from the north, down into Kenya and Tanzania. They are the only tribe that still holds onto its traditional ways of life. Other African tribes have acclimated and become more developed. No one understands or knows the Maasai, and because the Maasai don't settle down, other tribes don't have any interest in getting to know them. Add to that, the Maasai believe that God gave all cattle on the earth to them. They have consequently spent years roaming the plains taking any farmer's cattle they run across, which has not been a good relationship-building tactic.

As I've mentioned before, the Maasai subsist on drinking the blood and milk from their cattle and only for very special occasions will they kill a goat and eat the meat. Another custom is that a man will never eat food in front of a woman. They eat separately, and this makes me sad to think they have never known the joy of a family meal.

This day is an altering moment for this tribe. In the past, when one of the Maasai died, the family would coat the body in butter and leave it for the animals to devour. Then they would immediately move the entire tribe to a different location, start over, and build new huts. Mama Adia talked with them about burying their dead. She said that if they buried their loved ones on the edge of their village, they would not have to move the tribe. Also, the family could visit the grave as a place to mourn the loss, or feel close to the one they held so dear.

The fact that this tribe has decided to bury the child shows a desire for permanence, and a willingness to consider a new way of life. But what is the fine line between bringing a people into the modern world for a better quality of life, and losing their culture, identity and possibly unity in the process? To me this seems to be a very gray area. Can you have one without the other? Can you help change customs that are harmful, without losing the remarkable things that make them unique? I wish I had the answer.

* * *

Several weeks later we ride past the sugar plantation again to see the Maasai. This time, when they met us in the middle of the dusty road, they take us in the opposite direction. We walk with them for a while until we come across a small building in the middle of the vast plain. They lead us up onto a small porch, where they have placed the same table and benches as before, with the table covered with a kanga. They are not allowed inside the building because they are Maasai, but they are able to borrow the porch so we will have shade from the piercing sun. We brought with us, the first VICOBA bank for a Maasai tribe.

The first order of business is to teach the women how to lock, unlock and use the bank. The men look on curiously. Next is the election of officers, the "President," the "Key Keepers," "The Witness" and the "Recorder" who will be in charge of documenting the transactions. This person must be able to read, write, and calculate numbers. This becomes an issue for a few anxious moments, as very few Maasai women have these skills. They search among the tribe, and with apprehension they settle on a young woman, a girl really, who proudly accepts the job. Finally, the moment comes to officially open the bank. Each woman is to bring forward 5,000 Tshillings as their contribution, which is about three American dollars. Each person is recorded and given a number. One elderly woman has only 4,000 Tshillings in her hand. There is much discussion, because she has no more money, and cannot join the bank with only 4,000. They speak amongst themselves in Maasai, while the woman is crestfallen. Suddenly, from within the crowd of them, 1,000 Tshillings appears, and they burst into applause, the woman bowing repeatedly in gratitude.

Between now and the next meeting, seed money will be added to the bank from the Center, and decisions made as to how many loans can be given initially. The women of the tribe must now decide what their businesses will be and how best to use the money.

Next comes the choir. The men join the women on the porch. Elections are held and a man is voted to be the head of the choir, as suggested by Mama Adia earlier, in order to keep the peace. There is talk about goals, and dreams of performing at weddings, seminars, and special occasions. The main objectives are twofold as far as Mama Adia is concerned; to raise money for the tribe, and to earn a newfound respect from the other Africans, which will help the Maasai assimilate.

After the business of the meeting is completed, they give us a concert. Their beautiful harmonic voices bring tears to my eyes, as I think about these nomadic people being given such a special talent. At the end we give them donations of Tshillings as we applaud, and they gratefully accept their first ever performance money.

We rise to leave, as we have been here for many hours, and they say, "No, no we have meal for you. Please sit around table."

They leave, and scurry behind the building. We gather around the small table, quietly waiting and wondering. A young woman brings us plates and spoons. I do not know from where they got them. Another brings a pitcher and basin, pouring water over our hands to wash them. A third brings two small pots and sits them in the middle of the table. They leave us to eat by ourselves. We sit in silence for a very long time staring at the pots, our hands in our laps. Each of us has the same questions, and the same thoughts in our minds.

Finally I speak, "Mama, have you ever eaten when you've been with them before?"

She shakes her head, no.

"Do you know what's in these pots?"

Again, she shakes her head, no. I have never been with Mama when she was quiet, and it makes us all the more afraid these pots might be full of blood and milk, which would be mixed together for us to drink. One more glance around the table, and I reach over and take a lid off. In the pot are stewed potatoes they'd grown themselves. We have a moment with Mama as she wipes tears. They implemented her agricultural training, accomplished this and then shared their bounty with us. With trepidation I reach for the lid of the second pot. Inside is not blood, rather, the most delicious and tender roasted goat.

* * *

We finally reach a point where CCS is no longer consuming every single waking moment of our time, and we have a weekend off to ourselves. Several of us decide we'd like to get away from the emotions and complicated difficulties of our current situation and have a little R&R. We talk to Pristine, the group that took us on safari, and they say they can take us overnight to camp at some hot springs. The thought of leisurely soaking our bones in the warm water, napping, reading, and sitting by the campfire at night, sounds like just what we need. We sign up immediately. Friday afternoon we load our backpacks into a van that had seen better days, and squeeze ourselves in among the gear to find a seat. Along with us CCS kids, we have two guides; Evans and Living, a driver named Deo, and Omar, our cook.

About thirty minutes down the road, we pull off to stop, "We forgot someone."

"What? How do you forget someone?" We laugh.

"Belle decided to come at the last minute. Mussa is bringing her to meet us."

We are excited to see Belle again, as she isn't a part of CCS, but went on safari with us. While we wait for her to arrive it begins to rain. Pour actually. Really, really pour down rain. Belle climbs in soaked to the skin and we quickly slide over making room in the already cramped quarters. We turn off the main road onto a dirt one which heads out toward the plains. It is raining so hard our driver can only see several feet in front of the van. We begin to swoop up and down in large puddles in the road, and we hold on, trying not to bang our heads on the windows or the ceiling. It is pounding down so hard on the roof we find ourselves shouting to be heard.

"It's raining inside the van!" Alexa yells.

Water is gushing down the sides, in through the tops of the windows. We all bunch toward the middle with people sitting on top of each other trying to stay dry.

The plain begins filling up with water and we watch with sympathy as people caught out in the storm try to make their way home. The going is slow and several times we are almost stuck. We bounce through what may not even be roads, until one big bump causes the back door to fly up and all of our sleeping bags tumble out into the rain!

We stop and the boys run out to retrieve them, quickly shoving them in the back. Soon the roads themselves begin to disappear, as the entire plain becomes a flood. Another bump and the back door pops open again. Out go the sleeping bags again, and out go the boys in the rain to get them. This time the wet sleeping bags come up front in with us, and Omar holds the back door closed for the rest of the drive. Against the thundering noise of the rain, we shout-whisper in the back so Deo cannot hear us, "Are we even still on a road?"

"We're in the middle of nowhere, what if the van stalls, or we get stuck in the mud?"

"Or floats down the plain like a river."

Darkness begins to fold over the area, and our new concern is finding our way.

"Does the driver even know where we are? How can he identify any landmarks?"

The possibility of sitting in the damp van all night is looking more and more like our reality. We inch our way along until the boys see a building. We head in that direction, and the driver decides we will stop there and wait out the storm. He pulls up beside the porch and goes back and forth, again and again, trying to park as close as he possibly can to keep us from getting wet.

Several other people are taking refuge on the porch, including two women. I walk over and introduce myself. Through their broken English and my broken Swahili, I learn they had been at the market and were on their way home when the storm hit. This is their village, and the building we are sitting in front of is a community center. We all sit on the porch for several hours talking and getting to know each other. The rain is not slowing with the flooding not subsiding any time soon. The water is about two feet high now. We will have to sleep on the porch.

The African women would not hear of it. "We cannot have you visit our village and sleep on the porch. We will speak to the chief. At least you should be able to get into one of the rooms."

They take Living by the arm, hike up their skirts, and the three of them walk out into the very storm they are seeking shelter from. Tears mist my eyes at the tremendous giving nature of these people.

The women and Living come back to report the chief is not at home, but they left him a message. Omar begins preparing food.

I touch his arm, "Omar, you don't have to cook, we can just eat these carrots and fruits."

He is emphatic, "Oh no, you must have a proper dinner."

He puts potatoes on to boil over a gas stove he'd brought with him. The rain begins to slow down making it easier for us to hear each other. Belle digs through her bag and pulls out her iPod, along with some small battery-operated speakers. She is our DJ, shuffling through all kinds of American music even though she is from Singapore. We open a bottle of wine and our tragic event turns into a porch party.

"Deo, this is the season of short rains, does this usually happen?" I inquire.

"No, not this time of year. I don't know what's going on."

The chief of the village wades through the water and welcomes us. He brings a set of keys, and opens the door to one of the small rooms so we can stay inside. He says, for our protection, he has also called a night security guard to come watch over us as we sleep. Evans disappears from the dance party for a very long time and Jen finds him in the small room on his hands and knees scrubbing the floor.

"Why are you doing that?" she asks.

"Because I don't want anyone to wake up sick tomorrow. You cannot get sick. This floor must be clean for you."

She could not convince him otherwise so she comes back out to the porch. The smells of delicious aromas remind us that it has been a long time since we've last eaten. Omar is making mashed potatoes and he stirs and mashes for almost 45 minutes to remove every single lump. Finally, they call us to dinner in the small room. As I come through the door, I see the most beautiful table has been set up with a tablecloth, utensils, tin plates and beautiful serving dishes. A sob wells up in my chest, which erupts into a cry. I fall into my seat with face in my hands tears pouring down my cheeks. I completely lose my shit. I am overcome with love for every African I have met since landing on their soil.

My friends gather around to comfort me, "Their hospitality is too much. I don't know how to accept it. They give everything. I am so humbled by their graciousness. I don't know how to take being cared for with this intensity."

My friends agree, and we have a solemn moment of thanks before we dive into the most delicious camp meal ever.

After dinner, the table is removed and mats are laid out on the floor. There is barely enough room for all of us, wedged together spooning on the floor. As soon as the door is closed, with so many bodies in the tiny room it becomes incredibly hot. Someone is coughing all night, another snoring. My sleeping bag is wet. I don't sleep at all.

At first light of day we rise, pack up, and clean up the area. The boys work on the back door of the van, and we try to find places inside the van to lay out our wet clothes. Jen drapes her shorts over the sleeping bags in the back. The rain had stopped during the night and the water receded to a manageable level, so we go on our way.

We bounce along the road again. Before each large puddle Deo stops the van. Living, with the legs of his pants rolled up and leaving his shoes in the van, walks through each puddle to determine if we can make it across. We pick up a little speed, but go over another large bump and up flies the back door again spewing all the sleeping bags and Jen's shorts in a huge puddle of brown mud. By now it's just comical. The sleeping bags are moved up front, and this time Craig holds the door closed. We almost get stuck as we bang and scrape on top of a huge rock.

I look out the back window, "Uhm, guys, we lost the spare tire."

The boys get out, retrieve the tire, and after examining the undercarriage decide the only place for the tire is, of course, in with us. Finally, out of nowhere, large trees appear, an oasis in the middle of the plain. We have arrived at the hot springs. The springs are serene and beautiful, but it is too cold to swim. It is still early in the morning and we will have to wait for the clouds to part and the sun to come out.

We want nothing more than to curl up into our sleeping bags and take a nap, but the bags are hung out on the trees to dry. I take a walk to explore the area, and discover a stream full of warm water as well. We soak our feet and give ourselves pedicures. We clean weeks and weeks of red dirt off our feet. At CCS we have to wash our feet before we go to bed every night, because we can't put those dusty feet in our beds. Our feet are always filthy.

We use rocks to exfoliate the dead skin. It is pure joy to have truly clean feet, and we begin to feel rejuvenated. Eventually the sun breaks through and the day warms up. Some of our crew decides to go swimming, but I am still cold and want to wait. Living comes over to me and asks if I will hold his belongings while he swims. Then he gets down on one knee and asks if I will wear his ring.

"Hahaha, yes, husband, I will take care of your ring."

The guys pitch our tents for us and we stay another night, enjoying more gourmet meals by the springs.

Our trip had not turned out exactly like we'd planned, but each of us was moved by the events that unfolded, and we decided we would not have wanted it any other way. We were different when we arrived back at home base. We had truly experienced Africa.

* * *

It is 7:00 a.m. on a Wednesday and I dig through my pack trying to find the most conservative thing I have brought with me to wear to court. At 8:00 a.m. I will climb into a van that will drive me an hour and a half to Arusha, Tanzania where the courthouse is located and the trial is set to commence. I am nervous. What will happen? Being previously married to a trial lawyer for 18 years taught me a few things, but how will I deal with the emotions of it all?

You might be thinking I have somehow gotten myself into trouble, and given my exuberant personality, your thinking is not far-fetched, but the trial this day does not include me. Today, I will merely be an observer of history in the making, living history going on at this very moment, at the International Criminal Tribunal for Rwanda. This trial, known as the ICTR, run by the United Nations, is about the atrocities that occurred to the people of Rwanda, by the people of Rwanda, back in 1994, seventeen years ago. To us, a lifetime ago, but to the survivors who live with the disfigurement, the loss of loved ones, and the damage, it was only yesterday. Our trip to Arusha is one more layer in the cross culturing that CCS is giving us in Tanzania.

In the spring of 1994, in the course of one hundred days, one million people were slaughtered with machetes and other crude weapons. The Hutus obliterated the Tutsis in an unbelievably short amount of time. How is this even possible? Surely it could only be through organization, advanced planning, and plenty of hate media, the kind that only a government would have the resources and the power to pull off. The United Nations Security Council created a tribunal to judge the people in power responsible for the Rwandan Genocide, and decided to establish the proceedings in neighboring Tanzania, a peaceful country.

We pull into the parking lot, and are told we must leave all belongings in the van. Photos will not be permitted and we will not be allowed to take anything inside with us to observe the trial. After some convincing and pleading by us, though, we are allowed to bring a pen and a note pad. We go through security, are given badges to wear that grant us entrance, and are led upstairs to Courtroom Two. An armed guard ushers us into a small room with a huge glass wall facing the judge, defendant and prosecutor. Headphones are placed on each chair for us to listen to what is happening ten feet away, on the other side of the glass. I have goose bumps all over my arms. I can't believe I am actually watching one of the most important trials in current history. How in the world did I get here? I am often amazed where the turns in my life have taken me. I'm having one of those "moments".

Court is already in session and they are prosecuting the Minister of Planning, Augustin Ngirabatware. The judge, William Sekule, is addressed as Mr. President instead of Your Honor, and the lawyers wear the black robes and the white ruffled bib of an English court. The session is operated in English, but Ngirabatware speaks French and the transcriber keeps asking for pauses for proper translation. They are asking Ngirabatware if he recognizes a telegram he received on

March 22, 1994. My first thought is; can I even remember what I was doing in March of 1994? Then I realize these events must be inscribed on his mind, and surely he has thought about them every day since.

The lawyer then passes out copies of a certain document to everyone to prevent "shenanigans" from opposing counsel. We look at each other and giggle at the word shenanigans; stopping abruptly the moment we realize they can see us through the glass as well. At that moment my pen runs out of ink. Damn, I forgot I was in Africa. The rule here is that if anything can go wrong, it most assuredly will, along with a million other things that couldn't possibly go wrong, but do. I have no other pen, because I don't have my purse. I will have to rely on my memory. Uh oh.

Afterwards, we are led out of the courtroom, and sent to a conference room where we are given information on the tribunal and its importance. Before now, if a country decided to obliterate its own people, the world just had to put up with the carnage because those in charge of the country would say, "this is our country, you have no say and we can do whatever we want."

With the creation of the tribunal, all of the countries that make up the United Nations, in a united front say, "No, we will not stand by and allow you to commit crimes against humanity. Genocide will no longer go unaccounted for globally."

Fifty-three trials have been completed, eighty-one people have been arrested, and eleven are still hiding out on the run. As a result of this accountability in Arusha, there are tribunals for other murdering countries currently going on in Hague and the Netherlands. The message sent all over the world is this: no one is above the law.

The tribunal was also the first to arrest and convict a Head of State, and it was the first time that rape was officially added as a part of war crimes. The ICTR has also collected a huge archive now from which we can learn how to prevent genocide in the future, most importantly how it has helped bring closure to the people of Rwanda as they experience justice being meted out daily. The tribunal established ten sites in Rwanda where the local people can go hear what has happened in court each day. They also began broadcasting the trial on radio not only in English and French, but in Kinyarwanda as well, for those in the villages. Hopefully the healing has begun.

When I get back to home base I get on the Internet to look up Ngirabatware and I discover he has a Doctorate in Economics and was formerly a professor at the National University of Rwanda before being appointed Minister of Planning. Geez, this is an intelligent man who was previously an educator. What are the steps that could take a human being from there to here? I decide at that moment, that I must go to Rwanda when I am finished at CCS to study this further.

Now I cannot abide dwelling on such a horrid note for long, so I sit and remember several amazing Africans who are building up humanity rather than tearing it down. First is a young man named Living (my husband from the hot springs), who after realizing the small children in his village were not being educated, started a school himself. He works for Pristine Trails part-time, and CCS, to support himself so he can run the school at a minimal cost to families. We never saw him in the mornings because he was teaching class.

Next is Daniel, who while waiting to hear about test scores as he tries to get into medical school, is volunteering at CCS for the semester. Daniel could be doing anything during this time, but has chosen to be a translator and assist the CCS teachers who go out every day into the classrooms where only Swahili is spoken.

And finally, there is beautiful Cocaya. Cocaya is educated and certified to be a tour guide, one of the best paying professions in Tanzania, and she also knows sign language for the hearing impaired. She chooses to work for little pay and stay with her students at the deaf school.

"But, Cocaya, don't you support your mother and siblings?"

"Yes, but who would help my deaf friends acclimate to the world if I leave? They would be closed in a box within themselves, with no hope. No way to communicate with the world. Of course I will stay."

This is the Africa I have grown to love.

* * *

Back at home base, we gather to eat lunch and I am concerned, "Craig, you look as though you've seen a ghost. Are you okay?"

He stands beside us stoically without moving, holding his plate. It had been the first day of his job placement, and he is pale faced. Something has rattled him to the core.

"Here, sit down." We make room at the table.

"Craig?" Jenn takes his arm and guides him, gently pushing him down into the chair. We sit silently, hoping our collective quiet will force him out of whatever has seized him up. We glance at each other.

He quietly speaks, "…the prisoners were…they were right there… walking among us… I never taught before… just a… library worker… so many kids speaking Swahili and… and criminals… I don't think I can…" His breath runs out.

We give him knowing nods, intently pushing the food around on our plates giving him more time, honoring the gravity of what he has just experienced.

Nancy speaks in her consoling voice. "Of course you can, Craig. You have everything you need inside of you to do this."

He blinks. Slowly he turned his head to face her and in a barely audible voice says, "Thank you."

On my way to Tanzania I was talking with a man in the airport, and as travelers do, we were sharing stories about where we were headed to that day. When it was my turn to explain, his eyes went wide, and his mouth fell opened,

"Why? Why would you do that? I am astounded!" He took his hands and counted on his fingers. "Why would you take your hard earned money, go to an undeveloped country, live under harsh conditions, and work for free? Why?"

Whoa, well, when you put it that way…it was my turn to be stunned. Volunteerism has always been a part of my life, growing up and then when I had my own family we volunteered as well. I never even thought to evaluate the motive, or thought of it from that perspective. I wish I had been fast enough to come up with a great philanthropic debate, an oratory which would rock his world enough that he would sign up somewhere immediately, but what came out of my mouth was, "Why not?"

Kristen comes to lunch one day at CCS with her laptop, which she drops on the table almost with a slam. She is crying, huge tears pouring down her face.

"This is so unfair; why would they do this!?"

She shows us her profile on Facebook, where a friend of a friend had posted an article about how volunteerism is selfish and does more harm than good. Her friends were all commenting. She is furious and crushed all at the same time.

"They say we only volunteer to make ourselves feel better, and what good does a few weeks or months accomplish anyway because the people should be doing it on their own." She cries out, "It's a little late for this, don't you think!? I'm already here, and it took a lot of planning and a long time of saving to pay for CCS and my flight. Why would they send it now!? That's just cruel. Don't they understand how much help these people need?"

If she was a guy, she probably would have spit at this moment, she was so angry and hurt.

My heart is broken for her, and I touch her arm, "No, Kristen, they don't understand. How could they? They haven't been here, and evidently the person who wrote this has never volunteered before. Your friends were careless, yes, but don't be too hard on them because maybe they've never known the beauty of giving selflessly. What you're doing is good. You followed your heart and it led you to Africa. It doesn't matter how long you're here, you're improving the quality of life for the people of Moshi every day, and that's all you need to know."

Volunteering does make you feel good. Absolutely. It makes you feel good because you grow so much from the experience. You are never the same person after you give of yourself for nothing in return. You can't be the same. It is impossible to be unmoved. But volunteering is not easy, never easy. It's messy, uncomfortable, and complicated with lots of gray area and usually little resources. It's often the jobs no one else wants to have anything to do with. There are frustrations, limitations, and unmet expectations for everyone involved, both the helpers and the helped. That is just the way of it. Volunteering requires sacrifice and usually heartache, but it is still always worthwhile.

I'm a runner. I run a race, and I feel good. Is it selfish for me to run because it makes me feel good? If someone was choking in a restaurant and I did the Heimlich on him or her, I would feel great about it. Is that selfish? Should I have not done it because I was going to feel good about it later, or because that person should have known better than to swallow a shrimp without chewing? Should I not help those in need because they should be able to pull themselves up by their own bootstraps?

This is not a new conversation. This debate has been going on for a lifetime, and that's okay. We should not be afraid to constantly re-evaluate. We should have the debate. We all want Africa to stand on its own two feet, no one more so than those of us who are here fighting for it. But until it does, we cannot abandon those in need. Someone has to be here to teach them a better way, to look beyond simply surviving, to think critically about tomorrow.

Despite his fears, Craig went back to teach every day. The first few weeks, it was always with a knot in his stomach. He was teaching at Magaresa Prison. It was a nursery school for the children of prisoners, prison guards, and also members of the village. He learned that the prisoners were so close to their release date, that they wouldn't do anything wrong to risk being thrown back in, so he was not in danger.

The prison was run by the state, so the school had more resources than most, but they also had more children. Some days he would have sixty to ninety kids, which he would then split with another teacher. He planned each day what to teach the next, and asked everyone's advice about the secrets to teaching. He worked hard on learning Swahili, and eventually Daniel came to act as a translator, which made everything much more effective. When other volunteers had a day off they would jump in the van with Craig, and assist him for the day.

Christmas time is the end of the school year for Tanzania, and the children take their summer break.

Craig came to lunch that day. "I lost some of my kids today. They'll move up when they come back in January. I'm so sad."

The next school year started back and new kids poured into his classroom. Three months had flown by and soon it came time for Craig to return to the United States. "I don't know if I've really done anything."

His last day was emotional for him. He had grown in ways he never anticipated. He said some tearful goodbyes in the classroom, and sent the kids outside. A few minutes later, Craig's boss asked him to come into the next room, which he assumed was for an exit interview. When he entered the room all of his students and the other teachers were there with a huge surprise party! His boss said that he had made such a tremendous impact on the school that they would miss him terribly. The children clung to his legs and cried as he got into the van. It took every effort he had not to completely lose it in front of them.

He was reeling from emotion as they pulled out when the driver said, "Craig, look."

Lining the sides of the road, on the half-mile drive out of the prison, was every single one of his former students, clapping.

* * *

Many of the volunteers at CCS build in an extra week at the end of their service to climb Mount Kilimanjaro, which is the highest free-standing mountain in all of Africa. I've had the joy of seeing it every morning before the clouds cover her face for the day. Many people come to Africa specifically to climb the mountain. It takes six to seven days to reach the Ice Cap, and at 20,000 feet, a majority of the slow climb is acclimating to the altitude. Some people manage fairly well, and for others it is much more difficult. It doesn't seem to have as much to do with fitness level, rather how well your body handles the altitude when you reach such heights where there is very little oxygen in the air. I encounter many people as they come off the mountain exhausted yet glowing, saying it was the hardest thing they have ever done in their life but they are ecstatic with their accomplishment.

There is nothing I love more than a personal challenge and I wage a war within myself for two months as to whether I should climb. The argument for: maybe this would be the thing to snap me out of my stupor, the argument against: my asthma. I have spent my entire life trying to get oxygen into my lungs. Why would I deprive myself of the very thing I fight for every day? People with asthma do successfully climb the mountain, and you can pay a little more to have a porter carry an oxygen tank, but for me, when I added my age plus asthma plus 20,000 feet, survival won the debate. I am really disappointed, but soon discover there is one trail that can be taken as a day hike. I can climb up to the first base camp on Kili and spend at least a little time on the mountain that inspires me each day.

We hike straight up the mountain for several hours, stop for a picnic, and then get back on the trail. After lunch it begins to rain lightly. Then it starts to pour, and quickly becomes very cold. I hate to be cold. When I am freezing, that is all I can think about; I can't even enjoy the moment. All I have with me are summer clothes because I am living on the equator. I silently become increasingly miserable, when I begin to feel a stinging. Earlier in the day, ants had crawled up my pant legs, and bitten me ferociously. I brush at my legs until I realize this is not ants, rather it is hail beating down with a vengeance!

Incredulously I ask the guide, "Does this always happen?"

"Not this low on the mountain. In all my times up here, this is a first."

We were prepared for rain, but not for cold. My hands and feet go numb, and we try to quicken our pace. Our "mountain top experience" is desperately seeking shelter on the porch of the base camp lodge. I want off that mountain as fast as possible and once we start back, my trail running days kick in, and I begin to haul it down the mountain. The others yell at me that it isn't safe to run on the trail, which has now become a river, but I don't care. I don't slow down until I'm below the hail line, at which point the others have followed suit and run past me all the way to the bottom. In the van on the way back, the shivers set in, and we all look ridiculous, soaked to the skin with our teeth clacking, and bodies shaking ferociously.

So many bizarre things keep happening. Maybe it isn't Africa after all, maybe it is just...*us*. Eventually we start laughing at this thought and can't stop. How could we have ever thought it would turn out any other way?

* * *

My three months of service are coming to an end here at CCS and I am at a loss as what to do next. I fully intended to settle down here, but this is not the place for me and something is driving me forward. I am perplexed at this and also sad because it means I can't help realize a lifelong dream of one of my children. The oldest of our six is my stepdaughter Katie. Years ago her godmother lived in Africa and went on safari. Katie grew up hearing her stories and seeing photos of the amazing animals. It had been placed in her heart early on to one day go to Africa. I was excited to be able to make that happen for her.

"After I volunteer and get settled, I'll bring you over and we can go on safari."

Now I must write an email and tell her I don't know where I will be, and that I'll just have to let her know when and where I put down roots. I was also looking forward to deepening our relationship through having the experience together. Being the oldest, it was hardest for Katie to accept a stepmom, and our relationship has been tenuous at times. She's an amazing, determined person, who sets a goal and goes after it until she reaches it, never giving up. I long to be good friends with her, not just a parental figure in her life. I feel awful having to disappoint Katie, and I'm afraid it will give her one more reason to disconnect. Ah, me. Somehow, in some way, I want to make her dream of experiencing Africa come true.

I must also write Myriah. She and her husband wanted to meet me in Africa as well, but this would have to be planned months in advance, and now I don't know where I will be, so planning is impossible. I hate to let them down, but I don't see a solution right now.

At dinner one night a conversation develops among the volunteers around the table.

"What happens after you're done at CCS?"

"I'll go back to school; I have two years left until I finish."

"My job is waiting for me and I'm sure the work is piled up."

"I have to decide if I'm going to stay with my boyfriend or not."

"My sister is having a baby!"

I've said many goodbyes on this journey, both in Costa Rica and Africa. It comes as a part of the experience of being an expat. Expats learn to say farewell because eventually everyone around them goes home. Acquaintances always go back for the joys, excitements, complications, and every bit of the disorder that makes up a life.

"I have to tell a roommate to find a new apartment."

"I'm going to take the GRE, and hopefully I'll get into grad school."

"My mom is really sick, so I'll be taking care of her."

Initially my new friends are hesitant to leave. It's nice to take a break from trying to keep your head above water and instead live outside of the routine of daily life. Being able to step away and evaluate life from a different perspective can be rejuvenating and enlightening. But as the time draws nigh, each one of them begins to talk more and more of home, upcoming events and anticipating seeing loved ones. There is something so precious about the life we create around us that it draws us back to our home, whether it is the ideal life or not.

"I'll be living with my parents until I find a job."

"I'm a bridesmaid in my friend's wedding."

"I want to continue teaching, so I'll have to apply again."

"What about you, Lucetta?"

Being included in this particular casual conversation startles me. A wave of emotion pulls me under and tosses me. I can feel the color running as it fades from my face. A stinging in my eyes, I try to speak but nothing comes. Heart beating. A realization. I don't have a home to go to. I don't have a life back there that needs me.

I am fully aware that I am unbelievably fortunate now, to be on the journey of a lifetime. I am living out everyone's dream. Utopia. This presses on my chest. Everyone's dream, I understand that completely, and feeling the responsibility I try to honor it by being useful.

But this opportunity did not come without a cost. The moment my world came crashing down, I lost everything. Everything. The future I thought I had, which was all wrapped up in dreams and plans, was yanked away in a second, shattered in one moment, and I collapsed onto the floor. The life I knew, the life I lived, my life, no longer existed.

I understand that I am not the first person to have something bad happen to them, and even in my own life I have unfortunately experienced worse. Everyone has their own stories of tragedy. Not one of us is spared because it is an integral part of being human, and our souls are designed to be in relationship with one another, whatever form that takes. This means that the same way we learned to walk and talk, we must also learn to heal, because humans are human, and sometimes we let each other down.

When life sends me a dividing line; I must grieve the old existence, and embrace the new one. I must figure out a way to pick myself up off the floor, and create a new and precious life for the person I have now become.

In Tanzania I had an empty space in my being so cavernous I was afraid nothing would ever fill it again. I sat for months in the middle of my emotions, vacillating between numbness, sadness, and anxiousness about the future. My original plan was to live in Moshi for quite a while, and although I couldn't put my finger on the reason, it was not the place for me to stay. What then?

"Lucetta?" they ask again.

I look around the table, "I don't know." I have one week to find somewhere to be. In seven days I must find a place to lay my head.

Seri grins. "Well, I don't know about your long-term plans, but I do know what you are going to do this weekend."

"Really? What's that?" I ask.

"You're going to Nairobi with me. I want to kiss a giraffe."

I snap back into focus. "Wait...what?"

"Yeah, you heard me right, and you're going to kiss one too."

As humans, we can also give each other hope, a tiny breather where the spirits are lifted just enough to go on to the next moment, and then the next moment provides its own portion of hope. I seem to be living hope-to-hope. Having a plan for the weekend lifts my spirits. I remember Nurse Nancy's advice; I just need a next step. I am not accustomed to operating without a goal, wandering aimlessly through my life. When I leave CCS, I will need a quiet place to think, a room all to myself. If I could add to the wish list a bed big enough to make snow angels, and a safe place to go for a long run in the morning, then maybe I could sort out my life. My next step turns out to be a baby step. I do the only thing I have in me at the moment. I book a room at a hostel two dirt road's away.

Chapter Nine

It is 5:45 in the morning, and still dark as Seri and I stand on the corner. We wipe the sleep from our eyes as we wait for someone from the bus company to pick us up at six and take us to the bus to Nairobi. We were a little wary, as this sort of well-thought-out-extra service was not common in Africa, but they had offered to pick us up, so we agreed.

I am emotionally hung over because the day before I'd had a tearful exit interview with our directors at CCS, Mama Fatuma and Moses Pole Pole. They had been so thoughtful in their care for each of us that they made our experience all the more meaningful. I searched out the rest of the staff, who had become family as well, and gave them goodbye hugs. Poignant farewells among volunteers were always postponed until the last possible moment, so my friends refused to say goodbye, knowing I would be right down the street next week. That night I pack all of my belongings and store them under Seri's bed for the weekend. When we return from Nairobi on Sunday night I will move out of CCS and into the hostel.

This is our first time to travel on our own in Africa, no CCS, no tour company, no guide, just us. It is 6 a.m. and not a single car had driven by. Finally, at 6:20 we begin to walk down the hill toward the bus company hoping by now, the bus is running on TFT (Tanzania Flexible Time which often means an hour later). Of course, we arrive to find the place deserted, less one lone man sitting on the sidewalk. We greet him.

"*Jambo, habari za asubuhi na mapema*?" Hello, what is the news early in your morning? "The bus to Nairobi, *wapi*?" Where?

"Bus gone."

"What? Someone was supposed to pick us up." I hand him the receipt that says, Pick-Up at Rose Home. He stares blankly for a moment.

"I go. No one there."

"Yes, we were there. Why didn't you pick us up?" asks Seri.

"No, no one there."

"Yes, we were there, we even talked to the night security guard." Meaning, she could prove that we were there.

"My taxi driver say he go, no one there."

"What?" I inquire. "I thought you were the taxi driver."

"Bus gone. You go at 11:00." He kicks something invisible in the dirt.

"We can't go at 11:00 a.m. We won't have enough time in Nairobi so we must go now."

"11:00 is okay. You go then."

A little glimmer of the new and stronger me bubbles up and breaks through the surface for a moment. "No, it is not okay. We could have been here on time if we had known. We need to talk to your boss."

"Me the boss."

"Well then, we need our money back to go find another bus company to take us now." Whoa, where did this strength come from?

"I don't have money."

"Why not? Who has it?" Seri chimes in.

"My boss. You go at 11:00."

Seri frowns at his lies. "I thought you were the boss."

"Eleven is no problem. You go then."

"Sir, it is a problem. This is not okay. We want our money back."

"I don't have money."

"Who does?"

"No money."

It goes on like this for several minutes, and uncharacteristic for Seri and I, our blood pressure and our voices rise. By now the sun is coming up, and a small crowd collects around us. We are trying not to shame him, two white women fuming at a black man, but by now we are spitting mad because of all the lies. Every bit of cross culturing we've learned comes into conflict. I can't abide lying. It's wrong, completely unnecessary, and never helps anything. If he had just apologized in the beginning…it is obvious we are in the right and he is trying to save himself for forgetting to pick us up.

"You back at 9:00, the boss here."

Nine! We discuss this between us. What choice do we have? There are plenty of other buses, but if we take one of the others now we'll never get our money back, plus at this point we are standing on principle. We have to see this through. It would probably be good for us to go somewhere and cool down. We find a place that's serving breakfast.

We sit in silence, both of us taking deep breaths, contemplating the options.

Seri speaks. "If we don't get to Kenya until tonight because of this, we'll only have one day there. Is it worth a nine-hour bus ride, both ways, for one day there?"

"I don't know." I ponder the situation. "It doesn't sound very appealing, but when will we ever be this close to Kenya again?"

"And we'll get to Nairobi around 10:00 p.m." Exasperated, Seri thinks it through. "It will be dark. That is not a safe place for mzungu to be out at night, especially ones who don't know where they're going."

"We can't go next weekend, either, because it will be your last weekend, Seri. It seems if we don't go now, we can't go at all."

Silently she thinks for a few minutes, "I suppose we could stay in Nairobi an extra day and I could take Monday off from teaching, but I want to honor my obligation."

She looks sad. We are both so disappointed with the entire situation, especially the confrontation with the bus man.

"I will leave the decision to you then," I insist. "Because my term is done at CCS, so I could easily come back on Monday. I believe you've more than fulfilled your obligation with the many extra hours you've put in there, but I know that's not really the point, it's about the kids. Would Oliveri be able to cover you with teaching the children?"

"Absolutely, in fact, he would tell me to go and have this experience." She sits quietly for a few more minutes and I can see the moral dilemma swirl around her conscience, the now-or-never bringing weight to the struggle.

She shrugs. "I think we should go."

"Okay, at least we'll have air conditioning for the heat of the day on the bus and big cushy seats."

Three cups of coffee later, after killing time, we go back to the bus company and talk with the boss, who, it turns out, is a woman. She apologizes profusely, changes our return date and to make up for the debacle, gives us money for a cab once we arrive in Nairobi so we can avoid walking in the dark. Things were looking up.

That is until the bus arrives. We stand beside each other, staring ahead.

"Please tell me that's the vehicle which transports us to the real bus." I say, feeling hot, cramped, and contorted just looking at the mini bus and the total number of people packed in there.

"No, I would guess, according to the way things go here, that's the bus that is taking us all the way to Nairobi."

We climb into the small bus headed to Nairobi, and greet the driver in Swahili. The seats are so tiny and close together that our knees hit the seat in front of us and there is no room for our bags. They could either go on our laps, or on the floor with our feet on top.

"It's okay, we can put them in the aisle once the bus fills up and we're on our way." I mention to encourage Seri.

More people wait outside the bus. The smell is stifling. If a person must choose between washing their body with the little water they have available or drinking the water for survival, they will choose to live every time. I understand this and I have compassion, still the smell of these unwashed Africans lingers and is difficult to ignore. The driver comes back and begins folding down little seats in the middle of the aisle. Well, there goes our plan, but whoa, these people have to ride in those seats? No more complaining from us; we don't have it so bad. It turns out this bus is a shuttle, which means there are several stops. At each one, locals come up to the bus and tap on the outside of the window trying to get us to buy their goods. Seri, with her beautiful, gentle spirit tells them in Swahili that she can't buy, but takes time with each one admiring their work and encouraging them.

The highway, for some reason, is paved for one portion and is dirt for another, and this goes on the entire way. Once the highway is completed it will be amazing, but as it is our bus bumps and tumbles down the road creating a red dust cloud behind us. The landscape is beautiful and I am happy to see northern Tanzania.

There are quite a variety of people on the bus. Most striking is a very distinguished Kenyan man in a business suit carrying a briefcase, who is so tall that his legs are folded up to his chest for the ride. He looks us over, I'm sure wondering what two white women are doing on this bus. A beautiful young Muslim girl from Tanzania sits in the makeshift seat next to me. She looks to be about 14 years old and is so shy that she cups her hands around her mouth, whispers in my ear, and asks me questions about America and about being a woman.

In the back, one of the passengers drops his glasses and they slide forward on a quick stop. We all squirm as we try impossibly to look under our seats for them. Tada, we find them. We share our snacks with the young girl and at one of the stops her mother offers us some food she's made for the trip as well. During a pit stop, the bus driver almost left two people who were still in the bathroom, and Seri and I shout up to the driver, "*Mbili zaidi*!" Two more!

One man in the seat in front of us is self-appointed dust control manager. Every time a car passes and the red dust starts billowing in the window, he reaches over and shuts it, suffocating us in the heat.

Seri opens it again as soon as possible, because we don't mind the dust as much as the heat. His arm span reaches both sides of the bus, so we giggle with the people on the other side who are also in battle with him. Halfway through the trip, the young girl next to me can barely keep her eyes open. Her mother won't let her trade seats with me to take a rest, so I get out my camp pillow and she lays her head on my shoulder.

At the border we take our bags and climb off the bus. This is my first border crossing, and there are people everywhere. We follow some of the Africans from our bus to get in line for the exit stamp from Tanzania. Our bus drives away. What?!

"Is he leaving us?" We are more than a little anxious. A man behind us overhears, and points that we were supposed to walk down the hill.

"Your bus on other side."

"*Asante sana*." Thank you very much.

Seri and I stop in the middle of the crossing and have a moment of awe and appreciation. We are about to step into Kenya. Kenya. We'd heard about it all our lives, and never even once thought to dream about going there one day. It is crazy the path our lives had taken to get us to this point, and it is not lost on us this day.

On the other side we step up to the counter and smile as our passports are stamped: entry. Back on the bus, a few miles down the road, in the middle of nowhere, we pass several young men in sweatsuits running in unison. Kenyan runners! As far as we are concerned our trip is already complete. The camaraderie on the bus this day has touched our hearts. Though it is cramped and hot, we treasure the entire experience.

As we pull into the bus station late at night, the man in the suit speaks for the first time.

He looks at us. "Your Swahili is perfect. Really, it's beautiful. I've been listening to you all day."

"Wow. Thank you so much."

We shrug at each other in disbelief, who knew? We unfold ourselves out of our seats, smack the feeling back into our numb legs, and climb off the bus. A bank of taxis wait and we negotiate with one for a ride. In the car, after our greetings, we ask the driver to take us to Milimani Backpackers.

I am a little nervous about staying in a hostel. Traditionally they are for young people. Will I be the out-of-place old lady here? Will I seem ridiculous? In my previous life we always stayed in four-star hotels, where everything was pristine and picture perfect at all times. I've always wanted to learn to backpack travel. I want the local experience, not the resort experience. Besides, I am living without material comforts these days and it is just fine. What will it be like to rough it while on vacation in this large African city? Question: if we are in a dorm with other people, how will we keep our stuff from being stolen? We are in Nairobi after all, which is often called Nairobbery.

I am brought back to focus when our driver asks Seri, "Where did you learn your Swahili? It's very good."

"Thank you." She looks at me and holds up two fingers, mouthing the word, "Twice!" We grin at each other in the back seat, encouraged that our study and practice has paid off.

We pull up to Milimani and walk through the big gate. To the right is a small restaurant and bar. Among the crowd, seated at one table, are two older couples laughing and having a beer. Whew.

"See," Seri says, "you worry too much."

"I know. I never used to be this way. It's weird; I need to find ME again."

"Well, while you do that, I'll go find reception." We laugh.

We check in and are able to rent a locker for our valuables. We store our passports, cameras, and extra cash. The receptionist shows us to our room. It is a dorm, housing five bunks that sleep ten women. It's late and even in the dark, I can tell most of the beds are full. She points her flashlight toward two top bunks and whispers that they were ours. I toss my bag on top and decide it will sleep up there with me.

I quietly dig out my headlamp; find my toiletries bag and head down the hall to the community bathroom to brush my teeth. As I walk in, a man steps out of one of the showers and casually says hello as he takes his time to wrap his towel around his waist. Uhm, awkward. Does every hostel have communal bathrooms? Oh well, I guess we all have to take care of the basics. I go into the bathroom stall as the toweled stranger stands over the sink brushing his teeth.

Back in the room, I climb up to my top bunk and get settled in. I can tell I am going to be experiencing new things every single day now. Our morning had started at five, and every part of my body was exhausted. I whisper to the next bunk, "Hey, Seri."

"Yeah?"

"Thanks for making this happen."

* * *

Kissing a giraffe may not be at the top of everyone's wish list, but it was certainly in the top ten on Seri's, and while in Nairobi, it moved up to number one. How is it even possible to kiss such a tall, wild animal? The logistics alone are a hurdle.

I ask Seri, "What are we going to do? Chase them until we catch one and then ask if they would bend that long neck down for a smooch? Besides, it seems pretty gross to me."

"No, silly, giraffe saliva is a natural antiseptic, so it's perfectly clean."

"How do you even know these things?"

She laughs with a twinkle in her eye, "You'll see, it will happen, but first we are going to the elephant orphanage because we can only visit the toddlers between 11:00 and 12:00 p.m."

We find the receptionist at the hostel and ask for a trusted cab we can hire for the afternoon. She, in turn, asks us where we learned our Swahili because she thought it was so good.

"Thank you, we learned it in Tanzania."

"I thought so."

We walk into city center to find an ATM for some Kenyan Shillings.

We marvel at the paved roads, curbs, and tall buildings. It is very cosmopolitan and the people are stylish and beautiful. It is the New York City of Africa. We are experiencing reverse culture shock. We also feel very oddly dressed in our "Moshi appropriate" modest clothing, consisting of a knee length skirt and a T-shirt.

Seri muses, "We look like we just came to the big city from the sticks."

"We'll just put our ego aside and roll with it," I grin. "What other choice do we have?"

We climb into the cab and greet our driver named Paul. Seri gives him the list of places we want to visit today and we take off for the Sheldrick Elephant Orphanage. It sits on the edge of a national park, and the elephants can only be viewed one hour a day, during feeding and playtime. The babies are orphaned for a variety of reasons; mostly because poachers killed the parents, but also the mother might have fallen into a well, or sickness could have taken the parents.

Elephants are very smart and are also emotional creatures. If you blow your breath into their nose, they will remember your scent for seven years, and when they lose their families, they remember them too and are devastated. The orphanage replicates their living situation until they are old enough to make it on their own. In the wild, mother elephants constantly circle their babies, or calves, shading their delicate skin from the sun so it doesn't burn. At night they pat down the brush to make it soft, signaling it's time to go to bed. Then they snuggle up next to their babies to keep them warm.

At Sheldrick they use umbrellas to protect the babies from the sun. At night they take a mattress down from a ledge, pat it down, wrap them in a blanket, and keep them company until they fall asleep. They also routinely switch out the handlers so the elephants don't bond with them, and then eventually have to lose them too. Once the elephants do go out into the wild, they may run across relatives who take them into their herd. If not, somehow the others know they are orphaned and embrace them as a new member of their family. The elephants are free to return to the orphanage at any time. They have one elephant that comes by every few months, eats some free food, checks in on the new kids, and goes back out. I am now in love with elephants.

Next stop is the Rothschild Giraffe Center, also on the edge of a national park. The Rothschild giraffe almost became extinct so the center started protecting and taking care of them. Thanks to their efforts, the numbers are up and there are now four hundred and twenty of them living in the wild.

At the edge of the land they've built a two-story information center, and on that building is a porch, which is the perfect height to be eye level with a Rothschild.

And on that porch are pellets, which are made of oats.

And if you take those pellets in your hand, a giraffe might come over to eat them.

And if you put those oats between your teeth…

Wait for it…

Wait for it…

KABOOM! A French kiss! Giraffe love, that's what I'm talkin' bout! Nothing could be better.

Back in the car, Paul laughs at us as we go on and on like school girls about how awesome the experience was. We ask if he's ever kissed a giraffe, and he emphatically replies, "No and I never will."

While driving to the next stop, he inquires, "You learned your Swahili in Tanzania, didn't you?"

"Yes, how did you know?" Bewildered, we ask, "Paul, why does everyone keep mentioning this to us? No one says anything about our language skills in Moshi."

"Because in Kenya we speak English, and we only learn Swahili as a second language. We can understand a little, but don't speak it very well. You speak better than we do, *and* you're white." He grins.

"Oh, we had no idea! About the Swahili that is." Laughs Seri.

I agree. "I guess that explains all the comments."

We are so thankful for the language lessons we've been provided by

CCS, and can't wait to tell Mama Fatuma the news because she'll be so proud of us.

We move on to spend some time at the museum and plantation of Karen Blixen, the acclaimed author of the story, *Out of Africa*. It is a sad tale of her time in Kenya in the 1920s. In the midst of her own loneliness and grief, she treated her African workers with dignity and love. And among other things, opened a school for them in which they could learn to read. Today, there are many places in Nairobi named after Karen to honor her kindness.

Riding with Paul again, we quiz him on his Swahili. I ask him, "Have you heard the phrase, *Poa kachizi, kama ndizi*?"

"No, what's that?"

"Cool crazy like a banana."

"What!?"

"It's a rhyme the Tanzanians say when something is cool."

He looks back, "Say it again, I want to learn it."

"Oh my gosh, what kind of turned around world is this, that I'm teaching Swahili to an African!" We laugh as the lesson begins.

Walking through the city of Nairobi, we begin speaking exclusively in Swahili because it is so much fun to have the locals practice. On the street, Kenyans try to get us to buy their wares while engaging us in conversation. "*Hapana asante*." No, thank you, we say as we walk on.

One shouts out to us, "Hey, where'd you learn—"

"Tanzania!" we yell back and wave.

We are country bumpkin rock stars!

* * *

After another bumpy ride, for many hours, we make it back to CCS late in the evening. I must say my goodbyes again, for my bed has now been given to a new volunteer arrival.

Alexa grabs me at the door, "I'm going back to the States, and I have something to leave with you." From behind her back she pulls out two brightly colored T-shirts of hers that I have been admiring. She smiles, "I know you love them, so they're yours. And they're washed and ironed."

"Alexa! Thank you so much! I feel like I just took a trip to Saks Fifth Avenue."

Smiling at my good fortune, I move myself to the nearby hostel and fall into my very own big bed in a private room all to myself

I awake early in the morning because the sun is beaming in the window. I'm thrilled to have my own space for the first time since arriving in Africa three months ago, yet sadness catches up to me for a moment as my volunteer time is up. I miss CCS, my friends there, and the meaningful work we did each day in Moshi. It feels like the emptiness you get the day you come home from summer camp.

I smile. Ah…I don't have to get up and go to my volunteer job today. I lie in my bed relishing the thought of having a few moments to myself. What shall I do with my one wild and wonderful life today? I should go for a run. Then I'll wash my laundry in a bucket and hang it on the line. I'll sit on the porch while my clothes dry in the sun and write a blog post about my journey so my family knows I am still alive. Yes, this is a beautiful day, and I am okay. I got myself to Africa, I did a good job at CCS and now I am ready for the next step of my peregrination.

I pull on my running shoes, and put my ID plus a debit card, in my hidden zipper pocket. I head up to breakfast provided by the hostel. A staff member brings me a cup of hot tea, a hardboiled egg and a piece of white bread. Because I am famished, I savor and appreciate every bite. I say goodbye to the owner and take off for a run by myself.

Chapter Ten

I sit on the floor, facing Neema, holding her stiff baby in my arms. Her sister, Keta, sees what I see and lets out a bone-chilling scream, "Noooooo!" Neema keeps rocking and stares in silence but huge tears begin to fall down her cheeks.

I wrap the boy back up again and turn my attention to Neema. Again I touch her arm, "Neema, my heart is full of love and sadness for you. What is his name?"

Keta whispers, "Samwel."

"Ah, sweet Samwel," I instinctively rock him. "You are loved...you are so loved." Now tears pour down my cheeks.

Keta bellows in anger, stomping around the small room, "It malaria! We have no money for mosquito nets. He was throwing up and shitting all over the place. Aaaaaagh noooo!" She doubles over in the pain and disbelief of it all.

After she catches her breath I ask, "Keta, where are your parents?"

Wiping her tears with the back of her hand she says, "Our mother die of AIDS and we not see our father after. We live here three years trying to live."

Tenderly, I inquire, "What about the baby boy's father and *his* family?"

Keta now moves to the floor wrapping her body around Neema and holds her sister in sync with her rocking,

Hesitantly she speaks, "Boy gone, he bad. He find out we live here alone and he come one night and take Neema. I small enough to hide.

She have much pain because she cut when she was twelve. More pain when she have baby because she was sewn up."

The tradition of female circumcision can make sex very painful especially when it includes sewing up the vagina. This makes birth almost impossible in the best of situations.

"*Oh mimi ni hivyo pole sana.*" Oh I am so very sorry. I speak in her language out of respect. I feel my heart pouring out love for the plight of these young, yet incredibly strong women determined to survive.

I try to tamp down the despair I have regarding female circumcision as I speak again, "Neema, it is by God that I am here with you today for I too lost a child. A baby girl."

She stops rocking and looks at me through tear-filled eyes. She speaks her first words, "What happen?"

My heart is broken for the baby, for Neema and her rape, for Keta, the violation of the girls due to tribal customs, their mother, their survival. I already have a giant lump in my throat and my heart is racing, can I do this? Can I even tell this story? Yes, I must, for it may help Neema feel less alone.

I take a deep breath. "I was married at twenty years old and had a child when I was twenty-two. She was the light of my life. When she was nine months old I left her out front with her father while, at his request, I ran inside to get water for us. He must not have realized or remembered she was there. She crawled over to the truck, and without knowing it...he...he ran over her." A sob erupts from my chest.

In silence, their eyes wide, they wait for me to continue. "I came back out just minutes later and found her. As I ran to her it was clear, she was dead. I let out a blood-curdling scream. He was still backing down the long driveway and had no idea. I screamed and wailed. It was over. Finished. No way to take it back or fix it."

I bring Samwel to my shoulder and hug him closer as we all cry together feeling such immense loss.

"How you know she dead so fast?" asks Keta.

"Uhm, uh because the truck ran over..." Breathe, just breathe. "...

because the truck.... ran over her head and her brains were spilled on the driveway. I didn't… I didn't even know if I could pick her up or if she would fall apart."

Silence.

Neema reaches out and touches me this time, "You are sister."

"Yes." I hold her hand. "Sadly now we speak a new same language, don't we?"

"What was her name?" Keta lovingly asks.

"Leah."

Hopelessness rises up in Neema as she laments, "*Samwel, Samwel, jinsi mimi kuishi bila wewe!*" How will I Iive without you!

I lay him in her arms. She begins rocking again, her face buried in his body.

I stand up. "Keta, do you have *any* relatives in Moshi?"

"Yes, our Auntie not too far away. They no take us in because they have five children, one room."

I feel like they will need some help here with the burial and support in moving forward over the next days, weeks, and months. "Keta, can you go get her? I will stay and help Neema."

"Yes, ma'am." She wipes the snot on her sleeve and hugs her sister while stroking her hair, "I will bring Auntie; she know what to do."

I sit down beside Neema and hold silence with her. Our souls are now inextricably entwined. I vacillate between her grief and my own. The *why* question comes back up, as it always does. Why? Why do things like this happen? But I know there is no concrete answer.

A thousand memories rush into my mind, one specifically that moves me to action.

"Neema, when my Leah died, the police and ambulance came, but we had to wait for over an hour for the Coroner to come because the ambulance can't transport a dead body. The police…they scooped her brains into a baggie." I'm not sure she gets all this; it may be lost in translation. "During that waiting time we washed her little body and wrapped her in a clean sheet that I retrieved from the house. I am very thankful to this day that I could honor her so. Would you like for us to wash Samwel?"

Her eyes close and I wait. After a moment she nods.

I stand. "I passed a kanga shop on the way here. I can go buy water and fabric. Will you be okay here if I run very fast?"

"*Ndio asante.*" Yes, thank you.

I take off running out of the shack. I'm so thankful I've been in Moshi long enough to know where everything is. I hit the bank and quickly pull out the maximum it will allow at the ATM. I run to the kanga shop and find a beautiful piece of regal fabric. I barter the price down and ask if they have any small scraps that I could use as a washcloth. I take off for the market and buy two large bottles of water and soap. Loaded down, my pace slows to a fast walk. I make it back to Neema as quickly as I can.

As I anticipated, she is still on the floor rocking. I immediately open a bottle of water and have her drink her fill, "We must take care of you as well."

Searching, I find a pot and pour in one of the bottles of water and the soap. I take it over to Neema and ask tenderly, "Are you ready?"

"Yes."

She hands Samwel to me. I lay him on the rug between us and unwrap the blanket from around his little body. I hand Neema the washcloth and the soapy water. As she washes him she sings a hauntingly soulful love song in Swahili to her son. I realize tears are pouring down my face. As difficult as it is, this is one of those moments when we know we are fully alive, feeling the full range of human emotion. Experiencing all this life has to offer, the full breadth of it. We swaddle Samwel in his new cloth, covering his face to keep the flies away. Neema holds him to her breast and begins rocking again. There is comfort in the rocking, a small soothing in a moment of such devastation.

Suddenly she hands him back to me. There are wet spots on her shirt. Her milk has let down and is flowing everywhere. A cry of sadness pours out of her throat for he will never suck again. I, myself, had this reminder every four hours after Leah's death. It went on for several weeks, the most unbearable and cruel reminder that she was gone. I hand Neema one of the washcloth scraps to clean up with, as my heart breaks for her all over again.

I place him back in her arms wanting her to have every last moment she can with him. I take the pot and scrub some of the foulness off the floor, then dump the dirty water outside. I come back to sit silently, cross-legged on the floor with my hands in my lap. I know well the hopeless anguish of living on this planet without your beloved child, the one who came from your womb. I play with my ring and another idea comes to me.

"Neema, do you see this tiny ring on the end of my pinky finger?" She nods. "This was Leah's baby ring and right before we closed her casket, I decided to take it with me to remind me that she really did live, she was not just my imagination. At the time, I had on a dress with no pockets so I stuck it on the end of my finger to take it home, and this is where it has been now for twenty-eight years."

She rolls my finger round in her hand feeling the small gold ring. "It pretty and nice to remember."

"Yes, I am thankful to have it with me still. Do you have anything special of Samwel's you could keep with you?"

The tiniest hint of a smile forms on her face, "Yes. My cousin make monkey. On his bed in corner," she points.

I go to Samwel's little pallet on the floor and feel around. There I find a small monkey with a long curly tail, carved out of wood. I bring it back over to Neema.

"He love to hold and suck the tail in his mouth." She smiles a real smile this time and my heart lightens.

"What a beautiful way to remember him, Neema."

A thought comes to me suddenly and I look all around the shack for a string or chain of some kind. Their belongings are so sparse I'm fairly certain none exists here. Think, think, what could you use? Aha! I reach down and untie one of my shoelaces removing it completely from my shoe. I take the monkey from her hand as she looks at me questioningly. I string the lace through the curly tail and walk around behind her.

I place the makeshift necklace around her neck and tie it at just the right length. I come back around and clasp both of her hands in mine under his body. "Neema, this is done in memory of your beautiful baby boy. May he play with Leah in Heaven forever."

New tears emerge and pour down our faces spilling all over Samwel.

After a while Keta returns with Auntie and there is much wailing and holding. I step back to give them space to fully embrace each other in the solemnness of this grim moment. Eventually Keta asks about the fabric and Neema tells them the story. They are very grateful and thank me profusely. I begin to feel that my contribution here is complete, and I think of getting back to the hostel.

I look around the shack and ask, "Do you have a knife to cut my shoelace?"

Keta retrieves one from the corner as I remove my remaining shoestring. I cut it in half and lace a portion in both of my shoes. I probably can't run, but this will walk me home just fine. I'm not sure I have a run in me anyway.

I kneel in front of Neema. "I am sad not to help you further, but I must go to Rwanda and back, then leave the country because my visa is up."

I pull the money from my zipper pocket and place it in her hand, "Here is enough money to buy mosquito nets, food, and help with the burial. There should also be enough to buy a real chain for the monkey, or maybe a ring like I have so that his memory stays close forever. I love you and I will never forget Samwel." We hug and weep.

I turn to Keta. "I am so thankful you ran out to ask for help at that very moment. You are a good sister to Neema. You will survive this pain. You will, both of you, for you are strong survivors."

And to Auntie I say, "Thank you for helping them. The next year will be difficult as their hearts begin to heal. I am glad you are near."

Gently I back out of the shack feeling a deep, deep sadness at the leaving. I turn and walk away. Down the road my anguish overcomes me and I pull off the road into the brush, double over and hurl my guts out. My hands cover my face holding down the loudness of my sobs as I fall to the ground and sit in behind a tree. I can't believe that just happened! Oh my God. Oh my God. It hasn't been this real for me in many years. How can I live without my Leah? How *have* I lived without her? Why did this happen? I still don't have an answer. Oh my God, what is my life even about? I cry sobs that come from so deep within my soul they turn me inside out. I have not felt this agony in so many years that I am surprised at how it pierces my heart with urgent physical pain.

I don't know how long it takes to collect myself. Slowly I rise and begin to move forward. During my walk on the way home I manage to begin to breathe deeply. Some part of my long-time buried despair has come to the surface, out of nowhere in this cathartic experience. I begin to marvel at how often things happen so perfectly in the moment. Many would say it was a coincidence that I was running down the road when Keta came out to cry for help, but I don't buy that. I don't believe in coincidence for too often it's inexplicable. I believe there is something bigger happening here. And even though my heart was broken a thousand times today, I am thankful I was the one chosen to be there to help.

I round the bend to my hostel and go directly to my room. I pick up my soap, shampoo, a camp towel and head straight for the shower. I strip down and jump into the cold water with no hesitation. I cry and scrub until my skin is raw. I attempt to wash away the filth, the stench, the memory, and the pain.

I put on comfortable clothes, grab a bottle of water and go sit on my little front porch. Here I have a view of something bigger, a larger picture, Mount Kilimanjaro. I sit.

And I sit.

There will be no laundry today, and no writing. My heavy heart says, I can't tell this story. Not now anyway.

As the sun begins to go down on Kili I work my way to gratitude. Clearly I had some unresolved pain come to the surface today. It was buried so deep that I didn't know it still existed. Interesting that my runaway journey, ran me right into my most painful memory in a way that I couldn't run from it again.

I'm grateful that I had those months with my precious Leah, grateful that after her death I began to live out of the strength of a survivor. From that day forward, nothing could tear me down or devastate my soul so completely. The pieces that had been broken off or hidden away, are all collected, repaired, and sculpted into someone who is more impactful and empowered. I have been given a supernatural inner strength on which I have relied many times. And today I was able to share that experience in a meaningful way to give strength to another woman. I am also incredibly thankful to have given birth to two more beautiful children, and later embrace four stepchildren as well. One was taken, yet I was given a bounty. I am blessed, so incredibly blessed.

And I am okay. I am, and will continue to be okay. As strange as it sounds, at the end of this day, I can say my one wild and wonderful life is truly magnificent.

* * *

I sleep soundly after the emotional exhaustion. In the morning I rise and go up for breakfast. The owner is there and we chat while I have my tea, hard-boiled egg and white bread.

"Where are you headed to next?" he asks.

"I'm going to Rwanda to learn more about the Genocide, and return here to say goodbye to a friend. Then my visa is up so I'm going up to Egypt and will travel down the entire eastern coast of Africa."

He shakes his head, "No, you won't."

What? I take a bite of bread to stall, while my nerve endings bristle again at a man telling me what I will and will not do. "What do you mean I won't travel down the continent?"

"I mean you won't go to Egypt."

"Why?"

"Because there has been an uprising there, with marches and riots. It's unsafe. You should not go."

I'm shocked. "I didn't know about this because I don't have access to the news."

"It's crazy up there right now, Cairo is called a 'war zone' and thousands are protesting in Tahrir Square and trying to overthrow their president. They say it gathered steam on Facebook."

"Whoa. I didn't know. It's unbelievable that an uprising was fueled through social media. I really wanted to go to Egypt. This makes me sad, but thanks!" I grab his hand. "You're right, I'd better change my plans."

One step at a time, a next best step, that's all I need right now.

* * *

Africa is complex. For every difficulty there is an instance of beauty. For every heartache, there is a moment of tenderness, and for every occasion of progress there is one step back. It's gets under your skin, this culture, these people, and the life. There is an intangible so captivating and magnetic about this continent that once you've been here, it seems you can never get it out of your system. It pulls at your heartstrings, drawing you to think, reflect, be changed. Many are taken by this place because something has pierced through and broken them, yet has also strengthened them while here. I am quite certain I will never be the same.

I am curious to experience more of the surrounding countries, but now I am solo and paralyzed by my fears. I give myself a stern talking to. Other women have traveled Africa alone, which means you can too. Did they possess some sort of superpower that you don't have? No, they just decided to do it and made it happen. Buck up. I begin to research a way to get to Rwanda by bus. It is almost impossible from Tanzania, and the word on the street is there are problems at the border, which do not allay my anxious state. I finally relent and find an airline that flies the route, but only two days a week. I book a flight online. My reservation is confirmed, and the airline will send an email about payment. The email never arrives and I try to make payment happen on the site, twice, to no avail. There must be a problem with the website. I'll have to pay at the airport.

I'm up early to meet my taxi and make the 45-minute drive to the airport. I go through the first airport security check to get to the ticket counter.

"You must go office. Outside. Pay ticket."

"Oh, okay." I go back out through security and find the office. The woman at the desk has a gorgeous smile and speaks very good English. She checks her computer, which takes forever to boot up, and her pretty smile fades. "Looks like we've cancelled your ticket for non-payment."

"I tried to pay online, but it wouldn't take me to the right page."

"I'm sorry. The flight is booked now."

I sit still, running over the options in my head. If I can't get on this flight, the next one isn't until next week. My visa is running out in Tanzania, and I won't be able to come back through and meet Seri in Dar as promised, and I have no way to contact her. It is now or never. Why does this keep happening?

"Could you check to see if someone has cancelled at the last minute?" I am trying to be hopeful. We wait for her Internet to come back up, and while we sit, she asks me,

"What are you doing in Tanzania?"

"I've been volunteering in Moshi."

"Really? Thank you!"

"Oh," I am taken aback, "you're welcome. I was able to observe the International War Tribunal in Arusha, and I want to go to Rwanda to visit the Genocide Museum."

She smiles. "Let me see what I can do." She turns to her computer. Fifteen minutes later she finds me a seat.

"Thank you so much!" I hand her my credit card.

"I'm sorry, we can't take credit cards, we don't have the machine."

"I don't have enough shillings with me."

"There's an ATM down at the end of the airport."

"Okay, I'll be right back." Time is almost up, so I take off running.

OUT OF SERVICE blinks on the machine. Of course it does. I lug my bag back to the office.

"Where can I find another ATM?"

"I'm afraid that's the only one, the next closest is in Moshi."

Forty-five minutes away! I realize then that Rwanda is not going to happen and that's all there is to it. The sadness must be evident on my face because the woman asks, "How much cash do you have, I'll book you a one-way ticket."

She clicks away on the keyboard, and gives me the total. I count my money.

"I'm sixty dollars short."

By now an hour and a half has passed and the flight is about to leave. Why hadn't I been more persistent about tracking down the on-line payment? I always just let things roll. Why can't I be more aggressive when it counts? I'm about to miss this opportunity because I didn't follow through, find a way to call, or something, anything! I am so disappointed in myself. She watches me, silently, as though reading my thoughts.

"I'll tell you what I'm going to do," she says, "I'm going to book you on this one-way flight. When you land in Rwanda, get some cash and book your return. On Monday when you come back, you bring me sixty dollars."

I am stunned. Tears pool in my eyes. Sixty dollars is six hundred in Africa. Her job will be on the line if I don't come back and pay her. She is taking a huge risk by making my trip possible.

"You would do that for me?!"

"Yes, now run! Go through security and I'll meet you at customs with the boarding pass, hurry!"

I toss my money onto her desk and take off through security again. On the other side she shows up with my ticket.

"Thank you! I'll be back on Monday, I promise." I wave as I heave my backpack onto my shoulders and run.

The door closes behind me and I settle into my seat, thinking about the kindness I have been shown. It feels good to be trusted. Whew what a day, and it is only ten a.m. I look out the window to say goodbye to Tanzania when I notice the mountain range is on my side of the airplane, the left. Wait a minute…the mountains should be on our right. We're going the wrong way. Did I get on a different plane in the confusion? Did she book me on the wrong flight? At that moment the captain's voice came over the speaker and gives us the current temperature at the port of Dar Es Salaam. Unbelievable! I turn to the woman beside me.

"Are you going to Kigali, Rwanda?"

"Yes, I am."

"Do you know why we're headed in the wrong direction then?"

"I didn't know we were."

I flag down the attendant, and ask him where the flight is going.

He leans in, "We go to Dar Es Salaam first, then to Kigali."

"But that's the opposite direction; you could have picked us up on the way back over. That would have made more sense."

He smiles. "I know."

* * *

I land in Rwanda and make my way through the airport to the information desk to ask for an ATM machine. I want to be sure I have the benevolent woman's cash in hand no matter what happens while I am here. At the desk, I experience the record for the fastest marriage proposal to date on my trip. The attendant writes his name, telephone number and email on a slip of paper and begs me to marry him. I smile and tell him I am flattered, but all I can commit to right now is a trip to the ATM.

I arrive late to the Discover Rwanda Youth Hostel; I arrange a cab driver for all day tomorrow and dive into bed grateful that I made it into the country thanks to the lovely woman at the airport. In the morning, Mishek, my cab driver, picks me up at nine. He speaks Kinyarwanda and French, the languages spoken in Rwanda. Fortunately, he speaks bits of English and Swahili as well.

"I'd like to go to the Genocide Museum. I want to learn more about what took place then."

He nods, "Nyamata and Museum."

"What is Nyamata?" I didn't know that word. He holds up two fingers.

"There are two parts?" I am a little confused.

"*Ndio, Nyamata na museum*, you go?"

I hadn't read that in my research, but the third time he gave me the same answer I said, "*Ndio tafadhali, nyamata na museum.*" Yes, please, Nyamata and the Museum.

He lives here, so he must know. We drive 30 minutes out of Kigali. I began to feel uneasy. I thought the museum was located in town so I asked him several times, "Memorial?"

"*Ndio, ndio.*" Yes. Yes.

We pull up to the back entrance of a building, which is draped in purple fabric. The parking lot is empty with one man sitting in a chair by the door. My driver hands me over to him. He speaks English.

"Welcome to the Memorial Genocide site of Nyamata."

I stare at the big metal door, which is bent and twisted, and my eyes scan down to the tile floor, which is destroyed with a hole blown out. A grenade had done this. My heart stops and I look back at my driver full of questions and he solemnly nods for me to follow the guide. We step inside out of the sun. A pungent smell fills my nostrils. It's musty and sickly cloying. I am looking toward the ceiling as my eyes adjust to the dark. There are holes in the roof, hundreds of holes with the sun piercing through each one.

"Bullet holes." My guide must have seen the question on my face.

My eyes drop to follow the tiny beams down to the rest of the room. I gasp and then cover my mouth. My heart pounds like a hammer. This was a church. A church! On each and every bench are piles and piles of clothing, old clothes, dirty and stained with blood. This is the site of the massacre of ten thousand people. I was not expecting this. I didn't know I would actually stand in it, feel it, smell it, and touch it. I don't know if I can do this.

In Rwanda, in the spring of 1994, Hutus killed over eight hundred thousand Tutsis in a span of one hundred days. Many Tutsis sought refuge in churches, believing the Tutsi-hating militias would not enter the site of a sacred place. They hid in every possible space, in cupboards, under floorboards, thousands of them, trying to escape the atrocities of this war against them. Many priests, nuns and church officials fled Rwanda when the killings began. Others stayed, luring the unsuspecting inside, complicit in the bloodshed.

The militia did come into the sanctuary one day during that April, their guns firing toward the ceiling. What followed were some of the most gruesome acts upon men, women, children and babies, of torture, rape, mutilation, and death by machete. A bullet would have been a welcomed way to die. A few survivors made it out alive by lying perfectly still and pretending to be dead. Their wounds turned to scars, but the ones in their heart remain festered, barely healing, their stories too painful to recount.

I am unprepared for such an in-depth experience of the most heinous crimes against humanity. How could this happen? I cry tears of sorrow studying the articles of clothing, realizing they were once filled with a being just like myself. One who wanted to be acknowledged, to experience life, realize dreams, love and be loved. My guide stands beside me in silence. I don't know how long he waits.

"There is more to see..."

He takes me to a lower level. Downstairs are personal items and ID cards making it all too real for me. Outside, in the front of the church, my guide takes me down another small flight of stairs to the site of the mass burial. I'm thinking the graves might be covered over, large drawers possibly. No. Instead it is shelves upon shelves stacked full of tibias, fibulas and skulls. Bones everywhere, anonymous, their individuality prematurely lost forever. How does a country recover from this? How is this degree of hatred extinguished, so that healing is a possibility?

"There are fifty-thousand people down here, collected from the surrounding area."

I turn toward him and gently inquire, "Are you Tutsi or Hutu?"

He speaks softly, "I am Rwandan. We are all Rwandan now."

Some may feel this is a controversial way to memorialize the appalling actions of that spring. I'll admit it is difficult to see, but Africa is real and raw by nature, the truth in your face. The intended purpose is accomplished, searing the images in my mind, making me remember, question, prevent. As seen now, the memorial won't last forever. The sun and the rain make their way through the bullet holes deteriorating the clothing. This stark and shocking lesson will one day be gone. Hopefully by the time that happens we won't need it any more.

* * *

I'm not quite sure what to expect next after my visit to the church. Mishek, my driver, pulls up to the Kigali Memorial Centre, which is a beautiful building with a fountain in the front, and gardens on the side. It is designed as more of a traditional museum and I spend two hours inside reading the exhibits, observing the photos, searching for answers.

In Rwanda, in the 19th century, the Belgians came in to colonize Rwanda and used eugenics to racialize the Tutsi and the Hutus, meaning they artificially created an ethnic race where there was not one before. If you had more than 10 cows, you were Tutsi, if not, you were Hutu. ID cards were issued, and what were previously social classes became fixed as inappropriate ethnic classifications. The Belgians convinced the Tutsis they were superior, and the Tutsis oppressed and indentured the Hutus for many years, treating them horribly. Time passed, the Belgians left, and new generations of Hutus rose up, eventually gaining some positions of power. They, in turn, began a campaign of hate mongering against the Tutsis that was reported at the time, as rivaling that of Hitler. It included leaders of government, politicians, clergy, people in the media, and even Rwanda's favorite pop star.

On April 6, 1994, an airplane carrying the presidents of Rwanda and Berundi was shot down as it prepared to land at Kigali. Both presidents were killed when the plane crashed. The assassination was the straw that broke the camel's back and the Hutus unleashed their anger in an unfathomable way. The victims had become the killers.

Seventeen years later, in the aftermath, we're left with the carnage still apparent in the lives of the Tutsis. And in the lives of thousands of Hutu's who fled the country, afraid they might be convicted, whether involved or not. They live as refugees outside of Rwanda afraid to come home. The United Nations, though it denied help for the Tutsis during the Genocide, created the tribunal, which holds the main perpetrators accountable.

For the smaller crimes they use a system, which has always been in place in Rwanda. Called Gacaca, it is a judicial way of local justice used in the villages, with elected judges from the community. The goal of Gacaca is to find the truth, for that is the only way healing can truly come about. Those who confess, show remorse, and help find the bones of those they killed are given lighter sentences or folded back into the community. This takes a tremendous amount of forgiveness. I read a story of a perpetrator who killed a woman's husband and all of her children. After his confession at Gacaca she said, "I have no one now. I will take you into my home and treat you as a son." The healing power in that kind of forgiveness is undeniable.

Attendance at Gacaca each week is mandatory, as are many things in Rwanda. Umuganda Day is the last Saturday of the month and it is a day of required community service throughout the entire country. They have cleaned, repaired, planted, painted and rebuilt the entire country through this required workday. Plastic bags are now outlawed in Rwanda because they are so bad for the environment, and a visitor can even be fined if your luggage is searched and you are found with one. Ethnicity has been formally outlawed in Rwanda as well, in the effort to promote a culture of healing and unity. One can stand trial for the mere discussion of the different Hutu and Tutsi ethnic groups.

Rwandans believed that women bore the brunt of this war and should have more power in the restoration. They reserved seats for them in Parliament, and after the last election, they now hold the majority. There is a tight rein, a clamp down on anything untoward. Some say with all the mandates; it is a dictatorship cloaked in democracy. I don't know enough to have a valid opinion, but my first impression is that whatever is happening, it's working for now.

Mishek delivers me home to the Discover Rwanda Youth Hostel.

"*Asante sana.*" Thank you very much. I wave as he drives away. I would have missed the important component of Nyamata if he had not insisted on taking me. I walk out to the porch, and find the other guests are also collecting there at the end of the day. I grab a beer and using the honor system, record my purchase on the notepad placed at the bar.

"Hello. How was your day?" someone asks.

"Rough. I've been immersed in the Genocide." I pull up a chair. "Tell me about yourselves, why are you here? I need to take my mind off the topic."

"Well, I'm afraid I can't help you then," says a young Canadian woman covered in tattoos and piercings. "I'm a photographic restorationist. I'm preserving the photographs of the Genocide for the museum."

A Belgian woman leans forward. "Me either, I'm working on my doctorate, studying the colonial period in Rwanda. I'm interviewing the elderly people to find out their take on the hatred."

Another Belgian says, "For my master's thesis, I'm studying the effectiveness and relationship between donors and the Rwandan Government. Your country is a leading contributor by the way."

An American man speaks, "I'm a lawyer, clerking for the Chief Justice of the Supreme Court. My job is to help raise the standards of the judicial system."

"I'm American too," smiles a young woman. "I work with KIVA, overseeing micro loans for people to start small businesses now in Rwanda."

"I'm from Holland, interning at the Dutch Embassy."

My jaw drops open at the first of the introductions and never closes.

"Oh my gosh! Who ARE you people? I feel like I'm in the presence of greatness, found on a Rwandan hillside...in a youth hostel?" They grin.

These people, staying for six or nine months at a time, are working on the larger picture, the bigger issues, trying to change thought processes, traditions, and laws, from the top.

I feel small. "I'm just on the ground trying to help one person at a time."

Next to me, a man named Ryan chimes in. "Don't look at me; I'm just a loser tourist."

We laugh; raise our glasses and toast to change and healing.

Back in my room I check the international news on my laptop, which I have decided I will now do regularly before moving locations. I am surprised by one article. It reads:

> A Rwandan genocide fugitive, Jean Mary Vianney Mudahinyuka, was handed over by United States, Chicago, Authorities today following a deportation order of immigration fraud. He is expected to begin a 19 year sentence which he was given

> in absentia. He was instrumental in the deaths of many and also killed families himself. Known to be violent, say Authorities, he assaulted a U.S. police officer.

I am proud of the United States for bringing this man to justice. Many countries have assisted by helping with housing, providing seeds for planting, AIDS education and antiretroviral drugs, counseling for victims, and help for orphans and children born of rape.

This is how Rwanda heals, on many different levels in many different ways: one person with the courage to forgive, another with a new idea, or someone willing to give their time. The world wants them to succeed, to create a stable, viable society in which the Hutus and the Tutsis can live side by side as one again. They don't have to do it alone. Everyone can take part, everyone, even Ryan the tourist. For he had come to trek gorillas, which is Rwanda's number one source of income.

* * *

He looks straight at me, his face revealing nothing. Our eyes catch. His stare is benign and uninterested, as one might observe a stranger in passing at an airport. Why me? Why would he glance in my direction? He stands. He is tall, over six feet, I would assume. He moves toward me. I shake, both with fear and excitement, my heart racing. He heads straight for me, and my eyes widen into a stare locked on his every move. Am I in harm's way? Closer now. Closer, my chest heaving as I try to breathe. Within several feet of me he reaches out his strong arm, and as he comes by, he uses it to push me out of the way. My eyes following, he walks on, not looking back. *He* is a silverback mountain gorilla and I have spent the last twenty-four hours trying to get to him.

The trek to find gorillas, I discover, begins the moment you decide you would like to have a wildlife experience like no other in the world. Only 54 permits are granted per day. That's all. Most people who come hire a tour group to take care of their flight, the permit, and transportation details a year in advance. I didn't know about gorilla trekking a year ago. I didn't even know I would ever be in Rwanda.

My new friends at the hostel tell me that sometimes it is possible, if it is just one person, to get a permit at the last minute due to a cancellation because if people are sick they can't be near the gorillas. The primates are so genetically close to humans that they can catch our diseases, yet they haven't built up any immunity. I ask them how I would find out about such an opening.

"Just hop on a motorbike taxi and have them take you downtown to the permit office."

"A motorbike taxi?"

"Yeah, they're cheap and easy because they weave in and out of traffic jams."

"Do I have to provide my own helmet?" I point to the one she holds in her hands.

She laughs. "No, I brought my own. I'm here for six months and my inner Larry David wouldn't let me put a public helmet on my hair."

"I'm headed that way," says Ryan. "Hop on a bike and meet me downtown, I'll show you where the permit office and the bus station are located."

I walk to the top of the road, and flag down a bike. I don't have an inner Larry David so I put the potentially germy helmet right on my head and off we go, weaving dangerously through traffic like a video game.

Downtown, Ryan points to a small alley. "Down there and turn left. That's where the bus station is, believe it or not, and across the way, down the hill is the permit office. Good luck."

I walk into the office of the Rwanda Tourism Board with low expectations. It takes half a day to get to the park and I'm required to be at the entrance at 7:00 a.m. for briefing or I forfeit my ticket, so I would need to leave the day before and stay overnight nearby.

"Would you possibly have a permit for two days from now?" I ask.

"Sorry, we don't. Sold out. Would you like me to check the day after?"

"No, that's the day I fly out."

"Oh, wait we do have one for tomorrow, and looking at the clock I'd say if you hurry, you'd have just enough time to go pack a bag and catch a bus up to the mountain."

I stand there thinking quickly: I've heard you have to take two buses to two different towns of which I do not know the names; then get a ride from there to a lodge, somehow get to the entrance by 7:00 a.m., and hire a driver ahead of time to take you from the park entrance to the start of the trek to see your family of gorillas. That is so many terrifying variables. I don't speak the language, and if I mess up anywhere along the way I lose the chance to see the gorillas. My heart is pounding. No time to plan. No time to book a reservation, so possibly no place to sleep tonight. It's ridiculous how this keeps happening, choosing between now or never. This is a crazy way to live a life. I pace back and forth. I'm afraid to navigate these unknowns alone. I'm here, though, and I'll never have this opportunity again.

"Yes, I'll take it."

I run to flag a taxi bike and ask him to wait for me to throw some things in a bag. We race back to the alley bus station. I squeeze myself into the first mini bus and I smile as I sit in the familiar fold-down seat in the middle of the aisle with my pack on my lap. I breathe deeply. As we head up the mountain, I look out the window at the beautiful landscape of cultivated hills, and listen to the lilting sounds of Kinyarwanda being spoken around me. I have a few more modes of transportation to figure out, and hopefully, even if the lodge is at capacity, they will at least have a couch for me to sleep on.

I am the only white person on the bus, and no one seems to mind. An hour into the ride, the man beside me starts to nod off. His head sways and ends up on my shoulder. He must be exhausted. It is not an easy life here and there is no telling what his living conditions are, or what difficulties he faces just to survive. Others look at me surprised that I let him stay there. I smile back at them as though to say, it's okay. He sleeps soundly for the rest of the ride and I have time to reflect with peace for all that I have in my life.

My mini bus stops at a small town and by asking enough people piecing together Swahili and English, I find the next bus down the street. It gets me closer to the park. Off that bus I flag a motorbike and he takes me the last leg of the trip. Ah, so far so good, right on schedule. As we ride through the countryside, beautiful Rwandan children stand at the side of the road waving and smiling the entire way. I feel as though I am in a movie scene or the star in a parade. I eagerly wave back acknowledging their love.

A room is available at the lodge! It's tiny and their last one but I don't care because I have a place to rest my head. I drop my bag, immediately head to the lobby and begin quizzing the other guests as to whether they are going gorilla trekking, and have they hired their driver from the entrance to the trek? Each driver comes at a cost of eighty American dollars, round trip back to the entrance of the park. If you find people to share the car, then you reduce your cost. I round up four people, and we hire a driver. Having someone to share the experience with is going to make the day that much more enjoyable.

As I lay my head on the pillow in my room, I am filled with joy that I had the courage to say yes and make this happen. My lesson: follow your yes's until you get a no. Even though I was terrified and anxious most of the day, I did it. I did this! And sitting on the other side of it, I can say that every single difficult, emotional moment was worth the price.

I am up at 5:00 a.m. for the big day, and witness a beautiful sunrise. A surge of empowerment shoots through my body. The lodge serves food early, knowing we will need sustenance for the hike. My new friends meet me for breakfast and we express our excitement and fears at being near these massively strong wild animals.

Our driver takes us to the park entrance and we find the site of the briefing at 7:00 a.m. We are assigned to one of the seven family groups on the mountain, and are told we will stay seven meters apart from the gorillas at all times for safety and to respect their space. Upon first sight of the family, the clock will start ticking and we will be given one hour, and one hour only to observe.

We drive 45 minutes through the countryside to the base of our trek. Our two guides meet us, and although the gorillas are peaceful, each guide is carrying a rifle for our protection. The gorillas live between 7,000 to 14,000 feet in elevation so we hike an hour and a half straight up through farmland to Volcano National Park, the edge of one of the last high rain forests in the world.

Once in the forest the vegetation becomes incredibly dense. We roll down our sleeves and pant legs because of the stinging nettles. The others brought gloves, but not having any, I brought socks to protect my hands. Our guides use machetes to create a path for us leading toward the general area of where the family was last seen. We thrash our way through the forest. The radio finally crackles and the trackers say they have spotted the family. Our guide begins to make unusual guttural noises, announcing to the gorillas we mean no harm. The trackers guard our packs, as we are not allowed to take anything with us into the area, but a camera, with no flash.

I hear a guttural sound being returned. We pull back the brush and there is a mama playing and wrestling with her young one! The clock starts ticking as I gasp a cry of joy. These gentle giants roll, tumble and snuggle with each other. The love between the two is palpable and so beautiful to watch. We follow them up to another spot where they gather with the rest of the family. We quickly learn that the gorillas have not been given the seven-meter rule, which is how we have several close encounters with them. They go about their day, not caring that we are there, but brushing up against us from time to time. They are so incredibly powerful that it is scary and exciting at the same time.

I watch with a sense of wonder and awe. They are so similar to us, that it causes self-reflection. We are watching a different version of us. They are not so far away from being us. Although a life in the wilderness free of the pressures of supporting one's self, paying bills and going to work each day seems idyllic, and even though my life is so uncertain right now, I am still thankful for being born a human being in this lifetime.

A tear rolls down my cheek as a mama holds hands with her child. She snuggles her up and rocks her. It is easy for me to understand why Dian Fossey and Jane Goodall made a life's work studying these amazing primates. It is truly one of the most thrilling, and shortest hours of my life.

We hike down to the park reveling in the awe of our experience. I make my way in reverse back to Kigali, and to the hostel. I collect my things and head to the airport. I'm flying back to Tanzania and taking a bus to meet Seri in Dar Es Salaam, the capital, and then will have to leave the country as my visa is almost up.

When the flight lands in Tanzania, my sweet airport friend greets me and I hand her 151096 Tshillings. I give her the biggest hug ever and tell her I was also able to trek the gorillas thanks to her.

"Thank you so much for trusting me, a stranger, to owe you money."

She smiles, "You gave to us and we give to you. This is my dream for the world."

Chapter Eleven

"Seri, I'm old enough to be your mom, and yet, your wisdom, compassion and boldness has moved me miles down the road in the journey to myself. I'm pretty sure you were born forty years old." I grin through my tears, as I hug her goodbye.

"Well you, woman, are an inspiration of your own, always making good come from bad. You could fall into a pile of shit and grow a rose."

"I can't believe you got up at 4:30 a.m. to say goodbye to me. And you," I point at her. "It's not enough that you raised money and made the time to come here and volunteer for three months, oh no, because you are Seri, you raised double and took twice as much time off. So speaking of miles down the road, I'm going to somehow make my way to Cape Town to see you before your volunteer stint there is over and you head back to the States. I promise."

"Awesome! I like a 'see you later' goodbye much better. Love you, *dada*." Sister.

My journey starts at 5:00 a.m., at the bus station in Dar Es Salaam. It is still dark as I climb out of the taxi anxiously surveying fifty buses all packed together on a huge lot, rows and rows of them with hundreds of people swarming around and in between. I have my ticket in hand, but how in the world will I know which bus is mine? Fortunately, a porter appears. Thank goodness, I'll gladly pay him money to get me to the right bus.

We agree on a fair price, yet on the way, the porter tries to increase the fee several times. I say no, we have already agreed on the price.

I almost cave in but I know this is what they do, and I am trying to become stronger in how I show up in my life.

We weave in and out of people, frantically trying to get to their buses on time, loaded down with all types of bags and goods they had purchased in the big city. In all of the confusion I keep my eyes firmly on my bag he is carrying, making sure no one takes it from him. All the while he continues discussing more money, and I continue to say no. We stop at a bus and I confirm with the driver that it is the right one. I place my bag in storage under the bus hoping it will still be there when we reach Mbeya. I turn and hand the porter my Tshillings and he immediately takes off into a run, disappearing in the crowd.

"Hey, *yangu fehda*!" I yell. My money! My change!

I can't follow him leaving my belongings behind, and he knows that. He ripped me off and had gotten his price. I am so angry! I'm stewing as I get on the bus. It wasn't a large amount of money, but still it wasn't right. It takes a lot to make me mad, and after having lived with abuse in my first marriage, I am learning that nothing gets under my skin worse than being manipulated. My heart is pounding and sweat pouring down my back as I sit and wait for the bus to fill up. I try to calm myself. I know I couldn't have found the bus without him, though small consolation it is when I am feeling so violated.

I watch the Tanzanian people I have grown to love get settled into their seats for a long day of travel. I think of their gentle kindness, their hospitality for one another, and their indomitable spirits. A smile breaks out on my face. I've become accustomed to being the only white person and they return my grins with curiosity. I look forward to the rest of the day and seeing the landscape of southern Tanzania. Plus, this bus has air conditioning, a screen in the front for videos, and trashcans so I won't have to haul my trash around. It feels luxurious. As soon as we leave the station, the driver puts in a video of a live concert of Celine Dion from the '90's, because they love Celine Dion in East Africa.

We drive straight through to lunchtime and stop. The line at the squatty potty is very long, giving me time to prepare. With no access to running water, a squatty potty is a hole in the ground, often with cement around the opening. It could be housed in a building or in a hut of its own, like an outhouse. One enters the potty, straddles the hole and pops a squat. I have learned, through mishaps, the way to best experience the squatty. People often miss the hole when squatting, so I roll up my pants or skirt above my knees before I go in so they don't drop in the excrement as I squat. I take out a wet wipe and then place my bag so it rides my back without falling to the ground. When it is my turn to enter, I place the wet wipe over my nose to block out the stench. When I'm finished, I hold my breath, use the wet wipe, throw it down the squatty, and run!

The line is so long that I don't have time to get food. Back on the bus I open a bottle of water I brought with me. Staring out the window of a bus for fourteen hours with no electronics gives one plenty of time for self-reflection. The marathon of running from my feelings has come to a grinding halt. There is nowhere for me to run. I am face to face with myself and I go through every part and parcel of my life. My time at CCS had been busy and full of everything and this is the first moment to really reflect on my life since leaving the USA.

I'm headed to No Man's Land. It is a bridge over the Songwe River between the borders of Tanzania and Malawi. A bridge suspended between two different countries. It is a void, an empty crossing-over from one land to another, and one culture to another. There is a feeling of uncertainty, as one walks through this limbo. For me, the lonely pathway is about leaving the known, for the unknown.

I begin with feeling grateful for all of the experiences on my trip thus far, and the fact that I am out here living this life. I am in Africa. Awesome. How did that happen?! This soon leads me to thinking about how I got out here, which then leads me to why I am here and before I know it, I am in a full-blown slump. Complete and utter loneliness set in with sadness, which leads to a giant pity party for I don't know how long.

In this sadness I begin to question every path that got me to this place and before I know it, I am angry with myself for so many decisions I've made in my life. I begin to identify patterns that I loathe about myself, and the voices in my head say I will just continue to do the same stupid stuff. Now that there is no one around to blame or create circumstances where I can place a "well I did it because of what they did," I am realizing that some of those patterns are mine and it had nothing to do with other people. I'm angry at myself that I married my first husband who turned out to be abusive and angry that I left my daughter outside for three minutes, never to see her alive again. Infuriated that when I married again, I never pursued my own career, leaving me with nothing now. I feel like an idiot, a weak and compliant person. I feel trapped thinking I cannot change. I spiral downward into self-punishment.

At some point the woman across the aisle must have read my thoughts. I realize tears are spilling down my cheeks as she reaches over and touches my arm.

She holds her arms up, pumps her biceps and says, "*Uwe na nguvu.*" You are strong.

I put my hand over my heart and bow my head to her, "*Asante sana.*" Thank you very much.

The sisterhood of women and how we understand each other touches me. We just know. How perfect that she is here and acts upon her urge to comfort me.

I ponder what she said and think maybe I am strong. I did manage to get myself across the world. That took some strength and courage. And I am out here navigating on my own in a potentially scary part of the world. Yeah, that's kind of badass. I sit up straight in my seat and begin to feel better. If I did those things, then surely I can be strong and make new decisions for myself. And if I pull this trip off then certainly I can pull off other seemingly impossible things. I have always made every effort to do all I can, in any given situation. My intentions are pure, so why do I beat myself down? I have always made the best decisions I could, with the information I had at the time. And every single decision good or bad has brought me here. Tears pour again as I begin to find forgiveness for myself. I feel grace and kindness wash over me for the first time.

My thoughts drift to my first husband. Given he had some good traits, it took me many years to find forgiveness for his abuses. And what I now know from many years volunteering and sitting on the board of our local domestic violence shelter is that abuse is a learned behavior. He was abused and shamed as a child and this is all he knows. This is what love looks like to him. It doesn't make it right, but it does make it a little more understandable, which means I can have a little empathy for his plight as well.

My thoughts move to my second wonderful and fun husband. We raised our six combined kids in a loving home. After eighteen years he allowed himself to fall in love with another woman. I was so angry because I thought I was an awesome wife. I thought we were good. I thought we were better than good. As I sit here now with many, many hours to ponder, I realize there must have been some sort of void in our relationship that I did not recognize. There was something he must have needed that I didn't pick up on and he didn't express. I guess if that is the case, I was not the perfect wife for him, or maybe I was and then as the kids moved away I wasn't. I don't know, but I refuse to stay angry because anger turns to bitterness and bitterness is very hard to root out. Bitterness will eat me alive.

Life is what it is. I have done all that I possibly can to live a good life, full of integrity, trying to be the best person I can be. And now I am seeing a glimpse that my ex-husbands were trying to do the best they could. Our seasons ended and it was time to move on, creating something new. Yes, this is how I choose to look at it from now on. I will not operate from a victim's viewpoint any longer. I will claim myself as a survivor and move forward from here. Oh my gosh, I think I just made peace with my past. Ah, I breathe deeply, and as I exhale, years of self-loathing dissipate into the air. I feel my courage growing with a new resolve about how I want to show up in my life. I blow my nose and throw the tissue in the trash.

There is only one more unofficial stop in the day, which is by the side of the road. Men are the only ones who get off to use the bathroom near the small brush. Our driver takes the two trashcans, and I watch as he empties them down into the foliage of some bushes. Oh no! Out of sight, out of mind, I suppose. The Celine Dion DVD goes back in for round two, just in case we forgot, and we move on down the road.

I am excited that in a few minutes I will be in familiar Moravian family territory. My name "Lucetta" is a Moravian name for generations back in my family. We are a Protestant faith similar to Methodists and Lutherans. There aren't many in the United States because we are mission-oriented, thus we are mostly in developing countries, and the main reason most people in the U.S. have never heard of us. Except maybe we are known for our famous Moravian cookies and sugar cake. Our motto sums up how we operate within our faith:

In essentials unity;

In non-essentials liberty;

In all things love.

I think it's a beautiful philosophy. Southern Tanzania is full of Moravians, and I am about to stay in one of their hostels, a coming home, so to speak.

* * *

It is late and dark as we pull into the bus station in Mbeya, which for me is unnerving. Young men trying to get to our bags immediately swarm our bus. I get off the bus as fast as I can and push my way through the people to the undercarriage. I am four people back when, through the crowd I see a man reach for my bag! Instinct takes over as I literally crowd surf on top of people to get there in time. Just as the bag is coming out, I lunge with a final push and grasp the handle. The crowd surges back taking me with it, but I desperately hold on to that bag, fearing I'm pulling my arm off. The bus driver is trying to push the men back away from his customers and a small fight breaks out.

I back away from the bus for a moment to regroup. A young man approaches me.

"You need a taxi?" He speaks in English.

"Yes, to the Moravian Youth Hostel, do you know it?"

"Yes, come with me."

He leads me out of the crowd and flags a car. He speaks for a while with the man behind the wheel then opens the door for me. As I climb in, he goes around and gets in the back too, on the other side.

"You're not the driver?"

"No, he is my friend."

"Then why are you in the car?" I ask.

"I must show him the way."

"He's a driver, he should know the way. No, I won't take a cab with two men."

I open my door and start to get out. As I stand and look around a chill runs through my body. The lot is empty and dark. Friends or family had picked everyone else up. I have no choice but to take this offer of a ride. I take a deep breath, steel my nerves and get back in.

"I want you to know they are expecting me at the hostel."

"Yes, yes, we will take you, it's no problem."

My only consolation is that in a few minutes I will be in the safety and brotherhood of my people. We drive for quite a while, and I begin to feel on edge because I know the hostel is supposed to be relatively close to the bus station. More time passes.

The man leans forward to the driver, sneaks him some Tshillings and says, "*Kuweka kuendesha gari.*"

My heart pounds out of my chest. I have not spoken Swahili with them yet and they have no way of knowing I can understand. Keep driving, he had said. I am becoming more and more alarmed. I reach into my bag and find the only defense weapon I have, a pen, and place it in my hand. This could at least put an eye out if necessary. Besides, the pen is mightier than the sword, right?

"I am Moravian," I pronounce. "They know I am coming and they will be looking for me."

I am hoping this is true. My only defense is to make them realize they will be held accountable for their actions. We drive in silence and my head is alternating between it will be okay and dire warnings stinging my body. Think. Think. What did I learn about their culture during my time at CCS?

He places his hand gently on my shoulder. "Have peace."

Then in the dark his hand slides down into my shirt onto my breast, while his other slides down my pants. I immediately understand his intentions. Every alarm bell goes off in my head! I reach up and grab his wrist squeezing it as tightly as I can.

I look into his face and say in a loud strong voice. "*Mimi ni bibi yako. Gari yangu kwa hosteli.*" I am your grandmother. Drive me to hostel.

I firmly push his hands back to his lap and he slides away. They are both wide-eyed with shock that I speak their language. The driver nods, "*Ndio.*" Yes. He slows down and turns the car around.

The man, in a slightly sarcastic tone, says in English, "Grandmother?"

"*Miaka hamsini.*" Fifty years. I respond in Swahili to keep the driver in the conversation. I know that I look younger than I am right now, and that the Africans don't have much experience determining the age of a blond white woman, so they never would have dreamed I am that old. I also know the strong role that grandmothers play in their life, and the respect they hold for their wisdom. And if nothing else I was hoping to gross him out at the thought of "being with" his grandmother.

We ride in silence again as I hold my pen and my breath until I see the big gates with the Moravian symbol painted on the front. My place of refuge! It is 11:30 p.m. now. I pay the driver and the man gets out of the cab. The man grabs my bag, leans into the driver saying something, then finds the night watchman to check me into my room. I try to take my bag from the man.

"No, I've got it."

The taxi drives away while the man stands holding my bag. What? Why is the man still here? The watchman opens my door and the man walks into my room with my bag. I pick up the room keys the watchman has placed on the dresser, and discreetly put them in between my knuckles. I step out onto the stoop, which faces the parking lot, and look for the night watchman.

I gesture for the man to come out of my room and say loud enough for the watchman to hear, "*Kwaheri*." Goodbye.

He hesitates, fuming, but finally walks out.

Glaring at me, he brushes by and under his breath claims, "I'll bring a taxi and see you at 6:45 a.m."

Oh great, that will give him plenty of time to make a plan for retaliation and abduction. I run into the room, lock the bolt and slide down onto the floor, my back against the door. I am shaking and my heart is pounding. I take a few deep breaths. I can't move. Just get me to the border. Get me to the border. I jump at every noise outside.

Hunger pangs grow strong as I have not eaten since yesterday, but there will be no going out of the room to find dinner. As I calm down over time, I begin looking for the good. I escaped potential disaster, and I am safe for now. I am with Moravians. I have a bed in which to sleep with a mosquito net, and even though I am hungry, it is just for one day. Many Africans go to bed hungry every single night. I set my alarm knowing I will not sleep a wink, for I will be out at 6:00 a.m. flagging down my own taxi.

* * *

The sun is just coming up as I hear a beep go off in my pack. I hadn't slept at all and it startles me as I'd forgotten I still have a flip phone from working at CCS. I am shaking, waiting for more disaster. It is a text from Stephen in the States. Evidently he is hanging out with his workout girlfriends.

"THE GIRLS SAY I SHOULD START MAN-SCAPING. WHAT DO YOU THINK?"

I fall back onto the bed. Really? My life is in danger in Africa, and you're asking me if you should shave your parts? Really!? I was upset at first thinking, dude, I was abducted, seriously think about more important things! And then a smile begins to break on my face. This is so Africa, the crazy juxtaposition of things. He has no way of knowing my situation, and this is what is important to him in the moment. I begin to believe this happened at this time, in this way, as a gift to break up my anxious state, to remind me to think with a larger perspective. I have no idea how to respond, how much to say about all of what's happened to me in just a few characters, but I know I have to get going soon.

I chuckle and type, "I THINK IF YOU DID YOU WOULD LIKE IT"

I'll just leave it at that. I toss my phone back in my pack and begin thinking of how to make a safe escape from Mbeya.

I cautiously peek my head out of the door. I am still shaken from the events of last night, but things aren't quite so scary in the light of dawn. The security guard asks if I need a taxi, and when I say, yes, please, he takes off running down the long road. I smile, now that's the Africa I know. I walk toward the gate and on the left is a church, a Moravian church. A reminder that God was with me the entire time. I wish I could stay for a service and meet some fellow Moravians, but my Tanzanian visa runs out today.

I climb into the taxi and my anxiety ramps back up at the thought of going back to the bus station. My driver, a legitimate one this time, says he can drive me all the way to the border. It will be considerably more than the bus, but at this point I feel like it is worth the peace of mind. We negotiate the price, and I have him write it down.

A few miles down the road we stop for petrol, and he says, "You give me money to pay."

"Yes, but I take it out of this," pointing to the figure written on the paper. He is clearly disappointed that I know the scam of making mzungu pay petrol on top of cab fare, but he agrees. I am so glad I continually study my *Lonely Planet* guidebook. An hour and a half, and four security checkpoints later, we pull up at the border.

We'd beaten all the buses there, and so we enter an empty parking lot. Suddenly seven men surround our car, trying to open the doors, and banging on the windows. They are shouting and asking if I need to change money, or need a taxi to the next town over the border. It is terrifying chaos, the pounding and shouting.

I look at my driver, "If you get me into the customs building over there, I won't take out the cost of petrol."

He smiles. "Okay, are you ready?"

We get out of the car and the men are hovering around me like seagulls on the back of a ferry, shouting, trying to get my bag, and creating as much confusion as possible. My driver is doing his best to keep them at bay, as I keep answering, *hapana asante*. No, thank you. We near customs and they disappear into thin air. Inside, I receive my exit stamp and I am suddenly overcome with sadness at leaving Tanzania. I didn't renew my visa as I had earlier decided that I should travel to see other parts of Africa while I am on the continent. Perhaps I will find a place to settle down along the way.

Back outside I start the long walk to the bridge. The men appear out of nowhere and surround me again creating mayhem. This must be what it is like to be hounded by paparazzi.

"You must change your money on this side."

"No, thank you."

"You will lose your money. Change your shillings."

"No thank you."

They are all shouting at once.

"You can't change money over there, step over to my office, we will negotiate."

"No, thank you."

One tries to take my bag.

"I am trying to help you."

"NO, thank you."

Another says, "You need a taxi to Karonga. You pay me, I take you all the way."

"No, thank you." They keep talking and playing off of one another.

"You don't trust us? We are trying to help you." It goes on and on.

The last 24 hours finally boil over inside of me and I scream, "*Hapana acha*!"

It is the rude way to say, "No, stop!" They fall silent.

I'm on a rampage and I get in their face. "I know there is a bank just on the other side, so don't tell me about your black market money because I don't have to change it here, and you." I point to another man, "can't take me all the way to Koronga because you can't even cross the border, so I'm not giving you one single shilling. You're all a bunch of ...bullies! Go look that word up in English, and back away from me, NOW."

With his mouth dropped open, one asks, "How do you know these things?"

"Because she is an American woman," Says one of the others before I have time to answer.

I am slightly flattered, though I'm sure he didn't mean it that way. I turn and make my way to the bridge, unaccompanied.

I have a conversation with myself, "Whoa, where did *she* come from? I don't know—bunch of bullies? Really? That's such an old phrase—Yeah, but I kinda hope she sticks around."

I look up and see before me the 300-meter walk to Malawi. I am the only white person I have seen in days, and here I am walking myself across the empty bridge. My emotions are in tatters. I have with me all my possessions for the year, a knapsack and a roller pack, which is heavy and bulging. The scene is such a contrast. I am packing more belongings than most of these people even own, not to mention they've never seen a roller bag. I feel a little ridiculous. Half way across though, I remember that I am an American woman, and I hold my head high.

I get my Malawi stamp, change my Tanzanian shillings to Kwacha, and bargain a deal on a taxi to Koronga. Several checkpoints down the road we are stopped, and two Malawian policemen get into the back seat of the car. I look at my driver and whisper, "*Quanini*?" Why?

He looks at me. His hand is on the seat and he motions it as though to say, "Don't say anything." The hair stands up on the back of my neck. I sit in silence staring straight ahead, trying to be invisible. My mind goes to all sorts of horrible places. Twenty miles later at the next village, they finally speak to the driver. He pulls over and they get out.

I am so relieved until it occurs to me, "They just got a free ride on my money, didn't they?"

He had been holding his breath as well, and lets it out as he laughs and nods, "I think so."

At the bus station, when the taxi drops me, I encounter the same type of hysteria as at the border crossing, but at least it is a small station. I find a bus that will take me four hours to Mzuzu, the next town with transport. I climb aboard and wait for the bus to leave. The conductor comes back and introduces himself to me. We chat for a while as he tells me that many of the people in the front of the bus are his family members headed to a funeral.

"Oh, I'm so sorry."

"Would you like to meet them?"

"Yes, of course, I'd like to share my condolences."

He takes me up front and introduces me. I shake their hands and give them my love. I make my way back to my seat.

In a few minutes he is back by my side, "Will you marry me? You have met my family, so now you should marry me." So that's what that was really all about.

I smile and say I am honored, but I will never marry again. He gives me his email and phone number just in case I change my mind. I meet several other wonderful Malawians on the ride, such sweet people.

At the bus station in Mzuzu, taxi drivers accost me again. I tell them I need a bus to Nkhata Bay. This time their story is that there are no buses because it is Saturday and I should take a taxi.

I am laughing at this point. "Yes, there are buses, and they run every day."

"But you should have my friend take you because he can take you all the way to your hostel, and you don't want to get in after dark."

Ugh, after dark, he'd hit me right where it hurt. I bargain a price.

I look at the driver and ask, "You know Mayoka, and you're going to take me all the way, right?"

"Yes."

We drive through Mzuzu, and then an hour through the lush, green gorgeous Malawian countryside. We dip down into Nkhata Bay, which is a small village on the edge of Lake Malawi, and head up to Mayoka Village, my hostel. The road is dirt and really rough. After ten minutes of slowly bouncing over the ruts, the driver stops the taxi by a roadside market and gets out. He walks to the back and pulls my bag out of the trunk.

I get out. "What?"

"My car no go, need four wheel drive, you hike up that path, this man carry your bag."

"What? Do I have to pay him?"

"Yes, he help you."

"No, I have already paid you to take me all the way and you said you would. You pay him."

He reluctantly dips into his pocket and pays the young man a pittance. My new friend hoists my heavy bag onto his head. I grab my other pack, and we head straight up hill for a twenty-minute hike. I feel so badly for him, that I pay him again, once I finally reach my long awaited, hard fought destination.

I arrive just in time for dinner. I am famished, as I haven't eaten in two full days now. I sit staring out at the gorgeous lake, thinking, why can't I go home, get a job, and be a normal person? Why am I not getting a tug at my heartstrings for a place to stay here, or a job where I can be of service? It makes no sense to me. I feel as though I'm at Mile 22 in a marathon where runners often hit a wall, and feel as though they can't go on.

Why do I make these plans? I always dread them and half the time I'm scared out of my mind. I have to make these plans, though, precisely because I am afraid. I must get beyond being terrified and stand on my own two feet before I can move forward into my new life, before I can leave the No Man's Land I'm living in.

* * *

Mayoka Village is actually a hostel, but the Australian owners were determined to get off the grid and made the place ecologically friendly and self-sufficient as their own village. Their delicious food is organically grown and meals are prepared from produce that is in season. They have their own filtering system so the water is drinkable from the tap, though I'm not willing to test that. I have not had one drop of water pass my lips that did not come from a bottle. Even as I brush my teeth I use bottled water always, and the limited times I've had access to a shower I purse my lips, not letting one drop make its way through. I believe this is how I have come all this way without getting sick once.

The showers at Mayoka have hot water for a few hours each morning and they harness energy from lightning strikes to heat them. It's worth getting up early for a hot shower. They also have a compost toilet, which I have never experienced. It doesn't smell, which is an awesome relief for my nostrils, and the compost will eventually be used as fertilizer.

Mayoka is also very involved in the community and finds creative ways to support the locals. It sits on the side of a steep hill and overlooks Lake Malawi, the largest lake in all of Africa. It is so nice here that I decide to stay for a week and restore myself from the harrowing border journey. I wash my clothes in the lake and lay them out on the rocks to dry, as I enjoy a moment of peace in the warm sun.

At breakfast I sit beside a young American woman and she shares, "I'm in the Peace Corps and have a weekend off so I came here for a little rest, away from my responsibilities. What brought you here?"

I recount a short version of my story and she seems fascinated. Leaning in, she inquires if she can ask me a personal question. My response is, "Of course."

"I've met many people out traveling for long periods of time, and with the Peace Corps we are paid a pittance, so I've always wondered how people afford this?"

"Well, I can't speak for anyone else, but for me, I have taken the money that would have been a down payment on a house and am using it to travel and hopefully relocate." I grin. "The jury is still out as to whether this is a really good decision, or a completely crazy one. And other than my volunteer stint, I've been able to live on about $25.00 a day."

She sips her coffee, "Yes, I'm amazed at how inexpensive it is here, and in all developing countries."

"Even so, I'm constantly fighting fears about my money running out before my next career is started. I scrutinize every penny I spend. On a change of topics," I point to her pack. "I see you have that new book everyone is talking about, *The Girl With The Dragon Tattoo*."

She pulls it out. "Yes, it's spellbinding! I'll be done tomorrow if you'd like to have it?"

"Yes. I'm out of reading material and was about to visit the bookcase. What a score for me. Thank you!"

Most hostels have a book-share corner, where backpackers donate books they've finished and pick up new ones as they go on their way. This often includes Lonely Planet Books for neighboring countries, which people will leave behind as they cross a new border. This is perfect, because once we are done with a book we don't want to carry around any unnecessary weight. And with limited Internet and electricity, having a physical paper book is the only way to go.

Chapter Twelve

The one thing Africa has that we don't is time. As I leave Mayoka Village, a four-wheel drive taxi picks me up, and takes me to Nkhata Bay where I will catch a bus back to Mzuzu. The bus, it turns out, is actually a small car. I pay 500 kwacha, three dollars, for a seat and luggage is free. We must wait for the car to fill up with people before it will leave. I sit in the hot vehicle 45 minutes, wedged in between two men, until we are at maximum capacity. It is a tight fit. Right before we leave, someone brings a roll of laminate flooring, and after failing to tie it to the top of the vehicle they shove it in through the hatchback, up the side to the front. Now we are so squeezed that I sit upright on the edge of the seat with my face in between the driver and front passenger, the two men's shoulders touching behind me. The driver cranks up the volume on some American Pop music so I sing along, loudly. Fortunately for them, it is only an hour ride.

At the depot in Mzuzu, I find a taxi to take me to a hostel for the night, as the next morning, I will catch a real bus for a nine-hour ride to Blantyre. It is early on a rainy afternoon when the driver turns onto a slippery dirt road beside a field. It seems an unusual place to have a hostel, but it is in my *Lonely Planet* book, so I am going on the assumption that it is all right. It is called Mzoozoozoo, a clever play of words on Mzuzu. The place looks like an unkempt house.

As we pull in, the driver turns to me. "I'll wait to see if they have a room, and make sure you want to stay."

"It's fine, I called ahead and they have room."

"I'll wait." He says as he pulls my bag out of the back.

"Uhm, okay." I soon find out why. I walk in the front door and survey the room. The living room has been converted into a bar. There are five white men lounging in the room, each with a beer in their hands and several empty bottles already on the table. The air is a little creepy. They look crusty and worn, like they'd done too many drugs in the sixties and seventies. One stands at the bar with sunglasses on, a beer in his hand and snorkel flippers on his feet. Flippers? They stare at me, no one saying a word.

"Hello," I nod to snorkel man. "I called about a room."

"Yeah, it's a dorm," he says with a British accent, "but you won't have to share, no one else is back there."

Back there? I am a little nervous about being the only woman around, but I figure if they are this trashed early on a Sunday, they'll be harmless or passed out by nightfall. I thank the driver for his kindness, tell him I will stay, and ask him to pick me up at 5:30 the next morning. The men look at me, still in silence.

I turn to snorkel man again, "The room?"

"Yeah?" Pause.

"May I go there?"

"Oh yeah, yeah, right, right. Follow me." He tries unsuccessfully to flipper his way to the front door.

Now barefoot, he takes me out on the porch and around to the backyard. As we walk through the high grass, I search the recesses of my mind to remember what the LP guidebook had said about this place. "A favorite haunt of backpackers." Haunt, that was the word they had used. Now I also remember something about "sleeping in the room of the timbers." We pass a small shed where the bathroom is located and then he leads me to the timbers all right. He opens the door and it is a barn. The room has four beds with mosquito nets. It smells of mold and dirt, and I can see the outdoors between the cracks of the timbers. There are only sheets on the bed, no blanket. It is going to be cold tonight at this altitude, so I am trying to think of clothes

I have that I can pile on. Ah me, I need to get better about reading between the lines of the guidebooks. Placed on one of the other beds is a backpack with a man's toiletry kit. He must be checking out. I drop my bags, grab my laptop and walk into town for food and Internet.

I return before nightfall and discover a young woman at the hostel. She is a Peace Corps Volunteer and has a weekend off from working in her village. She is as relieved to see me as I am her. We sit at the bar and have a beer, all the while getting to know not only each other, but the crusties as well. One, named Phil, tells us they are self-proclaimed "harmless, chain-smoking alcoholics." Who, it turns out are very entertaining and quite nice. They are old rockers from London who came here many years ago and never left.

The electricity suddenly goes out in the evening so they light up the place with candles, and find snacks for us since food can't be cooked. We laugh and trade stories well into the evening. I am ready for sleep, and say goodnight.

Phil jumps up. "Oh, you're staying in the dorm room, I need to get you a blanket."

Thank goodness!

He comes back into the room with both palms turned up. One hand holds the blanket and the other tips up and down as though weighing something on a set of scales.

"You can have the blanket, or you can have the Phil, either one will keep you warm. I'm just offering it's your choice."

I laugh, "Thank you, Phil, I'll take the blanket, it's a lot less complicated."

I make my way back to the room and as I open the door I hear a rhythmic heavy breathing as though someone is in a deep sleep. It appears the man had not checked out. I quietly prepare for bed in the dark. I have a sleeping bag liner and decide this is a good night to put it to use. I am afraid to try the mosquito net because I envision it being full of dust and holes. Surely I can go one night without it and not get malaria. I climb in, and within minutes a mosquito buzzes my ear. I dive completely under the blanket, but he makes his way in. I fight the little bloodsucker for a long time, and finally decide to let the net down, just so I can get some sleep. Surprisingly, I find the net to be in very good condition, and I quickly doze off.

A dog starts barking at about two in the morning, waking the man across the room. He sits up, fumbles through his bag, lights a cigarette and lies back down. Should I be worried about the barn burning down? I watch the red glow for a few minutes, but lose track of where it is extinguished. The only solace is that it is pouring down rain outside, which also sort of means, inside. After he smokes, he goes back to sleep. At five I rise, wrap my backpack in a poncho and wade through the backyard. I never even laid eyes on my roommate in the timbers.

As I stand on the porch in the dark waiting for my ride, the front door suddenly flies open. Snorkel man is standing there in his shorts rubbing his eyes, his hair going in all directions.

"Oh brilliant, you're awake." He smiles. "I was about to come get you to make sure you don't miss your bus."

"Wow." I'm stunned. "Thank you, that is so thoughtful."

I realize I had done a pretty good job of misjudging and underestimating this place.

* * *

I move on to Blantyre, the second largest city in Malawi. My bus has people of several nationalities filling the seats, not just Africans.

A man suddenly stands up and with a smile say's to everyone. "I have a quiz for you. In ten seconds or less, what's the first thing you think of when you hear the word Malawi? Go. Anything? Anything?"

A German woman beside me offers, "Madonna, she adopted a baby from here."

"True," says the man, "and what's the next thing you think of?"

A man across the aisle says, "Farting, and the fact that in Malawi, it is a criminal offense if you fart in public."

"Bingo, this is also true and what I was looking for. So beware." He sits back down.

Evidently this law was on the books back in 1929, just like many of the crazy laws we still have on the books in the U.S. When it came up again though, rather than abolish it, the President wanted to enforce it. The Local Courts Bill reads:

> "Any person who vitiates the atmosphere in any place so as to make it noxious to the public to the health of persons in general dwelling or carrying on business in the neighborhood or passing along a public way shall be guilty of a misdemeanor."

I'm sure we all know people who could really rack up a criminal record in Malawi. Seriously though, how will they police this? What if someone let's one of those "silent, but deadly" ones? Who's going to take the blame? Will it be "he who smelt it, dealt it?" Surely there are more important things to clean up in this East African country. One concern I have is that there is potential for abuse. I'm afraid they may use this as an excuse to bring people in. The people of Malawi think the entire situation is ridiculous and that their government should be spending its time and money on other issues.

Malawians are not happy with their president. I ask several of them about this and they say he is selfish and not a man to be honored. This is the same president who bought a private jet while his country is in the middle of a fuel shortage, and there are conflicting stories as to why there actually is a fuel shortage.

It has reached the crisis stage and as I tried to book my bus trip from Mzuzu to Blantyre last night, I wasn't allowed to purchase my ticket in advance, because the ride was contingent on the bus company securing enough fuel to make the trip.

They said, "Show up in the morning, and if we have petrol, we'll go."

This morning the bus pulls out and we go on our way. Four hours into the trip, we pull over to the side of the road and sit. Twenty minutes later, I begin to breathe in the heavy, noxious smell of gasoline.

I look at the woman behind me and ask, "What is happening?"

She leans in. "Black mm…ma." She searches for a word.

"Black market?"

"Yes."

I doubt the bus company made a profit today, paying black market prices. When we roll into town I notice lines and lines of cars at every gas station. It reminds me of the American fuel shortages in the 1970s.

A few days later I call Linus, a taxi driver, to give me a lift to a shopping area so I can purchase some supplies. I get into his car and notice his tank is almost on empty.

When I ask him about it, he replies, "There is no petrol in the city anywhere. The stations are closed."

He takes me to the shopping center and as I get out I lean in the window, "Thank you. I'll call when I'm done because I don't know how long I'll be."

"I'll stay and wait. I have only enough petrol to take you back and then get home."

"Oh, okay. I won't be long then."

Back in the taxi, we head toward the hostel. During every stop in traffic, he turns off the car's engine. On the way up a hill the car sputters to a stop. No gas. We are about two kilometers from the hostel.

"I'm sorry." He asks, "Can you walk from here?"

"Yes, of course, but what about you? How will you get home?" I know he lives in a village outside of town.

"I will hitch a ride. The government has promised petrol on Friday."

"This is Wednesday. That means you won't make any money tomorrow." I make a mental note to call him and go somewhere on Friday.

Malawi is not all bad just because the government has its priorities twisted. The landscape is lush and beautiful. The country itself is called "The Heart of Africa" because the Malawians are so friendly and accommodating. I enjoy getting to know these precious people.

The highlight of my time here, though, comes not from a Malawian, but an American.

I'd checked my Facebook page one day earlier to find that Heidi, the director and instructor of my TEFL certification course in Costa Rica is going to be in Malawi! After teaching two more sessions in Costa Rica, she'd gone back to the States and worked. Then she accepted a fellowship from the U.S. government to teach at a university in Blantyre. We messaged and couldn't believe how fate was bringing us together again. We make a plan to meet for dinner when I get to town, which will be Valentine's Day.

"Teacha, teacha!" I yell when I see her across the restaurant. We hug and talk simultaneously, each of us so happy to see a familiar face.

We settle into a booth and Heidi says, "Hey, I remember that shirt."

I laugh. "Heidi, I'm still on the same trip, you'll recognize all five of my tops."

"No way! Six months seems like forever ago. Have you figured out what to do with your life?"

"Not yet. I say not yet because I'm not giving up hope that all will be made clear eventually."

We talk nonstop about the things that have happened in our lives since we'd met last August. When we said goodbye at the end of my course in Costa Rica, we assumed we would never see each other again, yet here we are, on another continent, halfway around the world in a remote country. We talk about Malawi and Heidi's high hopes for her students. We laugh about the crazy times back at TEFL, and the fun people in the class. It is like no time has gone by at all. Our meal is delicious, our bellies are full and we are content. We snicker as we try not to pass gas.

* * *

It is time for me to move on and I make my way to South Africa. The moment I step into Johannesburg I am in a completely different world. It is developed, has a western flair and there are white people everywhere. Before I started this trip, I'll admit I didn't even know that South Africa was a country in itself. I just thought it described the southern part of Africa in general. It is definitely its own country and quite different from the rest of the continent. Even the locals say, "There's South Africa and then there's real Africa." It is interesting to me that most South Africans in Johannesburg have never even been to real Africa. Many of my conversations with them are answering their questions and describing what it is like up in the eastern part. They have the means to go there, yet don't. I wondered why volunteers are coming from all over the world to help their continent, but they themselves are not.

I ask several South Africans about this and they tell me, "During Apartheid we were not allowed to travel north at all. It has not been that long and I guess it's just not on our radar."

As I spend more time in Jo-burg though, I begin to wonder if it isn't in part because they have no desire to help. Racism still lives on in South Africa, conspicuous in every conversation, and equally strong on both sides of the coin. After spending months trying to help black people though, it is disturbing for me to hear them being scorned by whites. I can't abide this, and know I cannot stay here for long.

South Africa is still in the beginning stages of reconciliation as we were in the U.S. in the '70's. After one day of staying at the hostel, I notice they put the whites in one building, the nice one, and the blacks in another. When I ask about it, they feign innocence and say they hadn't noticed. I move over to the "other" building. It will take time. There are those enlightened few who are doing their best to eradicate the disparities, but it takes three generations to wipe out racism, and that is only if all three generations want to be a part of the process.

In the meantime, tension is high in Johannesburg. It feels a little like a ticking time bomb. Violence is an everyday occurrence, and the people live in constant fear. They stay behind high walls with barbed wire on the top, security guards, and panic buttons in their homes.

They drive straight to their destination, go inside, come out, and hurry back into their walled habitat. I am saddened by it all, as it seems they are prisoners of their own lives. During the World Cup everyone had been on their best behavior because it was such an economic boom for the area. A new police commissioner was appointed two years earlier who really clamped down on the car jacking's and violence. It could be that it *is* actually safer now, but South Africans are still reeling from old anxious fears.

The hostel I am staying in is located in a very nice area with a mall five blocks up the street. I put my laptop in my backpack and walk up the street to buy an Internet modem. I nod hello to everyone I pass, which is only black people because all the whites have cars and wouldn't dream of walking the streets. I enter the retail kingdom and marvel that every single item known to mankind is suddenly at my fingertips. I buy a real coffee in a "take away" cup, and they even give me napkins! I use three, just because I can, and put one in my pack for safekeeping. As I stroll I am quickly overwhelmed with choices and excess. I've learned to live with nothing, and it will take an adjustment to live comfortably in this life again. The modem store does not have the right equipment for a Mac computer and says I will need to return the next day.

In the afternoon I spend a very emotional three hours at the Apartheid Museum. As I enter the museum I am randomly given a ticket that allows me through one door or the other. Depending on whether I draw a black or white ticket determines the experience I have for the first twenty minutes of my time in the museum. They've done a brilliant job of taking everyone back in time. I observe several people, both black and white, wiping tears from their eyes.

Nelson Mandela addresses the issues at hand in his quotes:

"No one is born hating another person because of the color of his skin, or his background, or his religion. People must learn to hate, and if they can learn to hate, they can be taught to love, for love comes more naturally to the human heart than its opposite."

"As I walked out the door toward the gate that would lead to my freedom, I knew if I didn't leave my bitterness and hatred behind, I'd still be in prison."

"There is no easy walk to freedom anywhere, and many of us will have to pass through the valley of the shadow of death again and again before we reach the mountaintop of our desires."

"As we let our own light shine, we unconsciously give other people permission to do the same."

I am moved by the experience of the museum. I make my way back to the hostel and the moment I walk in one of the long-term residents stops me. "I saw you walking with your pack today. Don't do that, you'll get mugged!"

I am surprised. "I didn't have a choice, I had to have my laptop with me."

"Well, just don't, and don't ever take a regular cab either. It won't be safe for a white woman alone."

It seems I'm not left with any options. I have just become imprisoned.

The next day I take my laptop up the street to the mall anyway, just as I had the day before. The store is able to sell me the right modem, but the clerk says, "In order to use this type of equipment, special software must be installed. You need to take a cab to our Data Care Center and they'll load it for free."

Oh boy, now what do I do? I decide to go back to the hostel and ask for suggestions on transport. On my way down the road, I see the side of a Crowne Plaza Hotel. I'd stayed at the Crowne many times in New York City.

Aha, they'll have safe taxis parked in front of the hotel. They would never let one of their clients get into a cab that wasn't known to be secure. I walk inside to the extravagant lobby and head for the concierge desk.

"Hello. How much would it cost for me to take a taxi to this shopping area?" I show her the address. "Also, do you think I could ask the driver to wait, because this will only take fifteen minutes?" I explain what I am trying to accomplish.

"Well, since it's not going to take very long and you want him to stay, I'll just call our driver."

"Oh, thank you." She must think I am staying here.

The driver finds me in the plush sitting area. He is dressed in a black suit with a tie looking very nice. I pick up my pack and follow him outside to a limousine! I laugh out loud with disbelief at my transportation security. He takes me to the Data Center, and as I came back out, he is waiting and holds the door for me. I feel like a celebrity. Upon arrival he escorts me back into the sitting area. After thanking him and giving him a tip, I walk out the side door and stroll across the street to my fifteen-dollar-a-night hostel. The juxtaposition of these two worlds reminds me how happy and content I am with so little of the material luxuries. My race toward them has slowed to a granny shuffle walk.

Chapter Thirteen

Back at the hostel I discover the best thing that's happened to me since landing in South Africa, and it comes in the form of safe, easy, worry-free transportation up and down the entire coast. It's called the Baz Bus, and it's a brilliant concept. I pay one price, less than the cost of a flight, and can ride from Johannesburg to Durban, and all the way down the 1,400 miles to Cape Town. Sign me up!

I purchase the "hop on, hop off" program, which means I can take as long as I want at each stop and get on or off, as often as I like. At each town I select one of the hostels on their route, there are several to choose from, and they drop me right at the door. When I am ready to leave, I will call the Baz Bus and ask them to pick me up and take me to the next town. I don't have to fight anyone at the bus station, worry about my luggage being stolen, or get ripped off by cabbies. This sounds like nirvana to me, and it is time for me to break out of the prison of Jo-burg.

I am sitting on a bus again for nine hours, which seems to be the magic number for getting anywhere in Africa. I stare out the window. Never before in my life have I had nine-hour blocks of time to think. Some people meditate for hours on end to find themselves. Me? Evidently I prefer sitting on a bus surrounded by Africans whose odor is at times, almost unbearable. As I sit, my thoughts wander to what meaningful volunteer work I might participate in next. The need in Africa is so great that it feels like anything I do will just be a drop in the bucket. I am dismayed at this thought, which concerns me because it is evidence of where I am emotionally. Rather than wanting to roll up my sleeves and dig in like I usually do, I just feel overwhelmed as though I don't have the energy to make my voice heard. I've always been a helpmate, one to rally the troops or fight for a cause. It has always been a big part of who I am. Can I live without that?

Time after time and village after village, I keep feeling the same way. I can't muster enough outrage to stay and help. I feel certain, or am hopeful anyway, that this is a temporary condition, but it is real nonetheless.

It begins to occur to me that maybe I have gotten it all wrong. Possibly the purpose of this trip is that of helping me. Fixing me. Allowing myself some space to sort through the past in order to move into the future. As women, we often spend so much time nurturing and caring for others that we don't always do a very good job of taking care of ourselves. I realize that's cliché, but still, it rings of truth. I can't find the heart I gave my husband anywhere. Can I have this experience without a noble intent? This is me as the halo fades. It seems shameful and selfish. Will it be sufficient for me to just "be" each day, and write? Is that a worthwhile life for now?

I am headed toward the eastern coast of South Africa. I arrive in Durban at dusk and find a cool hostel called the Happy Hippo. The owners bought an old warehouse and completely refurbished the entire place. Everything is brand new and hasn't been beaten up by years of weary backpackers.

I awake and do something I haven't done since October of 2010. I put all of my clothes in a washing machine, every single article of clothing whether it needs it or not. I am thrilled not to be beating my clothes on a rock. And even more amazing, every bathroom has toilet paper provided! Such luxuries.

I walk to the beach. The ocean has always restored my soul. Being by the water does something for me, and today is no different. I feel at peace and happy. My life has possibilities and I am no longer terrified. My waves of fear roll up on the shore holding me under, but then roll back out and I find respite for a while.

Back on the bus I move further down the Eastern Cape to an area called the Wild Coast and I can see why. It is beautifully unspoiled and untouched, not cluttered with urban sprawl or trampled by tourists. There is plenty of big, wide-open space. We pull into The Buccaneers Backpackers, which is in an amazing place right on the ocean. I sign up to stay in a dorm and when I walk in I discover it is coed. There are so many good-looking men in the room, mmmmm…bonus. Breakfast is served in a sunlit room with a view of the lagoons and the ocean, and because we are in the wilderness they also offer dinner if we sign up in the morning and pay.

A switch from running, I sign up for a 28-kilometer bike ride to a Xhosa Village and back. The adventure guides say it is mostly downhill. That doesn't even make sense, and yet eight of us fall for it.

We ride into the village and meet Mama Tofu. Yes, Tofu is her name and at age 94, she is the oldest living, licensed guide in South Africa. Speaking in very good English, she teaches us about the traditions and practices of the Xhosa (pronounced Cosa) Tribe passed down from their forefathers. Within the Xhosa culture each person has his or her place in the clan, and goes through many graduations and rites of passage ceremonies throughout their life. At each stage they sit with the elders for quite some time to learn from them, before the ritual of passing through.

To me, the most interesting thing about the Xhosa culture is they speak the "click" language. Even the word Xhosa begins with a click. There are different types of clicks formed in certain areas of the mouth for different meanings. The closest thing we have to understand how it sounds might be when one clicks a horse into a gallop. It is fascinating to hear it spoken and none of us masters even one click.

At the end of the tour, as we are saying our goodbyes, I walk over to her.

"Mama Tofu, you are ninety-four, have lived a long life and seen many things."

"Yes."

"Do you have any words of wisdom for me?"

She takes both of my hands in hers and looks deeply into my eyes, pausing for a long moment before she speaks. It is as though she knows me, her eyes searing straight through to my soul. I feel extremely vulnerable and uncomfortable as it seems that minute stretches into two or three or five while she stares at me.

"You." she pauses. "Are enough."

In the ninety-degree heat, I have goose bumps.

* * *

My plan is to follow the Eastern Cape all the way down to the southernmost tip of Africa, and the next stop is Storms River, part of the Garden Route. It is a small town, slightly inland and mountainous, not directly on the beach. A young man from Germany is on my bus and we get off at the same hostel. We are the only ones here as it is off-season.

"Hello, my name is Julian." He shakes my hand.

"Hi, I'm Lucetta. I have a daughter named Julien, but she goes by Tessa. She's twenty-four."

"I'm twenty-four."

I grin, "Must have been a very good year."

"Are you going to do it?" He is excited, "Are you going to jump?"

"No! Absolutely not." I respond emphatically.

"It's the world's highest bungee bridge jump, how can you pass that up?"

"Easy. I'm not crazy."

"I'm all by myself and no one else is around." He begs. "Please don't make me go by myself, pleeeease? I can't do this alone. Say you'll go with me."

And this is where he gets to me. The neurons in my brain do something they haven't done in many months; they fire into "mother" mode. He looks up at me with pleading eyes, which hit me right where it hurt. What if this was Tessa who wanted to take the highest bridge jump with only a rope tied around her ankles? She's certainly got the balls to do it, but still, I wouldn't want her to go solo. I would hope someone would step up and be there for her.

There is just one small snag. I am deathly afraid of heights. If only there was even one other person at the hostel, I could send them instead. Or perhaps, if this were the second highest bungee jump in the world I could talk him out of it. Neither of these are true and so cannot protect me from confronting myself again. If I had known that the theme of this journey would turn out to be that of constantly facing down my worst nightmares, I'd have never left the safe soil of the United States.

I know I have to do this. I must, for this is what my life is about right now. Facing every fear. I am nauseous as we ride in a taxi to the bridge. I can always bail out even at the last minute if I have to. I'll go with Julian as far as I can.

We pay our fee; each puts on a harness and waits to be taken out to the bridge walk. For thirty minutes we watch from the side of the hill as people jump. A big screen video is in place that allows us to hear the screams and watch the flailing up close and personal. It is not pretty. Our names are called, and it is time for our group of eight people to make the long walk out to the jump.

Our guide takes us down a dirt path to the edge of the bridge and stops us. "We will walk along the side of the bridge to the jump. This is only a five-minute walk. Remind yourselves it is only five minutes."

"What?" we look at each other. "Why does he say it's only five minutes?"

He takes us around a bend and suddenly we understand his warning. On the underside of the bridge is a wire cage walkway constructed to get us out to the point of the jump below the cars on the bridge. This wire cage is 216 meters high, which is the equivalent of a 60 story building, and we can see below as we walk across this rickety skyway.

"Julian! What have you gotten us into!?"

The guide laughs. "Many people say this is scarier than the jump."

The wire moves somewhat, up and down beneath my feet. I look to the left and see the ocean. I glance down. A mistake. The wide river, nestled between two mountains, now looks like a small vein snaking its way through the trees below. Immediately I am queasy and my head begins to spin. I think I might faint.

"Keep walking. Keep walking." The guide encourages.

I might throw up, what can I do about this? I cup my hands around my eyes like a horse with blinders at a race, willing myself to look only straight ahead. I shuffle along now, my pace slowed by my toes tenuously reaching out first to guide my way through the air-holed metal. There is a cool breeze up here of course, but I am soaked with sweat. In that moment, out of nowhere I suddenly remember my only reoccurring childhood dream. It is that of flying, arms stretched out soaring over houses and mountains. Something inside me shifts.

I can do this. I can do this. No. I can't. Walk. Breathe. The blinders are helping. Walk. Don't look down. My stomach calms slightly. Breathe. Remembering childhood dreams with arms stretched out, wind in my hair, flying and I was free, completely free like a bird. Walk. This is my chance. Reorder my thinking. I will not close my eyes. I will not thrash. Breathe. For twenty glorious seconds, I WILL CHOOSE TO FLY.

We get to the launch point and of course they call my number first. I'm simultaneously freaked out and relieved. If I had to sit and watch I would certainly chicken out, but as it stands I have no time to renege on my new instantaneous dream. I come forward and sit as they strap my ankles together wrapping them tightly. They guide me to the edge of the bridge, count down, and let go of my arms. In that moment…I fly.

A few seconds into the air and I realize, I am not dying. I feel the living in a heightened sense as I fall towards the earth. What happens in the moments of flying freely in an inhuman way is a complete repositioning of all of the self-confidence cells in my body. Floating downward, I experience an explosion of love for myself for facing my greatest fear head on, and I realize immediately that I will never ever be the same.

In the afternoon I buy Julian a beer.

* * *

Back on the Baz Bus I move on down the coast to Plettenburg Bay and end up in the tiniest room to date. I wander up to the rooftop to see what I can see. Up here, besides a beautiful view of the ocean, is a bar filled with hilarious men in the midst of preparing and "pre-gaming" for a bachelor party. They'd left the girls behind and brought all sorts of provisions for the evening to beat all evenings.

I accept an invitation to join them in a round of celebratory shots. Wait, I am attending a bachelor party. Yes, me, a girl. I witness a man in the last throes of singlehood. I also witness a man being sentenced to death. Yes, it is the same party. They have the groom in a prison outfit and on the back it reads, Death Row. One of the friends brings Plaster of Paris as well. What? They have the groom hold a beer glass in his hand and bend his arm. They begin wrapping the arm in a plaster cast all the way down including the drinking glass! I ask all the guys what he is supposed to do with that arm next week as he walks to the altar.

With surprise they look at each other and shrug, "We don't know." They raise their glasses and shout, "But a toast to the drinking arm!"

That's the thing about traveling. The unexpected always happens, and sometimes you brush up against, not just other people traveling, but also other people in the midst of living their lives. This night is intentioned to be the last fun night out this groom will have for the rest of his life. I ponder where he'll find his fun from now on, and what form it will take.

I don't know anything about this man or the woman he is marrying, but I can't help but wonder how much of himself he's about to give away. Love can be tricky. How do you maintain who you are and at the same time compromise for the sake of the relationship? Often we relate to each other in certain ways simply because at some point, in the early stages, it becomes fixed as a habit. Rhythmic patterns of behavior are formed without us even realizing, then before we know it, we are operating on autopilot. Never reevaluating the validity. So in the early days how do you know how much of yourself to give up, and how much do you fight for before the grooves are too deep? Do you always have to give an arm and a leg?

I awake in the morning and decide to leave my bed unmade. The sheets are all rumpled and the pillows tossed aimlessly. I just look at them, staring, without moving. He always implied it was lazy not to make the bed. I was always trying to prove my value and my worth because I was a stay-at-home mom. Adding lazy to the fact that I didn't bring one single dime into the household wasn't something I could live with. I realize, though, this is my life now and I can be lazy if I want to.

Really, what does that even mean? It's so subjective, and I've built my life around NOT being it. What may be lazy to one person may not be to another, and what is wrong with being lazy once in a while? Americans have built a billion-dollar industry trying to go on vacation to be just that, lazy. If I choose to leave my bed unmade in this lodge, on this day, does that make me less of a person? Could this be a small step in the healthy dismantling of perfectionism and overcompensation in my life? One more glance at the disheveled mess on my bed and I head out the door, guilt-free, to swim with three thousand seals.

Along a northern facing rocky shore lives a colony of thousands of brown fur seals. The thought of an opportunity to swim among them is exhilarating. The thought of jumping off the boat into the water at 13 degrees Celsius, on the other hand, is terrifying. I join a group of people from Sweden and our guide explains it like this:

"When we get into the water we will stay beside the boat. For two minutes I will monitor each of you and make sure you are okay before we head over to the seals. The water is so cold you will feel as though you cannot breathe. Actually it does take your breath away. Work through it, because your body will acclimate at about the two-minute mark. Do you understand?"

He was looking at them, but I was the only one with a dumbstruck look on my face. What the cuss?! Have I mentioned how much I hate to be cold? Ugh, the proverbial bad with the good. It's kind of like going to the doctor as a kid. You've got to take the shot before your mom gives you a treat at the end.

"Okay, I may never get this chance again." I say to myself. "Let's do this."

I jump into the water and as I come back up, I find myself gasping for shallow breaths of air. I am immediately numb. I have never experienced anything like this before. Our guide checks in with each of us and sure enough, after two very, very long minutes, which I think will certainly be my last, my body suddenly relaxes. I never would have believed this was possible.

Then comes the treat! A curious baby seal swims over to say hello. Mothers and fathers follow and soon we were surrounded by hundreds of them diving, rolling, and communicating with each other through loud calls. It is as though we've been invited to a huge happy party. Their playfulness is beautiful to experience. Becoming a human Popsicle is well worth the prize.

When I get back to my room that evening, my bed isn't made. The room looks unkempt, disorganized and sloppy. I don't like it at all. Not one single bit. Even the sheets don't feel the same as I slip into bed. I decide. "Tomorrow I will make the bed when I arise, and the next day, and the day after that..." This time though, I own it, it's mine. And as for the groom, I think he has the right idea. It appears he decided only to give up an arm.

* * *

Next stop on the Garden Route is the South African wine country. The quaint town of Stellenbosch, designed with a Dutch influence, has not only vineyards, but is home to a large university as well. The Baz Bus drops me at my hostel just after dark. As I walk in, I have to weave among a crowd of people to make it near the reception desk. Evidently graduation is in the next few days, so the place is packed to capacity. Several people are ahead of me, as I wait. In the front of the line are two African women, one of which is very, very large in stature. It seems there is a problem with her reservation.

"Ma'am, we have your reservation in the women's dorm, but all of the bottom bunks have been taken. There are only two top bunks left."

Silence falls throughout the room

"Do I look like I can make it to the top bunk? I need a bottom bunk."

"Well, the only thing I can offer is a private room that is a little more expensive. It sleeps two, but it's on the men's hall."

More silence.

"Do I look like I want to stay on the men's hall and share a bathroom with them? Oh no, that won't do at all. I can't stay with the men." She looks at her friend, then for some reason whips her head around in my direction, and continues, "I bet SHE won't have to stay on a top bunk, with the men."

Assuming she means because I am white, I shrug and give a small, friendly I'm-trying-to-sympathize-with-your-pain smile, while in my mind I am thinking, I am so glad I have a confirmed reservation.

"Ma'am, if you stay in that room one night, then tomorrow you can move and claim a bottom bunk on the women's hall."

"Hmmmph. Does it look like I have a choice now? No, it doesn't." She pulls out her wallet, tosses her money on the counter and huffs off to get her bags. The next two women in line gladly scoop up the top two bunks in the women's dorm. Finally it is my turn.

"Hello, I have a reservation under Zaytoun."

"Are you sure?"

"Yes, I have a confirmation number."

"No, are you sure you're Zaytoun?"

I laugh, "Yes, I'm pretty sure."

He looks slightly embarrassed, and lowers his voice, "Ma'am, I am sorry, but for some reason, from your name, we thought you were a man. We have you booked in the men's dorm, and we just gave our last two female beds away."

I burst out laughing! I get the giggles, and can't stop, "It's okay, really. It will be fine, I'm certain." I almost describe some of the crazy places I've stayed in the last few months, but that isn't really necessary. I go up to the men's hall and walk into my room. An African man wearing glasses is reclining on his bed reading one of the many newspapers spread around him. This is uncharacteristic of most African men I have run across. Ah, surrounded by the world of academia, how refreshing. We exchange pleasantries, and I go downstairs to eat the dinner I'd brought with me.

I wander outside to sit beside a beautiful koi pond, and have a clear view into the community kitchen. Inside are people preparing dinner from things they'd purchased at the market. I watch as bodies weave and bob around each other, trying to get to utensils, the stove, and the refrigerator. There are many instances of sharing, numerous spills, collisions and laughter. I am mesmerized for almost an hour and I realize a tear is running down my cheek. I miss the chaos of family.

In the middle of the night, I awake as another man joins us. Exhausted, he falls into bed and is quickly sound asleep. I stay awake listening to the rhythmic sounds of the men sleeping. The deep breathing, slight snores, and noises a man makes turning and moving in the night. I am surprised that somehow I've never really paid attention to this before, possibly taking it for granted. In the morning I pretend to be asleep just to hear the routines of a man in the morning as he prepares for his day.

After breakfast, we are all back in our room, packing up our belongings. We open the door to let in a little cool breeze as sweat pours down our brows. We hear the door across the hall open and suddenly the room darkens by a shadow blocking the light. There, the robust woman stands surveying the room, her mouth gaping open. Suddenly the loudest, longest belly laugh fills the room.

"Oh my Lord!" She slaps her side, and then raises her hands. "Come here, baby girl, and let me give you a hug!" As I approach she grabs me, pulling me into her soft ample bosom, and holds me with arms full of comfort saying, "Oh Lord, I promise, I will never whine again!"

* * *

I've reached a goal. I've made it to the southernmost point of the continent of Africa. To give you an idea of how large this continent actually is; you can put two and a half United States inside Africa. I started *halfway* down the eastern side and have still traveled over 4000 miles. I went about the same distance as driving from Seattle, Washington to Costa Rica. Crazy big. At the southern tip is Cape Peninsula, the meeting point of the Pacific and Indian Oceans, the Cape of Good Hope, a lighthouse, towering mountains and numerous animals.

My favorite is the adorable South African black-footed penguin. They appear to be very social, which makes them fun to watch. They breed in colonies yet are monogamous. They return to the same spot each year to breed, and it must seem like a huge reunion. The average lifespan is 10 to 27 years! The most amazing thing is that the pattern of spots on their chest is completely unique to each one, as a fingerprint is to us.

I have come all the way down here to be no one, to be invisible. To have no demands placed on me, no one needing me night and day. No one bringing their emotional needs for me to carry, shoulder, and return only when the owners are capable. I ran away, away literally, as far as I could go from America. More so, I ran from the rat race of the great surpass, of needing to watch this, study that, own more, keep up, and stay on top. The unspoken translation is: conformity by up-sell.

You know this. The same happens to you. It keeps you awake at night and makes you want to run away sometimes too. Well, evidently I did just that and here I am, at a southern tip of the earth. I reached the goal, and guess what has drifted ashore?

Nothingness. Just like I wanted.

I take a long deep breath… expecting... something... anything. A revelation maybe? A new lease on life? But do you know what I find?

Emptiness. Complete and utter blankness.

It has nothing to do with the scenery, which is gorgeous; it has nothing to do with the number of people, there are plenty. It has everything to do with my life. Lacking aspiration, I am just coasting daily, creating a void. As much as we think we want utopia in a world with no responsibilities, the truth is that is the very thing that makes us alive and human. It is what sets us apart from the rest of the universe. The ability to carry another's burdens, show compassion, work to change the world, give hope, lend a hand, and sacrifice for the things we believe in. These are the privileges we are afforded as human beings. It costs us, yes. The price is vulnerability, change and at times disappointment, heartache, and fear. The reward; not remaining stuck, breaking useless patterns, and living with meaning, which then leads to a deliberate life full of merit. I realize now that responsibility and purpose are spirit enhancers not soul crushers, and that a life without them makes one a desolate vessel.

God designed me with my own set of fingerprints. I forgot how cool this is. I am unique. I should value this, treasure it, and not let it go to waste. My very uniqueness is my greatest asset, and should be used for something bigger than me. Not in a way of conforming, or in someone else's version of who I should be, but in a way that is true to my authentic self. I will search for purpose, direction and my true north. If my intentions are pure, I am certain I will find them. I will discover my next season. No more running.

It seems no coincidence that my serendipitous realization comes the day I wrap myself up in a Cape of Good Hope.

* * *

I am discovering racism is alive and well in Cape Town too, and here it is multifaceted. The Dutch descendants don't like the English descendants, who don't like the blacks, who don't like the coloreds, who don't like the whites, who don't like the blacks, who don't like the Dutch. There seems to be no unity anywhere, yet I remind myself that Apartheid has not been over for very long. Still it hurts my heart.

One of the best things about reaching Cape Town is being reunited with Seri. You remember her, right? Seri of "Seri's Cross Culture Porch", of "kissing a giraffe", of "the ice climb up Kilimanjaro", and the list goes on. That would be plenty for any person, who could then race back to the States guilt-free, for hot showers and Starbucks and beds without nets, but that's not the stuff she's made of. Seri went straight to South Africa for another three months of volunteerism, with yet another school. This is a woman who is clear about her purpose and passion. She's a 90-pound fireball of activism for children, who believes in the importance of educating them to brighten their future. Her enthusiasm is contagious and just being near her, the glow of it rubs off on you.

I spew scattered unrelated stories from my trip all over Seri. I don't know if any of it makes sense, but she is the first person I've seen that I know, who can relate.

After we'd caught up with excited, rapid fire talk-over-each-other sentences about both of our experiences during the last few months, Seri says, "I think you should participate with me in a march on Human Right's Day. We'll march for Minimum Norms and Standards in the schools, from the city center to parliament where we'll remind the government that these kids must have the basics to get an education."

Of course that would be her normal conversation. And of course I can't say no.

Having Table Mountain as a backdrop, the rally starts with a concert and speeches about education. With mostly middle and high school students in attendance, the final count is over 20,000 people! The band Freshly Ground performs; they are the band that sang "Waka Waka" with Shakira at the FIFA World Cup, and they get the crowd so pumped up. Spontaneous dance circles spring up and the kids include us. They are amazed that we know some of the dances.

The students are so happy to have their say and stand up for their rights. It is inspiring. They smile and sing as they peacefully march in their school uniforms. Many of them made signs asking for the basic things their school needs, and the camaraderie for the common cause is palpable. This generation living in the era of Nelson Mandela is empowered.

These are the things needed in the schools out in the townships: water, toilets, electricity, enough classrooms, a library, textbooks, a playground, and an administration center. This is difficult for us to understand or even comprehend, but these are the things they don't have. We march to Parliament, but no one comes out to speak to us.

The students seem disheartened at first, but soon begin to feel strong about their efforts, "At least we sent our message. There's no way they don't know we're here."

"Yes, I think now they know we are serious, and just because we are young doesn't mean we can't stand up for our rights."

Maybe that's what this was really all about, the students claiming their own power. This sounds very familiar to a certain woman who marched with them and I'm not discouraged because the march ended up on Hope Street.

* * *

Cape Town, South Africa, reminds me of San Francisco. It's a cosmopolitan city on the edge of an ocean with a kaleidoscope of people and many exciting things to experience. One can go sand boarding down a huge dune, shark cage diving with the great whites, hang out with penguins, go to Carnivale, visit Robbins Island where Nelson Mandela was imprisoned, and one of my personal favorites: climb Lion's Head Mountain.

"Hello, everyone, I'm Tom, your guide from Cape Town. Welcome to the Full Moon Hike up Lion's Head Mountain. Does anyone know why you picked the right month to make this hike?"

"It's a super perigee moon," says the person next to me.

"That's right. It means the moon is larger and closer to the earth than it has been in almost twenty years, so this should be awesome! The climb gets progressively more challenging as we go up, with one part being an actual rock climb should you choose to take that particular path to the top. Keep your buddies nearby. Everyone got water?"

He looks at me, "Where's your group?"

"Just me." I grin. "Always just me."

"Okay, cool. Well, follow me." As we head up the hill, people asking questions soon surround him. As we work our way up the mountain I fall behind the crowd, becoming engrossed in the same thought patterns and questions that have dogged me the last months.

I'm at the tip of the continent, there's nowhere else to go and I am confronted with myself. What do I do now? What is my purpose? What does my life even mean? I should have these answers by now.

In a moment of complete exasperation, I look up and for the first time on this entire trip I cry out to the heavens, "What do You want me to do?!"

"I've given you a lifetime of experiences. Write them down and use it to help people."

I stop dead in my tracks and look around to see who is speaking to me.

No one.

I am alone.

The hair on the back of my neck stands on end.

In an instant I recognize the voice. I've heard it only two other times in my life, and I clearly know the source. A sob erupts from my chest that doubles me over and throws me down on one knee. I grab onto the rock to hold myself upright. Chills run all over my body, chills of awe. At the same time a frequency that can only be described as the purest form of love flows throughout my body. The voice that speaks to me is without judgment, not commanding. It is more like a statement. A helpful piece of information given in a slightly matter-of-fact way. The voice is also wrapped up in a tone of endearing love. It is there in one second, and in the next instant it is gone.

The low sun pierces my eyes as I look upwards and shout out loud, “Where…? How…? What people…?” But I know there will be no reply. There never is. He has given me what I need at the moment, and no more. The rest is up to me. I push myself off the rock beside me, brush my hands and steady myself to stand.

When my life fell apart, the pain was so deep that I went numb. An explosion of epic proportions had obliterated my heart. Walls shot up around it for protection and, God Himself, was not immune from the emotional standoff I was having with the world. But this separation from Him was new to me. I have known I was a child of God since I was old enough to have a conscious thought. I sought out His word, studied it, memorized it, and taught it as I grew older. More than words, though, was His steadfast unconditional love for me and mine for Him. He has always been my anchor, my strong force, my companion, and I’ve always understood that His place in my life couldn’t be separated from who I was. Even many years ago, when my daughter died, I didn’t turn away. I determinedly told everyone who questioned the tragedy, that God had a reason and one day I would understand. But this time, I didn’t question, I didn’t get angry, I didn’t do anything; I went blanket numb. And so I ignored Him, covering my eyes to His stars of light, denying even His comfort.

I would have thought by now He would have turned His face from me, but He waited patiently for my pain to ebb out, gently reminding me of His love by periodically placing people in my path to tell me. An American woman on the plane to Rwanda, an email from home, a new South African friend in Cape Town, and the wise words given to me by Mama Tofu.

I know Him, but I can't *feel* Him, and I operate on feelings. I know in my head He loves me and so has not turned from me, but I can't feel it. And if I don't feel, I'm like a little boat in the water without a rudder. I've been paddling around in circles. He knows this, of course. He knows everything about me. He knows all of the parts that make up my whole, and He loves me so completely anyway. At this moment, on the mountain, I can't imagine why.

The sob pours forth gratefulness that I am not alone, that He still cares for me and has a plan for my life that is greater than I could ever hope for or imagine. I let His love wash over me, and at the same time I am ashamed that He had to speak audibly to reach me.

I don't know how much time has passed as I stand here. The others are long gone up the path, but I am a rock climber so I know I'll be okay to make it to the top on my own. He gave me an answer to the long, sought out question that took me all the way to the other side of the world. I wipe my eyes with the tail of my shirt, and the snot with the back of my hand.

I watch the sun set beautifully in the west, turn and watch the moon rise in the east. I make a note to myself: If you go on a three hour hike up to the top of a mountain to watch the sun go down and the moon rise up, take someone you love with you because it can be incredibly romantic. And if you don't, even though you are up there with one hundred people, it can be incredibly lonely.

I remind myself of my earlier message and begin to sit in purpose and gratitude. I realize it is time for me to move on. Africa has given me all that it can, which encapsulates the irony of this great continent; I was supposed to help Africa and yet Africa has helped me.

* * *

Time to leave, so what's next? I'm not ready to go home so where do

I go? I'm wandering at this point; the race to my next life has turned into a trek. I have to be somewhere on this planet. I receive an email that my stepson will be in Thailand and I've heard many amazing things about the country, so I book a flight. Conflicting emotions of excitement and sadness well up inside.

Since I only have three days before leaving Africa, I need to make them count. I go down to the harbor in Cape Town, and find it is festive and fun. I catch a ferry to Robbins Island where Nelson Mandela was held prisoner for 26 years. I can't imagine living in that small cell, being mistreated daily and coming out as a warrior for peace. And yet I am not surprised because I experienced so much of this understated beauty while on this continent.

I climb to the top of Table Mountain. When you reach the top it is flat, like a table, and you can see for so many miles around that even the curve of the earth is visible. I am a climber and always want to get to the highest point of anywhere to see what I can see. Today I feel like I am literally standing on top of the world. I'm overcome with appreciation for where my life has taken me. If I had known where I was going I would have surely lost my way, but in my wandering I am finding myself, and that seems like enough for now.

Africa had become familiar. I was here long enough to embrace the energy, and the people. I learned to appreciate their thinking, their hurdles, and their indomitable spirit. Africa had stretched me, pushed me and challenged me in ways I never dreamed imaginable. I faced so many fears here. I became comfortable with being uncomfortable, which I realize is a valuable gift. It seems impossible for anyone to come away from here unchanged, and I myself am very different from when I touched down in Tanzania.

On the flight to Thailand, the airline has said I am only allowed to take one bag, period. They will not even allow me to pay extra money and take another. If I were flying from the United States I could take two, but because I am flying from Africa I can only take one? The few belongings I brought with me on this journey have now been cut in half and I've been unpacking my emotional baggage since I landed. Now I'm really stripped down to just me. I guess I'm going to find out exactly what I am really made of.

Part Four

Running Around

The truth is always an act of love.
—Emily Lewis

Chapter Fourteen

"Ma'am, I bring you dinner, you like some wine?" The flight attendant startles me back into the present.

"Oh, yes, please!" Whew, that helps.

As we take off for Thailand, I close my eyes to sit and just be still for a moment. I have spent the last several months living with a clamor of voices in my head. Which is mine? I have layers of all types of relationships in my life and they all combine to make me who I am today, for which I am grateful, but of that what needs to be discarded now and what should be reserved? Every once in a while I get a glimpse of the authentic person I truly am. Awareness pushes against the clamor and I am lifted. Then, just as quickly, I fade back into who the world would have me be.

There are several threads that keep weaving through my life of how people describe me. They keep coming up over and over, now even from people I've met who live all over the world. It is "you are a breath of fresh air," "free spirit," and "courageous." Is that who I am? I certainly don't feel that way, because I know the fears I live with. That is who I would most want to be, so why do I have such a hard time holding this at the forefront of my heart? Why can't I fully embrace this? I've always felt God designed me in a very unique way and I always saw this as an impediment because I felt so different from everyone else, but what if this is a gift? What if this is the most beautiful and sacred gift He could have ever given me?

My mission statement remains the same; I want to create something that benefits mankind, something that encourages people to claim their magnificence and live with hope. God wouldn't put this on my heart and then say, "No, you can't do this." What all of this means and how it will play out, I have no idea. Maybe I'll write. At this point, all I know is I want to help people find hope in their own life.

Then those past voices rush in and say, "You can't do that. You're not good enough. You don't have a degree in writing. Just go get a job. Any job. You don't even know how to earn a living. And no one cares to read about your life. You're no different than anyone else."

Somehow I must push through this noise. Banish these tapes that run over and over in my head preventing me from moving forward. Honestly, these are things that I have always thought were wrong with me. Why can't I just be normal? Get an accounting degree like my brother and go to work every day, earn a paycheck, have a career? I've always felt less than by not being designed that way. It seems my life would be so much easier if I were.

Recently, though, I've been getting glimpses that maybe it's okay. Maybe I can forgive myself for not being that person and learn to love and embrace the person that I am, all the parts of me. Maybe if I embrace me I will feel peace and experience true freedom to grow and blossom. Maybe then I could actually believe all the wonderful things people say to me. Maybe I could feel I'm an okay person instead of always thinking I'm a fuck up. The only obstacle between my dreams and me, is me. I am not afraid of taking the way that is not "safe" am I?

I consult my *Lonely Planet* book for Thailand and check the "Dangers and Annoyances" section to see what scams I can expect upon arrival. I figure out the currency and memorize the equivalent in American dollars. Upon first arrival in a new country, they know that you don't know the language, the money or the customs, so they see this as the perfect opportunity to make extra money for themselves. I am happy I have this insider information ahead of time because as I get into the taxi, my driver says, "Your hotel full. I take you to another." I know that he wanted to take me to a place where he would get a kick back.

"No. I want to go to my hotel."

"It full."

"That's okay. Take me anyway."

He argues with me the entire way trying to sound like he is worried for me and helping me, but thanks to my *LP* guide, I'm not buying it at all. It takes everything I have inside of me not to cower or give in and end up who knows where? I want to seem polite and accommodating as I am a sweet Southern girl, but I am learning to stand up for myself. I have only me now. If I don't stand up for me then who will? He pulls up to the Shanti Bangkok and my room is ready and awaiting my arrival.

As I pay and get my room key, I see a sign for a 90-minute traditional Thai massage. I calculate the exchange in my head and the cost is $13.00! I book one immediately. I have only slept four hours in the last 48 and my body is wasted. I drop my bag in my room and go in search of street vendors for food, hoping sustenance will give me some energy.

Back at the Shanti, I lay myself down on a massage mat placed on a landing in the middle of a set of stairs. A beautiful 26-year-old Thai woman named Num answers my questioning look, "No one come up these stair. It okay."

She begins to work months and months of African stress out of my body. She is so tiny, yet unbelievably strong. The Thai massage is a bit rough, painful, yet necessary. I go to another place in my mind and lose myself in the complete releasing of it all. Afterwards, I roll off the mat, crawl down the steps, barely making it to my room. I land on the bed unable to move, and fall fast asleep.

I awake at dinnertime and slowly move all of my body parts to make sure they still work. I pick up my laptop and drag myself to the restaurant in the hotel. A fellow traveler in South Africa told me about the Shanti. He said the accommodations were sufficient, the food was amazing and fresh, and they had unlimited, strong Wi-Fi. I was sold. I order my delicious food and crank up my laptop.

Num is there and comes to say hello. As she does, she sees my screensaver, which is a picture of my six grown children. She is remarking about how beautiful they are and at that exact moment my son Ford calls in on Skype!

Num is stunned that suddenly he is there in person, "He is *really* good looking, but his beard is Mafia. Here a beard mean mafia."

Another waitress pops over, waves hello and Ford grins. "Whoa, Mom. I'm coming to Thailand, those girls are gorgeous!"

We have a wonderful time together catching up and I begin to cry as I say goodbye. I love him so much and I miss him terribly. I miss all of my children such that sometimes I find myself pining for the way things used to be.

* * *

After dinner I return to my room, feeling a little stronger after delectable Thai food and love from my son. I decide I can handle the emotions of checking my email for I am about to spend time with my other son. Yes, one of the reasons I have come to Thailand, other than the fact that everyone recommends it, is that my stepson Adam will be here. We will intersect in Phuket, as he is on his own two-month journey around the world with his friend, Scott. I couldn't pass up an opportunity to see him. I can't believe I'm actually going to get to see someone from home in two weeks. My heart skips a beat just thinking about it. I'm especially excited to see Adam because he is such a fun traveler, and a prankster too.

My favorite memory of him was when he was eight years old. One afternoon the kids were all home from school and from one part of the house I hear a sister yell, "Adam, stop it!" In just a minute or two I hear another sister yell from a completely different part of the house, "Adaaam, quit that!" And then from downstairs, yet another sister screams, "AAAAdam, stop!" I'd had enough and had to put an end to this. I came around the landing at the top of the stairs to see Adam running up from the bottom. He stopped dead in his tracks.

"Adam Zaytoun! Your sisters have called you out from places all over this house, what is the common denominator here?"

He looked up at me and a grin broke out on his face, "That my sisters are intolerant?"

Stunned at his answer, I burst out laughing so hard I had to sit down on the stairs. I am in awe.

"I can't be mad at you. How do you even know that word, and enough to be able to use it in proper context!? Go." I wave him away. "Just go. Do your homework and leave your sisters alone."

Another time when he was young, there was a Hepatitis C scare at our local grocery store and everyone was required to go to the health department to be checked and cleared. All eight of us were in the waiting room, with kids climbing all over me. My turn came and the nurse called, "Lucretia Zaytoun." Adam fell out of his chair onto the floor laughing at the name Lucretia. For some reason he thought it was hilarious, and he called me Lucreesha from then on, until he shortened it to Creesh which is what he has called me ever since.

I am thrilled to have my own travel with him. Having six kids means it's not easy to get special, uninterrupted time with any one of them. He is on this trip with his friend traveling through Europe and Asia. I am honored that they would even want to include me on one of their stops. Couple of dudes roaming the planet freely, why would they want to catch up with Mom? It is beyond me, and I am flattered.

We've been emailing and Skyping to set up the details of our trip. I'd heard there was flooding in Phuket, a monsoon in which people died and some were still missing. I shared this with Adam and he was concerned. I told him I would keep up with it, and things would probably be fine by the time we met up there.

Back in my room I boot up my laptop and there is an email from him:

Creesh, 9:19 p.m.

I registered with the State Department to get text message alerts on my phone.

I received one this morning advising all US travelers in SE Asia, specifically Vietnam, Cambodia, Thailand and Malaysia to be advised that significant quantities of Japanese radiation from the earthquake have shown up in local food and water.

Yikes! It went on to say avoid fruits, vegetables, fish and rice. That doesn't leave much else to eat. I don't know what to do.

Anyway, I thought I'd make you aware. See what other info you can find out about this. Let's Skype later.

Adam

I am soooo disappointed! Does this mean I should leave? I begin to panic as I realize I ate all of these things today off carts on the street no less! Damn. I could have gone anywhere in the world and I chose to head straight for radiation. I begin to get angry with myself. It's just like you to go off on a whim and not get your facts down first. What is your problem? I don't know but I don't want to leave, I just got here. Dammit!

I go online and pull up the U.S. State Department website for travelers. I guess I should register. If something happens they'll evacuate me or at least they won't leave the country until they've found me, or I am accounted for. I have avoided this so far, not really feeling the need to let the government in on my personal travel, but now it seems the time has come to involve them.

I fill out the form, which is extensive and takes quite a while because the Internet is slow all the way up in my room. My anxiety ramps up with every question they ask, and I keep wondering if at any minute I will begin to feel sick from what I have eaten today. I research the earthquake to see if I can glean further information. I don't know how long it will take for the State Department to get back to me with a confirmation, so I go to the bathroom to clean up, take my asthma meds and get ready for bed. Whew, what a day, and wow, how is it midnight already?

I decide to check my email one more time before turning out the light, and there is a new email from Adam.

Creesh, 12:01

I just got another text alert from the State Department. It said,

"April Fool's, Creesh"

Adam

What the hell? I look at my calendar and sure enough it is a few moments into April 1st! Oh my gosh, he's done it again! He gets us every year on April Fool's with his elaborate tricks. I can't believe it! I'm usually on to him, but I am not tracking the calendar these days. I am simultaneously furious and relieved because I was fraught with worry and self-hate. I don't know what country he is currently in and what their time zone is, but he figured it out to the minute to pull off this intricate charade.

I begin to calm down and eventually start laughing at his clever nature. I can't be mad at him because he would have no way of knowing how dramatically he impacted my emotions and thought process. Thanks to both of my boys, it has become a family tradition to pull pranks on April Fool's Day. I smile and feel grateful to know I can now stay in Thailand, I can now eat the food, and that in two weeks I can kick his ass all over the place for this stunt.

* * *

I awake the next morning to muffled sounds next door. My small room is adequate for my needs, yet the walls are made of thin bamboo allowing every sound to seep through from the rooms around me. A couple next door are speaking to each other, not loud enough for me to decipher their words, rather the intimacy of their moment and the melodies of their voices in sweet morning conversation. You know, the dialogue that lovers have in the first few moments of waking while still tangled in one another's arms. The instant when awareness lifts one slowly from dreaming sleep to realizing where you are and what is happening in your world.

It is those first seconds in the morning that are so difficult for someone who grieves a loss. Because in your dreams that loved one still loves you, or is still alive, or you still have your job, or your health. And then the bliss fades as evidence rises to the top of your consciousness and your truth will not be ignored. It is those early moments that can destroy your progress and beg you to stay in bed forever ignoring your new reality.

But this couple has awakened to find each other. Side by side they lay against each other feeling the heat of a human being next to them, the familiar smell of the breath, the body in the morning, a sense of belonging. They talk for a while and then they are quiet. I picture them both lying still, completely relaxed in the moment, contemplating what's been said.

There is more conversation, and then silence. This time I imagine the quiet includes a kiss, one so light and tender that says, "I know you, I love you, and I am here." Soon after they rise and begin preparations for exploring Bangkok for the day, for we are all visitors here and this land is new to us. It is good to bring the familiar with you.

In Africa I tired of marriage proposals and being desired only as a meal ticket off of the continent, yet this morning I feel the pain of not being wanted at all. It unsettles my heart. Which is it? How do I want my life now? To be wanted or not wanted, to be loved or not loved? I don't know the answer, so I will just sit with it for a while. I am content right now to be alone so that is what I will do. Be alone. I don't have to compromise with anyone, I don't have to fight with anyone, and I don't have to do something I don't want to do just to save the relationship.

I also don't get to adore or be adored. I have no one to be a witness to my life. When I see something amazing, I don't get to share it. And in my most discouraged moment, I don't get to be held. I slide out of bed and collapse onto my knees, my face buried in the sheets, sobbing silently. Can I do this? Do I have it in me? I can do this. I can be alone. I am okay. I can be alone, not lonely. I will be all right, I will.

I grab my journal and pour my heart out on the page. After a while I collect myself enough to go down to the restaurant and eat breakfast. While there I inquire of the fellow backpackers the best places to visit while here in the city. The most recommended place is the Grand Palace, a huge Buddhist temple. To enter you must have your entire body covered completely or they will not allow you to enter the sacred temple. I have been traveling around the equator and I don't have clothing that covers all of my appendages in 90-degree heat with no air conditioning. Fortunately, there are Thai vendors in front of the temple who will rent you the appropriate clothing so you may enter. I rent covered clothing and close-toed shoes, putting my flip-flops in my bag. The palace is beautiful and full of rich history. I even get to watch the changing of the guard.

In the afternoon I wander down to Khao San Road, a backpackers area and famous party street in Bangkok. It is quite entertaining and very commercial. I'm glad I'm here during the day because I'm not 19 years old anymore and I think I will pass on the night scene.

Back at the Shanti I run into Num and she tells me about an outdoor market that only happens once a year. She asks me if I want to go with her. Yes! I'd love to hang out with Num. To go to a market with a local friend means I don't have to be on guard about where to go, what to do or not do, my safety, getting lost, not knowing the language, what to eat or not eat, or falling for a scam.

Num and I walk down the road together and chat as girls do. She shares that she'd love to go to the United States one day because she can earn so much more money for massages there, but it is difficult to get a passport.

Grinning, I suggest, "Well, Num, I could just arrange a marriage to my son Ford and you could live there forever."

She bursts out laughing and says, "Mafia man. Okay. Then you be my mom."

She calls me Mom from that moment on as we walk through table after table piled high with goods for sale. I stroll along looking with wonder at how much effort the vendors have put into fitting every single thing onto their tables. Suddenly out of nowhere a familiar aroma reaches my nostrils and I stop dead in my tracks.

"Num, this is crazy but that smell, it's a smell from home! It smells like home." Tears form in my eyes. "Have I gone crazy with homesickness? Where is this coming from?"

She is concerned for me. "Are you sure?"

"Yes, there is no other smell like this anywhere on the planet. It is from a company that started in my hometown. They make doughnuts. It's called Krispy Kreme."

"Oh, you mean these?" She spins me around and there right before my eyes on a card table at a market in Bangkok are Krispy Kreme doughnuts! I am ridiculously delighted to have a taste of home while halfway across the world. I buy a box and dive in, sharing the goodness with Num. How wild that the aroma alone is so ingrained in my being from the earliest days of my childhood such that I picked it out of a thousand smells at the large market.

We play around into the evening, watch some street performances and finally make our way back to the Shanti. Num gives me a hug. "Goodnight, Mom." I head up to my room, boot up my computer and compose an email.

Ford,

Hey. I wanted to let you know that I have committed you to an arranged marriage to Num. Just in case you have a girlfriend right now, you may want to let her know. Haha

Love, Mom

In the morning I stroll down to breakfast and sit at a table beside two men. I quickly determine they are gay. One gazes into the eyes of the other with such love and endearment that it surprises me. I guess, like most everyone else, I've mostly thought only about the sexual side of a gay relationship. Yet their conversation is so adoring and full of intimacy. They clearly have an emotional connection surpassing the physical. Well duh. Today I am enlightened. These two men are truly in love, caring for one another.

Sitting at the next table over is another couple, a man and a woman, doing the same thing. They giggle and talk, mesmerized, their faces only inches apart from each other. They lean in to whisper even when it isn't necessary, I am staring but I am not listening.

Why is one love wrong and the other is deemed perfectly beautiful? Procreation? Goodness knows there is enough of that going on to keep the human race alive. I love people, all people, and have never believed that being gay is a choice. How can I judge something I have never experienced, so how do I know what it is like for them? And here is another thing; I was born with asthma. When I was a little child in the early '60's, they thought our asthma attacks were all in our head. They thought we created attacks to get attention, meaning they also thought we could control it, so they treated us as mental cases. I remember being a five-year-old and trying to talk my lungs out of filling up with fluid, while at a friend's house that was full of cats. The science and the medicine had not caught up yet. We didn't know what we didn't know.

I am fully aware of what the Bible and other religions have to say about gays, but maybe we don't have all the information yet. All I can say is, at this moment, what I see before me is love. Pure love. And in the moment I am reminded that love really does exist. I have been so numb to these emotions I wonder if I have almost convinced myself they are imaginary, a farce. But here it is right in front of me, and I realize that everything happening in this trip is to move me forward.

* * *

I decide to visit the World's Largest Outdoor market, the Chatuchuk Market. It is huge and easy for one to get lost in the rows and rows of goods, food, and displays. I go because I never want to pass up an opportunity to experience something unusual when touring, even though I have no desire or need to buy anything. It doesn't give the same pleasure as if I were actually shopping, but it is interesting with parades and shows going on around the periphery.

Temple visiting is also what one does when in Thailand. So I take a tuk-tuk (a motorized rickshaw) to a famous temple and head up to see what I can see.

As I approach the door, a man with a security badge walks over. "Temple close. Ceremony until 2:00 p.m. You come back then. I bargain a price for tuk-tuk. He take you two story temple, you very high and see all around Bangkok, then come back."

He flags down a tuk-tuk driver and bargains a ridiculously low price to drive me to temples for the next two hours, so I agree assuming the driver would know good places to visit. He takes me to the two-story temple and it is sort of cool. Not exactly the view the security man had described, but oh well.

Back in the tuk-tuk my driver tells me of a Blue Sapphire Expo that happens only once a year and today is the last day. He wants to take me.

"No, thank you, I don't need any jewelry."

He pulls to the side of the road and turns around to me. "Sapphires, you must see, price so low and today last day."

"No, thank you, I can't carry jewelry with me anyway."

"You ship home."

Shaking my head, I say no again. I have beautiful jewelry in my storage locker at home, and even that has lost its luster as I have become quite content living without material possessions.

"You buy gifts for family. Big Expo you must see. I take you." He pulls back on the road.

I detest confrontation, but he is not listening to me. I debate with myself; you're being a pansy. You never stick up for yourself. And yet, you are only paying this man a pittance to drive you around, just go where he says. But this is my trip, my money and my day. I want to spend it my way. Maybe I haven't made myself clear that I don't want to go.

He pulls up to the "Big Expo" which is a small building, "I wait while you buy. You tell them I send you."

I grudgingly go inside. It is a jewelry store, a permanent jewelry store. Not an expo at all. And today is not the last day they will be selling sapphires. I wander around the store constantly having to fight off the pressure of the salespeople. I stay long enough to appease my driver, and head back out with nary a package. He is very disappointed that I did not buy anything.

In the tuk-tuk as we take off down the road he says, "I take you to tailor, you get suit made for cheap."

"No, thank you."

"For work, they make suit just for you, very stylish."

I know people often come to Thailand or Vietnam, buy several tailor-made suits and ship them home. They are good quality, very inexpensive and fit like a glove. It seems like I shouldn't pass this up, but I don't have a job or an office at home. I don't even know what I will do if and when I go back home. As it stands right now I don't have a reason to purchase a business suit.

"No, I don't want to go to the tailor."

This time he started yelling at me that he gave me a deal and I must go. The hair stood up on the back of my neck, at a man yelling at me. All of a sudden I remembered how my *Lonely Planet* book had spoken of this. Wait. This is all a scam! All of it! Even back to the security guard at the temple. He wasn't even a security guard, just a random guy with a badge. And the temple wasn't closed! Everyone gets a kick back from the jewelry stores, the tailors and sometimes even the Temples who ask for donation. *Lonely Planet* warned me. I am furious and feeling like a fool that even though I'd read about this, I STILL fell for the elaborate scam.

"No, I will pay you full price to take me to my hotel."

He pedaled furiously shaking his head, no.

"I will pay you full price."

"No." He keeps going.

I am outraged. I pull out the small pittance I originally agreed upon paying him and not one Baht more. My heart is racing. He stops at a stoplight and as he does, I jump out, throwing the money in his lap.

He screamed at me in Thai, then yelled to all of the people around, pointing his finger at me. "Cheating American, cheating American!"

I am so shaken at the unexpected nature of how my day has unfolded. This is a Buddhist country, aren't they all about Right Living and Honorable Deeds? I realize that every capital in each country has its share of tricksters, and touts, but this one stunned me. I flag down a new taxi and ask him to take me to the Shanti Lodge. I am not about to go back to the original Temple as I have lost my desire to stand inside its walls. I am done with this city for the day.

In fact, I'm done with this city for a while. Beside the registration desk back at the Lodge is a flier promoting Shanti Lodge Phuket. I love the Shanti and their food is amazing. I decide to get out of Bangkok and go to Phuket a week early before meeting up with Adam. I make a reservation and book a flight.

* * *

My flight is short and as my taxi pulls up to Shanti Lodge Phuket, my first glance reveals a beautiful pool with waterfalls, lush walkways and small bridges. Ah, yes, this is much better. I check in, drop my bag in my room and head straight for the restaurant. I had eaten my way through Shanti Bangkok's menu and I am excited to see what Phuket has to offer. I am famished yet happy as I open the menu only to discover it is exactly the same! I burst out laughing and the other patrons and wait staff look at me with strange wonder. For some reason this is hilarious to me and I can't stop laughing. When I catch my breath I explain to everyone that I have just come from Shanti Bangkok. As a result, many conversations ensue with fellow travelers about Bangkok, and with the wait staff about food at the Shanti Bangkok.

I believe this situation unfolds in this embarrassing way so I can make fabulous new friends very quickly. I meet an adorable American couple, Jeremy and Mira, traveling with Vita, a friend they'd met from Amsterdam. I haven't run across very many Americans on this trip and they move over to my table as we chat about the USA. It is glorious and warms my heart to have a moment of home. I pay my bill and the waitress invites us to attend a staff birthday dinner with them at a local restaurant later that night.

We decide to put on our bathing suits and go for a swim while getting to know each other better. We jump off the top of the waterfall and play in the spray below. This feels a little more like paradise than Bangkok. Good decision, Lucetta. Any time I actually make a wise choice I cherish this, holding it close to my heart, gaining strength. I am also realizing that no one seems to care about my age. My three new best friends are the ages of my own children, and they don't seem to care one bit that I am older.

In the evening we jump in a car with the staff and head to S&P Restaurant. It is a huge place full of only local Thais. I'm guessing the tourists don't know about the deal they have going here. It is a big buffet of all you can eat for only 130 baht (less than $5.00). On the buffet, along with many other things, is raw meat, fish and shellfish. I load up my plate and as I reach our table I see three large pots full of burning coals with a tiny grill on top. The table also holds a trough of water for steaming or boiling. You cook your own dinner at the table! I enjoy watching the Thai people in community with one another when they are not serving tourists. I love seeing their fashions, how they interact, and their customs.

Back at the Shanti, the four of us decide to have a glass of wine to cap off the evening and Jeremy and Mira share a dream of theirs.

Jeremy sips his beer. "We've got an old school bus back in Washington State and our dream is to put it on a piece of property and live in it, turn it into a house."

"Jeremy is extremely handy and I can find a thrift store bargain like nobody's business, so I think we could manage it, but everyone thinks we are crazy!" Mira takes a big swig of wine. "We haven't figured it all out, and friends and family keep asking questions about how will you this and how will you that...? And we don't have any answers. What do you make of this?"

"I am a believer in following your dreams. Don't let anyone else's opinion stop you. If it works out, awesome, if not, then recalculate, alter the dream or find another. You don't have to have all the answers now. These people are doing what they do according to human nature, they want it all sorted out in THEIR mind because it makes THEM feel better."

Her brow furrows. "What do you mean?"

"They want to be comfortable about your decisions and they want to know you're not going to get hurt, which if you really think about it, makes it all about them. As an example, in the late 1980s I had a dream of owning a bakery and I was determined to make it happen.

"My friends all said, 'You're a single mom without a penny to your name, there is no way you can start a bakery. You just moved back here, how will you have credibility and how will you get the money? You are setting yourself up to fail.'

"Maybe I was too naive to believe it couldn't work so I said to myself, what do I need? I need a kitchen to bake in and then I will deliver my goods. Where can I get a kitchen? I could ask my friend who owns a restaurant if I can bake in his kitchen at night, deliver in the morning, take the kids to school and go to sleep for the day. I set a meeting with the restaurant owner and as I shared my dream, I noticed there was an elderly man sitting at the table next to us, intently listening to our conversation. I felt a little uncomfortable and awkward at how openly he held rapt attention. After we made a deal, our conversation ended and the owner walked away. The elderly man came over.

"He took a seat at my table, 'Is there some reason you want to stay up all night and bake?'

"'Well, I don't really want to stay up all night but I need a kitchen and I feel like this is my only option.'

"He leaned back and smiled, 'I own the commercial bread bakery next door and I have a kitchen that is open during the day because I have a baker in there at night. I always like to help young entrepreneurs so I will rent it to you cheap, but if your goal is truly to have your own place in a year, then I won't rent it to you for more than one year, meaning, you will have to reach your goal.'

"I was out of my mind with delight! I baked away every day and went to every nice restaurant, hotel and conference center in town giving out tastings of my products. I got so many wholesale clients that within six months I was ready to move into my own location. Within two years I had served Oprah and Stedman pastries when they came to town for a Double Dutch Contest, made a seven-foot high cake for a Walt Disney movie, and won Small Business Person of the Year from the Chamber of Commerce! My point here is this: run after your dreams like a madman. Never decide you have to have all the answers first because you won't, and even if you do that doesn't allow for miracles. Never let anyone else's own fears stop you. If you want it, go after it, if it fails at least you gave it your best shot. And it may lead to something even more fantastic that you never would have found without that failure. Oh, I'm sorry I guess I got on a rant there."

"Whoa, that was an awesome rant." Mira glows as she high fives with Jeremy. "I think we are doing this, babe."

* * *

I steel my nerves and rent a moped. I work my way to the left side of the road, which is really weird and takes lots of concentration. I blend into the crazy traffic to visit Wat Chalong Temple. Afterward, I throttle my way up a hill to the World's Largest Buddha. Construction of the Buddha is almost complete. It is huge and truly beautiful, sitting on the top of a hill; he can be seen for miles. It is being produced as an 80th birthday gift to their king, whom they dearly love and respect. He is a humble man, has only one wife, and lives modestly. I enjoy the unusual freedom I have with the moped.

I hop back on and ride to the top of different hill overlooking the beautiful ocean. A small crowd gathers, as this is a favorite place to watch the sunset. Down below us sit architecturally modern hotels nestled in lush tropical greenery along white sand beaches. We hang out on the hill as we wait for the sun to make its descent. A family from England stands beside me and we chat to pass the time.

I spread my arms wide and smile, "Ah, the perfect vision of paradise."

The dad lays out a blanket to sit on. "Now it is, but that's Patong and just over five years ago that's where the tsunami hit."

"Oh, wow." Chills ran down my spine. "I had friends who were here that day."

The mom touches my arm gently, "Oh, I'm sorry, did they make it through?"

"Yes, and it's a surprising tale of fate as to how they are alive today."

"Will you tell us?" She takes a seat.

"Yes, please do." He points to the sun slowly setting. "We have time for a story." He pats the blanket offering me a seat.

I sit cross-legged on the corner. "My friends Leslie and Tom are Americans and their son was living and working in Sri Lanka at the time. They decided they would all meet in Thailand to celebrate Christmas together. On the morning of the 26th they had plans to take a ferry to Patong Beach for the day. They piled into a taxi to head to the ferry port. They rode and rode in the taxi for so long Leslie began to get anxious they were going to miss the ferry. After numerous discussions and translations with the taxi driver, they discovered he long ago missed the turn, driving right past the ferry port! Even if they turned around right then they wouldn't make the boat in time.

"'No problem, I take you to another,' the driver waved off their concern.

"They continued to ride in the heat of the small taxi, frustrated at the chain of events, suspecting he was just increasing his fare. Finally, they arrived at another port and upon buying their ticket learned they had to wait over an hour for the next ferry. They were furious that their day was being ruined by the incompetence of their taxi driver.

"They finally got on the ferry and were out at sea when a voice on the boat's radio said that a big wave had hit the shore and they couldn't dock. Questions and much confusion ensued on the boat. It took eleven hours for them to go around to the other side of the island and find a dock that was open. They didn't have many provisions on the boat so everyone was hungry and dehydrated in the heat. It was disappointing for all on board and they couldn't understand why this was happening just because of one big wave.

"It was well after dark as they landed and soon began to understand the gravity of the situation. My friends said it looked like the Night of the Living Dead as they stepped off the boat. People were wandering aimlessly, staring, wounded with blood everywhere, in shock and couldn't speak. As my friends collected details of what happened and pieced together the timeline, they fell into each other's arms crying tears of disbelief, yet gratitude. If their driver had not screwed up, and they'd made the first ferry, it would have been them wounded or killed on that beach! As it was, the tsunami rolled underneath them as they glided along out in the ocean on their late ferry.

"They decided to stay on the island and help rather than catch the next flight out. They gave up their hotel room to a Thai family with children who had lost their home. They worked as volunteers helping people locate loved ones, sleeping on pallets whenever and wherever they could. Tom is a commercial photographer and had his camera with him capturing it all. The photos were disturbing and heartbreaking. The good news is that my friends made it back to America and are alive and well today."

The daughter points to the top of the hill. "Mum, is that why they have escape routes over there with the big signs?"

"Yes, love, now they have paths from the beach all the way up here so people can run up to safety if it ever happens again." she turns to me. "I am thankful your story had a happy ending."

Looking below I observe, "It's amazing that five years later, you can't even tell everything was once obliterated down there. I hope the survivors' hearts have mended with such completion as well."

We sit in silence. I say a prayer for the hearts of those who endure because I know well the experience of tragic loss and how the very core of your being is forever altered. It's a balance of the scales. On one side is: I am stronger for having survived; my character and life experience is far richer and fuller. On the other side, a piece of my heart has been broken off and though the wound may heal, the empty space resides evermore unfilled.

The sun slips below the horizon igniting beautiful hues of reds, pinks and orange. I haven't thought about my friend's story in so long. It reminds me that everything that happens in life is perfect, even though perfect doesn't always feel good at the moment, and perfect can be very messy. There is something greater here at work in our lives, and I am reminded of the beauty in my life regardless of the empty crevices, for they also build the temple of who I am.

* * *

It had been a wonderful, restorative week with my new friends spending time at the calm environment of the Shanti. I load up my bags, say goodbye and grab a taxi for I am going to see Adam! We'd decided we will meet in Patong right before the big celebration of SongKran, which is New Year's Day in Thailand. On that day the entire country pours water on everyone to cleanse them from their past sins and bad luck as they start their New Year 2011. It is done as a sign of respect and good wishes for the New Year. They may also throw a white powder on you which signifies "we love you like family." Evidently it is a one of a kind celebration not to be missed. I grab a taxi and head toward the beach.

At the hostel I sign in, "Zaytoun, please."

"Yes, ma'am. Dorm room. I take you up now."

We go upstairs and I am the first to arrive in the room, which is always a bonus because I get to claim the bed I want most. As I begin to unpack the door opens and the desk clerk brings in my roommates. A sudden burst of familiar laughter fills my ears and my heart. I turn quickly to see Adam and Scott in my room!

"Creesh! We're in the same room, hahaha, did you plan this?"

While laughing and hugging so tightly, I reply, "No, I didn't."

The clerk, smiling says, "We see same name and put you together."

Tears pool in my eyes for being with Adam, and true to his tenderhearted nature he notices, grabs me and gives me another long hug. "Aww it's okay, Creesh." After all, this is the young man who dropped everything for his sister, Tessa, when her dog was nearly beaten to death.

"I know, I'm just so happy to see you and to see someone from home. It's been so long."

He wipes a tear from my cheek. "I'm happy to see you too. I get to see with my own eyes that you are alive and well. We have all been more than a little concerned."

"I can appreciate that and I'm doing well now."

I turn and give Scott big hugs too as I haven't seen him in several years. As they unpack we talk about their journey to this point. Scott was in France and Adam joined him on a two-month backpacking journey. Their biggest tale at the moment is they have just gone skiing in Dubai. Wait, what? I'd heard that Dubai built a ski slope indoors away from the intense heat, but I could never really wrap my head around it until they show me photos.

The guys begin to settle in and somewhere out of the blue I start to feel a little awkward. I know they want to hang out with me, but what will this be like to share a room? Will it be uncool if I take my asthma meds at night like an old person? What if I snore? What if they want to party all night and I want to get to bed? These guys are twenty-six years old; will I cramp their style? What if I say something lame or stupid and they regret this whole thing? Insecurities for approval rush through my veins, anxiety gripping my heart tightly, just like it always did in the past. I thought I was over this.

"Let's go walk and get the lay of the land around town, then get some dinner," Adam suggests.

"Good idea." Scott nods. "We need to get prepared for tomorrow."

Not certain exactly what he means by that; I agree anyway as at every new destination I first take a stroll to see what I can see and get the lay of the land. The entire town is packed to capacity and there is great excitement in the streets. The place is abuzz with anticipation for tomorrow's celebration. It feels a little like being in Times Square on New Year's Eve. We stop in a shopping area and I am looking at waterproof cameras, deciding if I want to spend the money for just one day of water deluge. Scott brought a waterproof GoPro camera with him so he was all set. The guys wander off as I investigate camera models and pricing.

As the salesperson goes to get another camera an Australian leans in. "You don't need to buy this for one day, just put your camera in a Ziploc bag and make the tiniest hole for the camera lens. I do it every year."

"Good idea, thank you." I catch up with the Adam and Scott to find they have purchased Super Soakers, big ones.

"Wow, are you planning to get into the fray tomorrow?" I ask as I admire Scott's water gun.

"Yes, and so are you," Adam grins as he pulls from behind his back a third Super Soaker for me.

"What?! I was just going to watch."

"No way, we're going to celebrate the New Year Thai-style."

"Well, all right then, thanks for the weapon. And you do realize you just armed me after pulling an April Fool's joke on me. I haven't forgotten. Just sayin'..."

Adam laughs. "Bring it, Creesh."

We work our way back to the hostel and after dinner, Adam gets out his iPad because we have Wi-Fi, "I have a Skype call with someone." He moves to a different table.

Scott and I continue to catch up, and after a few minutes, Adam calls me over. As I get close I hear him saying, "Dad, I have a surprise for you, your ex-wife is here."

On the screen I see his familiar face and in a second, what simultaneously pops out of my mouth is, "Hey, baby."

"Oh no! I didn't mean that." My hands fly up over my face. That was humiliating. It just came out after so many years. "I am so embarrassed!"

Adam starts laughing and says, "Run along, Creesh."

I go back to Scott and tell him what happened, "Haha, I blew it. The first time I've seen him since we've divorced and I called him baby. That was graceful."

"At least you didn't call him an SOB." Scott laughs.

"Na, we're cool now, we're friends."

Adam comes back to the table, "Nice one, Creesh. I was avoiding the awkward conversation with him that I was going to see you, so I thought this would be a big surprise. He said he'd heard a rumor we would be together. Turns out you created the biggest surprise."

Ugh, I feel so foolish. I had an opportunity to show the new empowered me, yet my body and mind fell right back into old patterns and ways of being, in less than a second. Later I tuck myself in bed and turn toward the wall signaling I'm not available for conversation. I fight the feeling of this setback.

In the morning, I put on my bathing suit under a little sundress. I tuck my camera in a Ziploc and cut a tiny hole in the plastic then wrap it tightly with rubber bands. Then I put the whole thing in a second baggie, adding an extra layer of protection when I'm not taking photos. Today is a new day and a new opportunity for strength.

We arm ourselves and go out to the front lines. People everywhere of all ages have squirt guns, buckets, and bowls of water. We are immediately soaked within minutes of walking out the door. Pick-up trucks drive the streets loaded with people and big barrels of water in the truck bed. They douse everyone with bucket after bucket as they drive by. Other trucks have water hoses and spray everyone in sight. It is a blast, and actually feels good as a refreshing break from the intense heat. It is good natured, boisterous fun and no matter who you squirt, they never get mad. I've never experienced anything like this before. Ever. It's the stuff my dreams are made of because I love to play. It is like summer camp on steroids and this is happening all over the country. We cleanse everyone in sight for as long as our water will last in our Super Soakers. Then we come back, dry off, get some food, refill our guns and head right back out.

Out on the street a man comes up to me and puts his gun inches from my face. He startles me as he shoots the stream directly into my mouth. What?

"Adam, that was vodka!"

Scott and I burst out laughing as Adam runs after him for a squirt of his own. We play like kids for 14 solid hours until we finally call it a day. We end up at a bar reliving our crazy adventures. Next to us are a couple of foreigners flirting with some beautiful young Thai girls. Later in the evening we overhear them planning to keep the night rolling by going to the guy's hotel room.

One of the girls goes to the bathroom and while she's gone, the other girl leans over to one of the guys and says, "Oh you go home with Daryl?"

"What?! Daryl? Noooo. She's a man?! Noooo!"

"Yes, Ladyboy."

"No." He slaps his friend. "We've got to get out of here, I feel sick."

We muffle our laughter as best we can until they leave the bar. Scott and Adam both agree they would have never guessed that was a man.

Bemused, Adam takes a sip of his beer. "This is accepted here in Thailand, but still, it's a weird situation."

Scott ponders, "I'm guessing they are born transgender."

I chime in. "I was talking with a local Thai woman about this last week and she said, yes maybe some are transgender, but there is one thing no one talks about publicly. In Thai culture the first born son is everything, the second born son is a drag on the family, so they will often raise him as a girl from the very beginning."

"Whoa I can't even imagine that, ugh…new topic," Scott says as he waves the bartender for another round.

Back at the hostel the lobby is festive and full of super soaked people from all over the world. Everyone is laughing and sharing stories from the day. We climb the stairs to our room, desperate for some dry clothes. Together we decide the best quote of the day goes to Matt from Germany, "I have a blister on my trigger finger."

In the morning at breakfast, we decide to take it easy for the day.

Excited, Scott offers, "Let's play on the beach and get a fish pedicure."

"Yes!" I'm inspired. "Even though I am afraid to put my feet in a fish tank full of little piranhas, it's just fascinating enough to make me want to do it."

Adam is not on board. "Do you know how disgustingly germy that is? You are also putting your feet in fish poop because there are hundreds of them pooping in there."

Scott and I wink at each other knowing we are not giving up until we convince him to do this with us. We wander to the beach, play in the surf and take amazing video with Scott's GoPro, we have lunch and hmmm, somehow stroll right by a fish pedicure spot.

"Adam, they eat the dead skin off your feet. How gross is it that you have dead skin on your feet?" I take unfair advantage of him being a germaphobe.

"Oh well, yeah, that's gross too, thanks, Creesh. Now I'm stuck in a dilemma."

Scott chimes in, "We're here, and you may never have this chance again." Scott takes unfair advantage of his adventurous spirit.

"Damn both of you." he grins as he tells the woman, "Three fish pedicures, please."

We cautiously dip our toes first and then plunge both feet all the way into the water full of hundreds of tiny flesh eating fish. It tickles like crazy! I can barely stand it and have a really hard time keeping my legs in the tank. We are laugh screaming as they chew away at our feet and legs. After several minutes we become more accustomed or maybe they have gotten the worst of the skin off. Either way, it becomes a tiny bit more bearable.

Getting out of the tank Adam asks the woman, "Do you have a hose to clean our feet?"

She is confused. "You clean feet," pointing to the tank.

"No, but what about the fish poop?"

Scott grabs his arm. "Come on, dude, let's go back to the ocean, we'll wash our feet there."

Walking behind them, I can't let it go that I finally have something over on Adam so I quietly mumble, "There's fish poop in the ocean too."

* * *

At breakfast I am preparing my heart to say goodbye to Adam and Scott. This has been so much fun and it warmed my soul to brush up against a little bit of home. Having familiarity come right to my doorstep is not something every expat gets to experience.

Stalling on the topic of separating, I ask, "What's the next plan for you wild and crazy guys?"

Adam chuckles, "Scott did so much research for this trip and he has each day planned out for us to see as much as we can, and experience the coolest stuff every country has to offer. I'm amazed. It's so awesome, Scott, that I will defer to you."

Scott sips his coffee. "Today we go to the island of Phi Phi Don, we'll play around the area tomorrow, then move to Ko Pha Ngan Island just in time for the world famous Full Moon Party."

Adam puts his hand on top of mine. "We've talked about it, Creesh, and we want you to go with us."

"What?!" I am stunned as I gape at both of them, "Seriously?"

"Yes. Do you have any other plans right now; any place you have to be for the next week or so?"

"No, I haven't made plans past seeing you, but don't you guys want to roam free and have an insane party at Full Moon? You don't need a mom tagging along."

"We've been having fun with you, Creesh." he squeezes my hand, which brings a tear to my eye.

Scott quips, "Yeah, we love how you one-up us every time with your crazy Africa stories."

"Oh no, I'm sorry, I don't mean to out-do you, it's just that you're the first people I've seen to be able to tell these stories of my life. Ha, I'll tone it down."

I'm slightly embarrassed, as I always want to be the cool mom, not one who is coming from self-importance. I'm just so excited to have someone be a witness to my life that it spews out every time.

Adam laughs. "It's okay, Creesh, come with us, it'll be fun. In Ko Pha Gnan, Scott has reserved a place big enough for all three of us, so why not come with us at least through that leg of the trip."

I taste my coffee, as emotional baggage climbs on my back like a rucksack. I'm on this trip to have my own experience. If I go with them am I falling back into my compliant ways and following them because it's easier? Am I just trying to be liked? I feel awkward about being a third wheel, and the last thing I need right now is to feel less than stellar, when I'm just now gaining speed. I'll be doing all the things they want to do. Is that good for me now or is this me going backwards? Really, Lucetta? You know how to make decisions now and you can hold your own these days. How about you remove the old rucksack and look at this from your present self. Deep breath. Present, hmmm, well, right now I'm having a great time hanging out with these guys. I'm incredibly flattered that Adam wants his stepmom around. I adore him so much. He and Scott have been childhood friends for so long that I feel like Scott is an extra kid of mine. Once they leave, I'll be completely alone again. Why wouldn't I want to spend every second I can with them? Of course I'm not going to pass up this opportunity. Arrgh, I am so messed up that I'm even having this conversation with myself. Okay, stop. Just stop right now, do *not* go into self-loathing.

The inner battle ceases as Adam says, "Creesh, what do you think?"

I look into the beautiful hazel eyes of this man I treasure, and say, "I'd love to, thank you."

Scott flags down the waiter for our bill. "Let's go pack up, we'll grab a taxi and make it to the ferry just in time. The only thing I didn't plan is accommodations for tonight. It's pretty busy this time of year, so places might be booked. It's a small island. Are we willing to risk it?"

A huge grin breaks on my face. "Now you're talkin' my language. Let's go see what happens."

The ferry drops us at Phi Phi and we wander around hauling our packs. We find one hostel that has some openings in the dorm room. We walk in and stop at the edge of the door. It's 16 bunk beds all within two feet of each other; the mattresses are plastic covered with no sheets.

I'm dismayed. "Oh well I have a sleeping bag liner I could sleep in."

"I know we're trying to save money, but I wouldn't mind paying more for a real bed," sighs Adam. "I didn't bring a sleeping bag."

Scott wipes sweat from his brow, "It feels like it's a hundred and twenty degrees in here, but should we grab it because maybe there is nothing else available?"

"I almost feel like sleeping on the beach would be better." I offer half joking.

"Cool, that's our plan B, let's go look for another place." Scott picks up his pack and we hit the streets.

On Phi Phi, no cars are allowed, only bikes and carts. We weave through hundreds of tourists and bikes. Many of the Thai locals determinedly push huge carts full of anything and everything one might need while touring. I reflect and then realize this is an island so most likely, all goods must be shipped in and distributed. Without trucks, they use manpower to keep the island afloat.

We pass a small hotel with a sign that says, "Vacancy, Air Con, Free Wi-Fi"

"Sold!" We yell and high five.

We drag our packs up the stairs, and I veer off into my own private room. I haven't had air conditioning in six months. It has a thick blanket on the bed so I can crank it down tonight. Ah, this is a slice of heaven.

I meet the guys downstairs and we stroll the island. We find a place that serves dinner on the beach as we watch the sunset and drink piña coladas.

"We're going to sleep like babies tonight." Adam relishes the thought.

"I've always questioned that phrase," I quip, "because babies don't sleep. They wake up every few hours. Seems like it should be, 'I'm going to sleep like an adult.'"

They laugh, "Good point." Then they high-five each other, "One-upped again."

Ouch, is that a good thing or not? Do I talk too much, or am I still in teaching mode as a parent? I know they are teasing but it stings a little because as a stepmom, I'm always looking for approval. With my own children, it's built in, there is an innate connection that comes from being blood related. And even though I want to be cool with them too, there is a peace that I won't be totally cast aside by those I birthed, no matter what. The relationship has some built in security. But with stepchildren there are no guarantees. The connection must be cultivated, tended to, and respected. And I'm a little concerned at being so fragile now since a part of my home world has shown up. Would I revert back to this if I returned to the States? I'm overthinking it all. Why not just be myself and quit taking things so personally. Don't get stuck in reverse; move forward.

I ask Adam and Scott for the updates on their friends. They have a pretty tight group that remained close even through college and beyond. Many of them are married and living the 'family man lifestyle' now. We take a trip down memory lane and laugh at many of the lunatic stories of their high school antics.

As we work our way back to the Pirates Lodge, Scott says that tomorrow is play day. We are going to book a tour of four islands in one day. The guys decide to go back out and see about the nightlife here, but I bow out because I have a Skype scheduled at the crack of dawn with Ma and Pa. Up in my room, I crank the air down to zero. I dive under my down comforter, and sleep like an adult.

* * *

I awake at sunrise after a restful night's sleep, go downstairs, get a coffee and sit outside in the sun. A moment washes over me. I am so fortunate to be in this situation and I will embrace the effervescence of my foolish and crazy life right now, all of it, the highs and the lows. For this IS my life, and I am the only one who wakes up every day and lives it.

Back in my room, I boot up my laptop, and hear the familiar sound of a Skype call ringing. I see both of my parents sitting downstairs in their house. I am flooded with love and gratitude for these precious souls.

"Hey, Cet, how are you?" My father asks, as my mom waves.

"I'm good, how are the two of you? And, Pa, how was your cataract surgery?"

"It was fine, your mother took good care of me, and I can see you clearly right now."

"Excellent. I'm in Thailand with Adam and his friend Scott. They're sleeping right now, but we can set up another Skype so you can see them. Adam would love it."

We catch up on the news of my entire huge family, which takes quite a while. We share how much we miss each other, and I assure them that I am fine and I'm healing.

My mom asks, "Have you found a place you want to put down roots yet?"

"No, not yet."

"Well, good, then there's a chance of you returning."

"Now, Janice," my father interjects, "She's got to make up her own mind, we can't impose our wishes on her."

"Well I can certainly hope now, can't I?"

I smile at how adorable they are. "I love you both so much."

Pa looks at his watch, "Well we better let you go so you can get some sleep too."

I laugh, "No, Pa, it's morning for me. It's already Saturday here. I'm living in the future and I can tell you it looks really bright."

"Well that's good to know, and in that case I guess I'll be excited to wake up tomorrow."

I blow them kisses, we say our goodbyes and hang up right before the tears spill over my cheeks. I miss them so.

I journal as I wait for the boys to wake up. We grab some food and make our way to a long tail boat with a guide and a captain. First they take us snorkeling to see the black fin coral shark. I put my face in the water and can't believe I am swimming with sharks, even though they are a little timid and mostly harmless. Still, it is a shark and it's just a few feet away from me.

Something clamps my leg and I flip over with a scream. Suddenly I see the culprit. "Adaaam!" I splash him as he laughs that he's pulled yet another prank on me.

Back on the long tail, our captain takes us to some cliffs with a path leading to the top. He explains we will jump from 14 meters, which is 46 feet high. Adam and Scott are beside themselves, as they love adventure, and are thrilled to jump off a cliff in Thailand.

"She's not going to do it," Adam tells the captain as he points at me.

"What do you mean?" I ask.

Adam puts his hand on my shoulder, "I know you're very afraid of heights. I don't want you to feel like you have to do this."

"I *was* afraid of heights, but not anymore. You bet your ass I'm going to jump."

"Wow, Lucetta, that's awesome," Scott smiles as he climbs out of the boat. "Let's go make this mountain our bitch."

I climb up the hill and jump without a moment's hesitation. Whoa, I never in my life would have imagined it would be this easy for me. No terror, no panic, just freedom. I feel my soul expand with joy knowing I will never have to deal with that fear again.

Soon we are onto the next thrill of the day. We float around another island and snorkel in some Viking caves. Underneath us are sea turtles and I am fascinated by how huge they are, thinking they must be really old. We boat over to Monkey Island, which is full of sightseers. We watch as a tourist hands a tiny monkey a bottle of Coke, which the monkey takes and drinks it down. We are very upset by what this will do to this sweet animal.

Adam says, "Tourism will kill off this island. It's wrong to exploit the animals for entertainment. Let's go."

Our final stop is Maya Bay, where the film *The Beach* was shot, starring Leonardo DiCaprio. The vision in our head of hanging out on the beach we saw in the movies is shattered, as we get close. There are hundreds of people on this small beach! We can't even find a place to anchor that's close enough to get out of the boat.

"This is like trying to find a parking space at the mall at Christmas." I remark.

Our captain knows the ropes though and fits us in somehow. We wade to the shore and look around, trying to recognize spots we'd seen in the movie.

Adam, once again, is dismayed at how tourism will eventually destroy this island too, "I'm ready to get out of here if you two are."

"Yes," I reply, "it's beautiful here, but not the experience I expected."

* * *

In the morning we get up late and race to the ferry. We are just in time, but there are no seats left, so we sit on the floor and this is where we will be for the next two hours. Halfway through the ride some people come in from the front and tell us there are seats up front now, outside.

"Yes!" We scramble and grab a place in the wind and the sun. We land at Krabi and wait for a van shuttle which takes us to a different van. After another 30-minute wait, we drive for an hour or so and transfer to a bus. Again we wait, and after a two-hour ride we reach a ferry, which we take to Koh Pha Gnan. It is full of young people coming for the Full Moon Party.

Scott reassures me. "We are not staying on the southern part of the island where the party happens, we are going to a very remote part of the island up north."

We find a taxi that has four-wheel drive because the roads are dirt and barely passable. Finally, the last leg of our trip brings us to the end of the earth, the place we will stay: Mai Pen Rai. It is nine o'clock at night and the moon is almost full. It is so bright we can see our utopia, Haad Sadet Beach. Adam carries my bag, along with his, as we literally climb rocks up to our bungalow. It's an awesome place, but I immediately smell mold inside, which is number one trigger for my asthma, so I take an extra hit on my inhaler. We stroll the beach, get food, and soon tuck into bed after a very long day of travel.

The sun comes beaming in the window across my face and wakes me. I walk on the beach and decide this place is so remote that I might stay here for a while. Maybe I should go ahead and rent my own hut, then I won't be a third wheel and I can choose a place that's not musty. I stop by the desk and they show me a few open places. I choose one that is a small cabin nestled under some trees in between huge boulders. There is a little porch up top with a hammock and a beautiful view. When the guys wake up I move my belongings over to the new place. On the door in my bungalow there is a sign from the management that reads:

Full Moon Party has gotten out of control.
Please be careful about drugs and robberies.
Don't take anything with you except money to get back (and party).
Boats will taxi you at 7:30 p.m. and 10:00 p.m.
They will return you at 2:30 a.m. and 7:30 a.m. Be safe.

Hmmm, well, the Full Moon Party wasn't on my bucket list until a few days ago. Do I really want to get into a major bash full of young people? Am I up for a night of full on debauchery? The sign on the door makes me a little nervous about this actually being fun. Yet, somehow my free spirit won't let me say no because I am here and it's a once-in-a-lifetime experience. I've reclaimed my "yes" to adventure, so I will roll with the crazy.

I go for a swim, clean up, and settle into my hammock to write. I look out and two men are in a kayak paddling out toward some massive boulders. At closer glance I realize its Adam and Scott. I watch as they climb straight up and jump off, move to a different boulder, climb up and flip off of that one. Each jump gets progressively more daring. They explore like twelve-year-old boys. It makes me happy to see them enjoy that kind of liberty, so I get distracted by taking photos, and never write a word.

* * *

"Let's go eat there." Adam points to a beautiful restaurant sitting on the top of a hill overlooking the ocean, beaming in the light of the full moon. "We could get a taxi."

Scott surveys the mountain. "It will take forever to get one of the few taxis out here on Full Moon Night. Why don't we just hike straight up the hill?"

So, naturally that is what we do. As we get seated, we watch down below as the 7:30 p.m. boat leaves for the party. They are boisterous and loud as they stumble to get themselves in the boat.

"I'm pretty sure they've been pre-gaming." I note.

"Yeah, Creesh, can we talk about that?"

"Pre-gaming?"

Adam laughs. "No, the party, can we talk about Full Moon?"

"Sure, what's up?"

He squirms in his seat. "I've heard some horror stories and I'm afraid something bad might happen to you out there. I've been thinking about it, and I don't want to hurt your feelings, but I don't think you should go."

My, "I'm Empowered Now" persona kicks in. "Adam, I appreciate how protective you have always been of your sisters and me, but I just made it through Africa by myself, I think I can handle this."

Now Scott squirms in his seat.

Adam leans in. "Creesh, I guess part of what I'm saying is that if you are there, I'm not going to be able to enjoy myself because I will be worrying and watching out for you."

"I can understand that, Adam, and I don't want to put a damper on your party. It would be weird for you guys to have an ole lady there anyway, although I assumed we wouldn't even see each other because of the crowds."

"See, now that would make me worry even more."

I smile. "It's okay, Adam, I'll pass. You two go have a riot of a time tonight."

He lets out a big breath. "Thanks, I've been thinking about it for days and was afraid you were going to be disappointed with me."

"No way, I admire your honesty."

Scott raises his beer. "Well then, a toast to family."

* * *

We hike back down the hill and the guys veer off to go get ready for the 10:00 p.m. boat. I go back to my cabin, take a cool shower, and sit on my porch to watch the boat leave. Other hired taxi boats pull up, groups of people jump in and they take off with a roar. I wave Adam and Scott off on the Mai Pen Rai boat as it charges away to the big celebration. I sit and stare at the gorgeous moon.

I expected to feel peaceful at this moment, but I realize I am the only person left on the entire property. I am the only person not attending this legendary event. "Loser me" takes over my brain as I feel I have lost something I can't get back, a chance to have this adventurous experience. I'm here alone because I'm too old, and I need to quit acting like I'm young. I should stop thinking I can still get away with doing all the things I did in my youth, and start behaving like a grown-up.

And I'm feeling a little cast aside. I know the guys didn't mean it this way at all, but I am and I can't stop the way it spirals me down into a deep dark pit. I can't take any more rejection in my life after just working my way back from such a big one. Why did I follow them here? I don't understand. I wasn't going to tag along and then I did. Am I still not able to make good decisions? I cry out to God, "Why did you bring me all the way out here to let me hurt like this?!"

I'm going to bed. I'll just wake up tomorrow in a new day and start over. I climb down to my bed and lay under the sheet. Eww, something smells putrid. Ugh, this is awful, I cover my nose with my hand. What the hell? I look under the bed, but there is nothing there. I climb back in the bed. Just go to sleep and figure it out tomorrow. At that moment the electricity goes out and which means the fan goes off. Oh my gosh, seriously? Mai Pen Rai cuts off the electricity from 11:00 p.m. to 7:00 a.m. This is like being in Africa again; I'll give this place one more night. The heat makes the smell even worse. I cover my nose with a T-shirt and finally begin to drift off when a boat comes barreling into the bay. The loud engines and the drunken partiers wake me up again. This goes on for hours.

What is this rancid smell? It's not me because I showered tonight. Maybe it's the sheets or the mattress, because it smells only around the bed. I will talk to the front desk tomorrow. I get up and search the cabin, but don't find anything that could be causing this horrific odor. I lay back down and will myself to end this day by going to sleep. More boats roar into the bay, full of drugged up, drunk people. This is becoming a nightmare of epic proportions.

At 3:00 in the morning another loud boat pulls up and wakes me. This time though, there are no screaming drunks. I turn over to drift back off when I hear someone coming up the path toward my cabin.

"Lucetta!"

It's Adam. I quickly rummage for some clothes, "Okay, just a minute."

He knocks on the door, "Can I come in?"

I open the door and he bursts in, "It was awful! Just awful, oh my God awful. I need a hug, I'm so glad you're here."

He grabs me and we embrace in a very, very long hug. The hug I'd been waiting for, for twenty-one years, a mother comforting her son.

He began talking rapidly, spewing the events of the evening. "We bought some drinks and it was fun for about an hour or so. It became insane with so many people crammed on the beach. There was so much trash and it was all washing out into the ocean, they are ruining that beach. There was so much depravity and indecency right there in front of everyone. I couldn't take it any longer. If I was 18 or 20 years old, and got passed-out drunk, maybe it would be different, but I had to get out. I missed the 2:30 a.m. boat and had to pay 1500 baht for a hired boat to get back, but I would have paid a million dollars to get out of there."

"Whoa, Adam, I'm so sorry it happened that way. Here let me get you a bottle of water and let's go up on the porch."

We move upstairs and sit, looking at the beach.

He calms a little bit. "What those people were doing was disgusting. I knew you were here and I started thinking how grateful I am for the way you raised me. I couldn't wait to get back to you. Creesh, you're the only mother I've ever known. Mom died when I was so young that I have no memory of her. I know I've never told you this before but you are my mom. It's the truth, you are my mother and I love you."

I burst into tears, taking in this moment. A moment I never thought I would have the joy of experiencing. I knew he cared about me, but I thought he was his father's son and I was just the person he had to put up with, and then eventually we became friends. I could have never dreamed he sincerely considered me his mother.

We sit and he holds my hand until eventually his stories wind down. He decides to head up the hill to his place, but not without giving me another big hug, thanking me for everything, and telling me again that he loves me.

I go back up to the porch for another conversation, "God, you are drawing me in. This is why I am here. This was set up so that I literally followed Adam to the end of the earth and then you gave me a gift, a meaning, something bigger than myself on this journey. You dropped this in my life to show me how much you love me and to validate my life's work of raising this family, to say that what I did was important. I thank you. I thank you."

I will be forever grateful for my 3:00 a.m. intruder. I climb back downstairs and fall into bed. Wait a minute it doesn't smell at all. What in the world?

* * *

I sleep in, and as I wake I go upstairs to the porch to see the ocean and relish the beautiful moments of last evening. Soon the desire for coffee brings me back to the real world. I go down to my room and lay some clothes out on the bed. The smell is back! I almost gag this time. That's it—I am out of here! I throw on my clothes and blast out the door to hear a funny animal noise under my cabin. I look over and there right beneath where my bed is positioned, are two huge monitor lizards curled up together. I walk over to get a better look and they talk to each other as they take off running. Hmmm, I go back into my cabin and there is no smell. I bust a gut laughing that my noxious misery was caused by two little monsters snuggling underneath my cabin. I decide it is time for me to move along anyway, and after I get my coffee, I check out of Mai Pen Rai.

I run into Adam and Scott at breakfast. "We're leaving today, Creesh."

"Yeah, me too. I don't feel like this is the place for me. I'm going to Samui Island because they have an airport and I think I'm going to a different country..."

Scott says, "We're taking a four-wheel taxi to the ferry, want to share the ride?"

"That would be awesome, thanks."

At the ferry, Adam grabs me and hugs me into tears once again.

I place my hand on his shoulder. "Adam, thank you so much for everything, everything."

"Aww, Creesh, thank YOU for all that you have done."

I hug Scott and he grins. "Yeah, thanks for hanging out with two gnarly dudes."

I laugh as I wave. "What you talkin' bout, you guys are the cool kids."

* * *

On my ferry I consult my *Lonely Planet* book to see where I should stay. I make my way to Lamai Beach and take a bunk at IBED Hostel.

This place is amazing. It's very new, clean and spacious. I'm in a women's dorm and every bunk has a small TV with headphones, a night-light, a lockable cubby to store valuables, a curtain around the bed for sleeping, and a towel rack. It's like a ship's bunk and they have thought of everything. It feels luxurious.

I meet several young women in my dorm who are also out on massive backpacking trips for six months or a year. We share stories of being scared, doubts about what we are doing, and thoughts of chucking it all and going home. One speaks of being so homesick she doesn't know how much longer she can hold out. Another talks about depression or the rough feelings that hit every time you change locations. There is always anxiety around finding the new location, getting there safely, and getting settled in. We comfort each other, and encourage one another to persevere. I am relieved to learn I am not the only one to have these feelings. No matter where you are, no matter the paradise, unsettled is still a very difficult place to be.

I explore the rest of the hostel to find they offer free coffee and tea, and have a kitchen we can cook in, which has real wine glasses, made of *glass*.

I sit in the kitchen area having a cup of tea, meeting fellow travelers. I talk with a lovely woman from London. When I tell her I'm from America, she asks me which state.

"North Carolina."

"My cousin lives in North Carolina, and thankfully she was fine in the tornado."

"What tornado? Where?"

"In Raleigh, several days ago. It hit right in downtown and she said it was bloody awful."

"What?!" I panic. "I have two children that live there!" I am shaking and I stand suddenly, causing my chair to fall backwards making a loud crashing sound.

With my hands on my head I yell, "Please, does anyone have a phone I can borrow to call the United States, please, I will pay you for the call, please." I start to cry now. I look back at the woman. "I can't lose another child, I can't."

A man walks over and hands me his phone. With a Scottish accent he says, "You know it's four in the morning there."

"Thank you. And I don't care what time it is, I have to know my children are okay."

I step around the corner and dial Ford's number. I am so thankful I have it memorized. It seems that time stands still as I hear the phone ring and ring. Please pick up, please pick up. Horrible thoughts of the possibilities run through my mind. My heart is pounding out of my chest.

At last the ringing stops, and a very sleepy voice says, "Hello?"

I fall to the ground weeping, "Oh thank God, Ford you're alive I'm in Thailand and I just heard about the tornado Oh my God I was so afraid and what about Liza please tell me she's okay too." My run-on sentence finally slows down.

"I'm okay, Mom, and so is Liza. The tornado bounced right over my block. It touched down on either side but not on my house. And it did the same for Liza. We are both fine. Dad is okay too and he came to check on us."

I am crying buckets now. "I am so relieved. Ford, I don't know what I would do if I lost you or Liza. I love you so much. I'm sorry to wake you in the middle of the night but I panicked."

"It's okay, Mom. I understand, especially after losing Leah. I'm sorry I didn't think to email you, but we just recently got our power back, which is how my phone is charged."

"Thank God for that too, because I would have really lost my shit if you hadn't answered, and I don't have Liza's new number memorized. Please tell her that I love her, and I'm glad she's safe."

"I will, Mom, and don't worry, we are fine here. We're looking out for each other. You continue to have a kickass journey. I'm proud of you and I miss you."

I don't want to let him off the phone, but I know he needs to sleep and I am burning up a stranger's cell time. I force myself to loosen my grip on the situation.

"I love you so much. Please be safe and let's Skype soon so I can see both of your faces. Goodnight, sleep well."

"I love you too, Mom, bye."

I collect myself and walk back into the room. I'm slightly embarrassed at my dramatic outburst. The London woman must have explained the tornado to everyone because they give me knowing looks and nods as I hand the phone back to my Scottish friend.

He asks, "Everything awrite?"

"Yes, thank you, they are alive and safe."

Still raw, I sit back down at the table and let out a huge sigh. From out of nowhere a shot of whiskey shows up right in front of me.

I look up to see Phone Man smiling at me, "This will help."

"Oh my goodness, perfect, now I thank you twice."

After giving him a handful of bahts to pay for my call, I decide I need some solitude. I put on my bathing suit and head over to the beach. I stroll along replaying my emotions from earlier. After seeing Adam and now having the scare of my life, I think about going home. I still don't know what I am going to do with the rest of my life, and if I go home, I will just be trying to fix things for everyone. I can't be the fixer anymore, that's not my role now. I rededicate myself to this journey. I'm not done here yet; it is not time for me to go home. Whatever IT is, is keeping me out here.

* * *

I want to go for a swim, but one tough part of traveling alone is when you go to the beach, you can't get in the water and leave your belongings alone on shore. I decide to look ridiculous and hold my bag on my head as I wade in, up to my neck. The cool water restores me, and I feel some peace. I sleep well tucked into my ship's bunk, after coming off the adrenaline of an emotional explosion.

In the morning I am talking with a young Australian woman. "I am road weary, physically and emotionally exhausted. I have moved locations every several days for three months. I feel like I need to go somewhere for a full month and not move or sightsee or travel at all."

"Have you thought about Bali?" she suggests. "We go there often because it's so close. It has big mobs of beauty and might be a great place for you to refill yourself. Oh, and there is a beach called Sanur that is quiet. It's the place many people go to retire. Might be iffy because of the old people, but maybe you'll want to give it a burl."

"Thank you. I haven't thought of Bali, but I will do some research."

I get on my laptop and look up Sanur, Bali. Perfect. I look up flights out of Samui, but everything is booked because of Full Moon Party. Ugh, well what about a train to Bangkok and I could fly out of there? Booked, no train available for days. Damn, I'm back to the bus. My PTSD around buses kicks in.

My new friend Maebh speaks up, "I am trying to get to Bangkok to fly back to Ireland, maybe we could take the bus together. I just have to find a place to stay for the night before my flight."

"I was going to stay at the Shanti Bangkok. We could get a room with bunk beds and share the cost."

"Perfect, let's do it." she smiles.

Well it feels a little better to have a friend on the bus. We book seats on the only thing available, an overnight bus tomorrow night.

In the afternoon I go visit an unusual tourist site called The Grand Rock. It is a natural wonder on the south coast of Samui, consisting of massive rock formations. Now one might ask, why would you walk all the way there to look at some rocks? Because these aren't just any rocks. Two of them are called "Grandfather and Grandmother" and they draw quite a crowd. Now I understand why. Grandfather is a huge penis, and right beside him is Grandmother, with an even bigger vagina! Eww, why couldn't they have just called them man and woman, that wouldn't have put weirdness in our head. The thought of these attractions being our beloved grandparents is a little off-putting, especially because Grandma also has a giant clitoris. It was all kinds of gross, but not repulsive enough that I didn't take a picture.

We decide to have a girls' evening out that night, and several of us go to watch Thai kickboxing. The boxers have this awesome ceremonial dance before they begin, then they proceed to kick the shit out of each other. They are unbelievably quick. Later in the evening they bring out women to box. They are so strong and it is inspiring to watch. When I settle my life down, I want to start strength building again.

Then I have a thought. "These women are beasts, so how do we know they're not lady boys?"

Maebh laughs. "I guess there's only one way to figure that out; check for Grandfather."

* * *

The next day I'm sitting at a roadside bus stop on my way to Bangkok. I took a van to a ferry to a bus, to a van, to this place where I will wait for three hours to catch the overnight bus to Bangkok. Yuck. I will leave at 7:00 p.m. and arrive tomorrow at 5:00 a.m. Apparently they don't have day buses, only night trips, so I can't see any of the countryside. Is that because of the traffic?

The bus finally arrives and I am encouraged because it looks very nice and quite comfy. It's like a cruise ship on land. As I put my bag under the bus, I think, well at least I don't have to worry about my bag getting stolen when I arrive. Maebh and I climb aboard and find seats, which almost completely recline for sleeping, blankets, and a big screen TV. They show a movie. Afterward, the porter comes through and leans over everyone closing their window shades, which seems weird to me because it is dark outside. And can't people close their own shades if they want to?

They show another movie and at the end of that one, they turn off all of the lights. Everyone goes to sleep. Passes out actually. One; everyone on the bus is young and had probably been up partying for days. Two; every twenty-something kid on this bus has prescription drugs to sleep. No one moves a single muscle, or even stirs in their sleep, except for me, the old lady who'd had a good night's sleep the night before.

After a while the bus slows down and pulls off to the side of the road. I hear the bottom carriage doors open and I assume this is a midnight stop and more people will be getting on the bus. I watch and wait. The bus takes off and no one gets on. That's odd. About an hour and a half later we pull over to the side of the road again. The undercarriage doors come up and once more, no one gets on the bus. I wonder what is going on, as I finally doze off for the rest of the night.

At 7:00 a.m. we arrive in Bangkok and make our way back to the Shanti Lodge. It is nice to have the lay of the land and be able to stay in a familiar place. I nap, eat delicious Shanti food, and in the evening decide to do a complete repack of my bags before flying to Bali. As I go through my pack I notice something is awry. My bag looks like it's been through a blender. What?

I begin inspecting everything closely. I pull out a small sack that stays buried way in the bottom, wrapped in socks, tucked under a flap. My heart begins racing as the sack feels very light. I open it to find my iPhone case, minus my iPhone. And the American Express card hidden there is missing as well. I have been robbed! Someone had to have plenty of uninterrupted time in my bag to find these items.

All of a sudden the entire scam became clear to me. The bus only runs at night so they can pull this stunt. They close the curtains and lull everyone to sleep. Someone must have gotten in the undercarriage at the first roadside stop and meticulously gone through every single bag. At the second pull over, I'm guessing they got out. It took much planning and many people to pull this off. I feel so violated and manipulated. Oh, this gets under my skin, and I am fuming. This is not right. I am beginning to think of Thailand as the Land of the Grand Scam.

Fortunately, before I left on my trip a wise person told me to make copies of the front and back of all credit cards and my passport. They said if one gets stolen you'll have the numbers for your card and the numbers to call. Thank goodness those papers were in my pack with me up at my seat. I borrow a phone and call American Express. They say someone *did* try to charge petrol on the card today but luckily it was denied at the station. They said they would cancel it and send a new card to me, at my parents' address. Whew, crisis averted, but I was still out an iPhone. Even though I'd shut it down I brought it with me because I intended to settle somewhere and then would activate it again. Ah me.

I am so ready to move on and get out of here. This country has been a rollercoaster ride for me. I have not bonded with Thailand, but then I have not invested in Thailand either. I did all of the touristy things because I wanted to hang out with Adam. And although touring is fun, it feels a little empty to me. If I ever come back, I'd like to go up north to Chiang Mai and dive into the region, meeting the locals. Staying put and immersing in the community is my plan for Bali. My world has been shaken again and I need a solid place on which to stand, before I can even consider running further.

Part Five

Running Empowered

Sometimes when you lose your way, you find yourself.
—Mandy Hale

Chapter Fifteen

As I land in Bali, I go straight to an ATM and get rupiahs. I obtain my visa, which is good for one month. I will stay here the entire time. I will not give in to the allure of traveling to different islands, although Sumatra coffee is my favorite…No. I will rest, run on the beach, and write. It is time to replenish my weary travel soul. This trip has given me so much, yet I feel as though I am a bunch of flowers that need to be arranged.

I check into Keke Homestay. Rather than backpackers or hostels, they call them Homestays here because the owners actually live in the main dwelling on the property. I rent my room for five days, to see if this is where I will stay for the month. Breakfast is included; the room has air con and my own bathroom, yes!

I drop my bags and head out to buy bottles of water and explore the area. Down the street is a home that has a laundry business in the side yard. Someone will wash my clothes for me? Incredible. The beach is beautiful and wide, lined with hotels delicately placed under the foliage, small shops and restaurants. I discover there is a paved boardwalk that runs for six kilometers along the beach. Yes, again! I have a place to run each day. It is calm and quiet here. I take note of the places that offer Wi-Fi. I discover a grocery store, and across the street is a yoga studio. Ah, this is turning out to be a very good decision. I see myself settling into a very healthy lifestyle here. My shoulders relax and I take a deep gratitude breath. I stop for dinner and then make my way to bed early in the cool of my room.

I wake in the morning and put on my running gear. I have breakfast on the porch with fellow travelers. Today's menu is hard boiled eggs, toast and coffee. I gather all of my reeking laundry and drop it off on the way to the beach. I run along the boardwalk. Halfway down I see a huge diamond on the side of the beach, really huge, the size of a building. It's gorgeous but I am perplexed.

"Excuse me, what is this?" I ask someone walking by.

"It is a wedding chapel. People come here from all over the world to get married. It's beautiful, isn't it?"

"Yes, it is."

As I run, though, I try to push away my cynicism around marriage. Am I jaded now after twenty-five combined years of marriage and two divorces? I have completely lost my ability to trust. I feel as though my heart has gone cold and shut down entirely toward relationships. I said "forever" two times and it wasn't forever. The first time I left because it got dangerous, the second time, I was left. It seems "forever" means from now on, until things change. So what is the point? Ah, me, I have more work to do.

I go all the way to the end of the boardwalk, watching families play on the beach. It does warm my heart to see they have brought the children for this occasion. Many couples bring their babies trying to hold onto the notion they can still honeymoon together. I laugh; they'll be at Disney World soon enough. I realize I am not disillusioned about families, and that makes me happy because family is a core of our human experience while living on this ball of spinning dirt.

I take off my shoes to dip my toes in the cool water. It occurs to me that I am standing on the edge of two worlds. Each one, the land and the sea, offer a very different experience. What a metaphor for my life right now. I can stay out here and live an unconventional life or go home to comfort and safety.

I go to the yoga studio and sign up for class. The room is on the second story with a glass window that stretches across an entire wall. Outside is a splendid view of tropical plants in a small field. It's a very nice place to disconnect and put my life on pause, long enough to reconnect with myself. I'd forgotten how important yoga is to my well-being. I feel like I'm with an old friend.

The owner of the Keke tells me they have one of the world's most beautiful sunrises here at Sanur. Sunrise is one of my favorite things in the world. Getting up early, on the other hand, is one of my least favorites. I set my alarm clock and lay out my clothes fireman-style so I can step right in, half asleep in the morning.

My alarm goes off and I fumble around getting ready. I make my way to the beach in the dark and park myself on a beautiful pagoda, situated out on a sand bar. The color around me begins to change to an orange glow. It brightens with every moment that passes, and there, like my sleepy eye opening, is the sun peeking over the horizon. It is magnificent, and I am awash with a moment of splendor.

A conversation simultaneously takes place in my head. I don't hear His voice this time, but something supernatural is happening to me that is inexplicable.

"Hello, my love."

"Hey, God, I've been running from you for the last two years, I didn't know you were here in Bali."

"I'm everywhere."

"I know, but I just found you here. I'm all alone, I guess it's just you and me now."

"It always was."

"What do you want me to do?"

"Write your stories, remember we already had this conversation."

"I know, but are you going to do anything with it?"

"Are YOU going to do anything with it? Maybe it's not about the after, maybe it's about the writing."

"I know I'm sure it will be healing and cathartic for me, but do I have the discipline and the ability to stick with it?"

"You tell me."

"Yeah, but you know me better than anyone."

"I know your potential better than anyone."

"My life is no different than anyone else's, do you think anyone cares?"

"I do, your children do, your siblings and parents do. Isn't that enough?"

"Yes, absolutely, you are right, but I just don't know what is going to happen to me."

"Why don't you just work on the task I've given you for now, and let me worry about the future."

"All right, I'll try." I wipe the tears from my cheeks.

The sun continues to change colors and awareness encompasses my mind. When I married the second time, I couldn't wait to spend every single day of the rest of my life with my new husband. If our split had not happened in such a dramatic, over-and-done, no-questions-asked kind of way, I never would have let go. I would have clung and clawed to hang onto the marriage no matter how unhappy he may have been. And that would have been an awful way to live, a soul crusher and slow death for both of us. Now, I am discovering myself in a way that never would have been possible, and experiencing things in my life that I could have never dreamed up. I cross over to gratefulness for exactly how this happened, despite the painful process. Unbelievable. I am in awe of my life.

* * *

I decide to break my own rule and take a day trip around Bali and up to Ubud. I won't have to haul my pack, or fly, or take a bus, but I can't come to Bali and not visit one of the most famous places. I hire a guide for the day and he picks me up on his motorcycle.

We stop by a batik store and I learn the process. Then he drops me at a Balinese show. It is fantastic! The color, costumes and dances are wonderful. We move from there to a silversmith, where I buy some tiny silver earrings I can wear around the clock. Our next stop is at a woodcarver shop, and I watch them carve a rain tree. Then we are on to Ubud, the artist's town I have heard so much about. It is lush and beautiful. The good thing about being on a motorcycle is that I can snap pictures the entire way.

My driver then takes me to the Sacred Monkey Forest, a mountain that protects hundreds of monkeys. They play and live their normal lives despite the numerous tourists wandering right on their home turf. I watch them with thoughts of the Rwandan gorillas in my mind. They play and tumble, mamas and babies, the same way as their larger counterparts. Many people buy bananas and feed them to the monkeys, but I don't think that's good. They may lose their instinctual survival skills. I guess, though, in this situation, they are not really living in the wild and will always have food provided.

We begin to work our way back to Sanur, and on the way stop at the rice paddies, something I am excited to see. The rolling hills are a gorgeous shade of green, surrounded in tropical beauty. This feels like paradise to me. We make our way back to Sanur just as the sun is going down. I'm glad I had this tour today because I got a broader flavor of Bali and I won't have any regrets when I leave here.

In the morning I rise and go run on the boardwalk. It is packed with people and it is 7:00 a.m! It looks like it is noon out here. What in the world? Maybe this is what the Balinese do on Sundays; go to the beach and rent bikes. I run a little further down and see several lovely ceremonies being held on the beach, with their incense and flower offerings. In the afternoon I park myself in a restaurant that offers Wi-Fi and begin writing. I will compile my journals and stories in a book. I write an entry in my journal:

TODAY I OFFICIALLY START WRITING
TITLE: UNKNOWN
SUBJECT: MY EXISTENCE
MAY 1, 2011

Well, I suppose that's a start.

* * *

I am finding the Balinese people to be smiling, happy and friendly people like the Costa Ricans. They always want to have conversations and are quick to laugh. Their greeting, rather than "how are you?" is, "where are you going?" At first I give elaborate descriptions of where I am headed, until I learn this is mostly nonchalant. Now I say, "Oh, down the street." I wave and move on.

They also seem to live in a state of peace with their life. There are offerings set out every day at the doorsteps of a home or the driveway. Businesses set them out front. Women weave small palm leaf baskets and fill them with flowers and other offerings. They do this every single day without exception. The offerings are for good luck and to keep any demons away. In the morning they are beautiful and by afternoon they have been trampled or run over. No worries, though, tomorrow there will be fresh ones to savor.

After my five days are up at the Keke, I talk with the owners about staying until my month is complete, because I love this place.

He bows. "So sorry, room you stay, rented several times in month. You stay room in house with us, share bathroom. It cheaper."

I look at the offered room and it will be just fine. It overlooks the temple on their property, which is beautiful. I'm used to living without air con, and I can share a bathroom, no problem. The price is very good and he gives me an added discount because I'm booking so many days.

He bows again and with a smile says, "Welcome to family."

The family consists of a mother, father, and three grown children, who speak very little or no English. They all live here and run the homestay, which stays at capacity most of the time. The son seems to have a permanent frown on his face. He doesn't speak much at all and I can't tell if his fixed expression is sadness or indifference. If I speak to him, sometimes, though rarely, he will say good morning. The dad, who speaks the most English, manages the business and the wife cooks. They are adorable together because of, or despite, the fact they've been married since 1967. The girls clean the rooms and construct the offerings for each day.

I wake in my new room the first morning to find the son a few feet away, outside my window. He wraps himself in a colored skirt to gather the offerings from yesterday. When everything is cleaned up he wraps himself in a white skirt to give today's offerings. At each point in the temple, another basket is placed, holy water is sprinkled and incense is lit for the good fortune of his family and the homestay. This seems to be his main function in the house. This entire process takes 45 minutes.

I wonder if he can see me in this big window. Do I have to start wearing pajamas? The glass is tinted and smoked to make it cooler in here, but is he going to be looking in on me every morning? I watch as he silently completes his last ritual. Afterwards, he puts on his normal clothes and has a smoke, while I realize I am the only one spying.

* * *

I fall into my own daily rituals of running, yoga, writing, listening to myself think, and meeting people in the community. A very important man in Sanur has died, and I am invited to attend the cremation. I thought this was their term for the ceremony honoring his life after being cremated, but no, I am invited to his cremation. In Balinese Hindu they believe that when a person has died, his soul is freed to be eventually reincarnated. They embrace it as a celebration because they see the physical body as just a temporary container for the soul. In fact, they believe that the soul can't be fully set free until the body is burned to completion.

I meet with the family as we gather at the home. This is not a sad occasion for them, as death is for us. Outside is a huge shrine attached to a truck, housing his body. When all are present, we begin a parade through the streets of Sanur. We walk in unison behind the shrine, all the way to the other end of town, where adjacent to the beach, is a place for cremations.

They remove his body and place it in a wooden box. Everyone walks by to say last farewells. After more rituals and words, his body is set afire. The box quickly disappears and what is left for us to watch is the burning of his body. This takes quite a while, much longer than I would have ever imagined. After it is complete, the ashes are taken to the ocean and spread with another ceremony. The love and peace these beautiful people personify is permeating my essence.

In the morning, at breakfast, I commune with the newest traveling arrivals. Two motorbikes coming roaring down the road, and pull up at the Keke. As both men pull off their helmets, I jump up and scream with delight. It's Adam and Scott! Turns out they've been in Bali, staying further south. They rented bikes and made their way to Sanur to stay a night with me. The Keke is booked so we find them another place. I show them the beach, we walk around town, have dinner and I get to hear all of their new stories. It is a perfect, marvelous surprise.

I reflect a few days later and become aware that when I was with Adam at times I fell back into those ways of being invisible or bland, not wanting to embarrass him in front of Scott. It was so easily done, the slipping back into old patterns and habits. It was seamless and I was right there before I knew it. I must learn, somehow, to hold onto my empowerment, to let go of my fear of judgment, and just be completely me, always, no matter what. I remind myself of how far I have come in the last year, surviving the greatest rejection ever. This gives me a surge of power. Yeah, by the time I go home, I'll be a total badass, taking names.

The Keke daughters are outside my window today clipping the grass by hand. They are out all day long in the searing sun, on their hands and knees, carefully cutting each blade perfectly. Where is the brother?

I sign up for Japanese yoga. I'm really excited, as I have done many forms of yoga, but never Japanese. I walk to the studio and climb the stairs. As I enter the room I see that only Asian women are present, and they are looking at me curiously.

The instructor seems intrigued. "You speak Japanese?"

"No, I don't."

They smile and whisper something to each other. Turns out, it is regular yoga *taught* in Japanese. I don't understand a single word. Silly me.

* * *

I'm changing, not only mentally and emotionally, but my body is telling me something as well. I haven't had a menstrual period in four months and at the same time I started hot flashing about every twenty minutes. It's miserable, but I guess it's good that I'm going through menopause out here, alone, where no one has to put up with it but me. And it's good that I'm flashing in a place where everyone else is sweating, so no one has noticed. But geez, I'm already living in 90-degree weather, and then my body has to crank it up another notch, or five. Some nights the heat and sleeping in soaked sheets keeps me awake. Aging is something from which, as hard as I try, I cannot run.

A twinge of sadness hits that I am no longer in my childbearing years. It only lasts for a minute though, because at fifty, I'm perfectly fine with not starting over, and six is probably enough. It does mess with me because it undeniably throws me into a new category of old. And don't give me that fifty is the new forty crap because now that I've crossed into the no-baby zone, I can't deny my age anymore. I'll have to start taking calcium for my bones and quit hanging out with younger men. New rule, forty-five and above, that's it.

Oh God, here comes another flash. It starts like a fireball in the center of my body, works its way out to my skin in seconds, and I am soaked in sweat. I'm flashing like a mother! No, that's not right. I'm flashing like an unmother.

* * *

Myriah emails me and begs for a Skype call because she really needs to talk to me. I go to a local restaurant that has Wi-Fi and tuck myself in the corner. It's so good to see her live on my screen, and tears well up at the sight of her beautiful face.

"Mom, what is your schedule? Where are you headed next?"

"My plan is to go to Vietnam, Cambodia and then India."

"Is there any way possible you could meet me in Hawaii? Tristan and I are going to be there for a week in early June. It's halfway, please meet us there, I need to see you."

I go through the dates in my mind. That only gives me a short time in Vietnam and Cambodia with no India. And if my toes touch American soil, will I get drawn back in? I'm a little worried about the aftermath.

"There is nothing more I'd love to do than to see you, but I'm afraid to come back to the States. I haven't finished out here yet."

"Mom, I understand. I really need to talk to you about my marriage. It's very unhealthy. I think I need to leave Tristan, and I don't know how to make that happen or how I will fully support myself." She begins to cry. "I just need my mom right now."

I was actually relieved to hear this news because I was in agreement about this relationship. I did not want her to marry this man in the first place. It felt very wrong. But when your daughter says she's in love and wants to marry, you get behind her, that's what you do. And who was I to say? They might have lived forty or fifty happy years together. And now she is about to make a very courageous decision, which will rip her heart and world apart. Divorce is so painful and brings out the worst in everyone. Death is final and you have no choice but to move on. Divorce is like scraping an open wound every day.

"Tell me the exact dates and I will be there. I will make it happen."

A deep sob breaks forth as she expresses her gratitude in broken sentences, "He'll be there, but we can go for walks on the beach and talk. Uh oh, he's here; I've got to go. I'll email the details of the trip. Thank you so much, I love you."

"I love you too, goodbye."

I sit and stare at the ocean. Life is so unexpected, and our journeys here are ever changing, growing us into richer versions of ourselves. Ultimately it is all perfect, even though perfect doesn't always feel good and can be very messy and painful. It all moves us forward in the expansion of our souls.

I begin to look around the restaurant. It's Friday night in Bali; there is a cool breeze, music, and the ocean. Everyone should be having the time of their life, but I look around the tables and people are barely talking to each other. Families and couples sit in silence with somber looks on their faces. Was there some sort of world tragedy on the news today that I missed? Or could it be that vacation in paradise is all just pretend. People aren't truly happy to be out of their comfort zone and they don't really want to spend that much quality time together. Truth be told, they'd rather be back home in their routine, even if it is miserable, instead of putting up a front in paradise. Maybe it's just me being cynical again, as I think it's all pretend. But these people? They're not even doing a very good job of that.

* * *

I receive an email from Myriah with the details of our upcoming trip. My sweet, precious daughter ends the email with a Mother's Day gift. She'd researched spas near me in Sanur and booked me for a massage and a sea salt scrub at the Puri Santrian! It is a beautiful resort about two kilometers from where I am staying. This is such a thoughtful gift, and the perfect way to spend Mother's day when you can't be with your children.

Wow, did I ever need that. As the masseuse scrubs, I think she takes off a pound of dead skin and dirt after months of few showers, and cold ones at that. It seems you can never really get clean in a cold shower. It is glorious to be massaged in oil as well. My skincare has not been the best on this trip, and when your daily moisturizer consists of SPF 50, well I'm a little afraid of the long-term ramifications.

I walk home from the spa by way of the boardwalk at the beach. I am dazed and glowing as I slowly make my way along. I begin thinking of my children. Each one of them is loving, compassionate, giving, and caring. After the beautiful chaos that was our life as they grew up, it is wonderful to see them mature and go after their hopes and dreams. They are each following their heart and pursuing goals that are true to themselves, rather than just going after stature, money or power. They are following their passions, even if it means they are broke half of the time. As a mother, I could not be happier and more proud of what they are about in the world. I count it a success if their father and I fostered this in any way, but mostly this is just who they are. They're creative, witty, industrious, and most of all, loving in a genuine, authentic way. I have been blessed beyond measure.

* * *

I log on to my laptop and there is an email from my mom.

Hi,

Just saw this from Wire Reports in our morning paper labeled Jakarta, Indonesia:

SE Asian leaders made little headway Sunday in helping Thailand and Cambodia end a deadly border dispute. The prime ministers of the two feuding nations held talks mediated by Indonesia's president as part of efforts to hammer out a cease-fire, but neither seemed in any mood to back down.

Don't know if you are aware of the news, but stay out of those countries. Glad you registered with the state department. Let us know your news on this situation. (you know moms always worry about their kids, young or old.)

Lots of love and prayers to you—Ma and Pa

Well, maybe I should go to Vietnam first and give things a little time to calm down. Then when I cross the border into Cambodia, I guess I'll fly just to be sure, and maybe this will make my mom feel a little better.

I Skype with my sister Martha and she urges, "You know, you can always come home."

"And do what?" I ask. "I still don't know my path."

"No one has wanted to tell you about this because we didn't want you to feel bad, but I can't hold it in, so I am speaking it now. You have always been the glue that connected our family. Whether you know it or not, you have always been the bridge and the one to keep us together. You are the one who cultivates redemption, restoration and forgiveness. Since you left we have all gone off into our corners, disjointed, and we are far apart for the first time. I just want you to come home. Come home and be the glue."

I am crying now, to be validated in such a powerful way, especially since I've always been the free spirit in the family. And I'm crying at the thought of my siblings and parents drifting. This tugs at my heart. "I love you, sis, and I have a feeling I will find my way home."

I understand now that this truly is a gift I've been given, the ability to bring people together and give them hope. This is the essence of my being and the thing I love the most. It's how I have always operated. Is there a way to use this? Can I incorporate this into my mission and apply this in creating something that benefits humanity? I feel an opening in my heart, and it feels like empowerment.

The days pass gently as I continue my rituals, and something in me has changed. I am no longer consumed with my past, my history, the what-came-before part of me. I am beginning to look toward the future. Even dreaming that a future might be possible.

At lunch today, I book my hotel in Hawaii and begin making plans for Vietnam and Cambodia. It seems different planning this part of my trip because I am no longer afraid or anxious about the travel. I have learned that I can make a home anywhere and can become comfortable with any accommodations if I give it twenty-four hours. I can get used to any neighborhood or any lifestyle, anywhere. This is a relief to me after living a posh life. It is liberating and gives me hope that no matter where I land, it won't be a wrong decision because I will make it home. I now know that it is not about the place, it is the life I create, and I feel I am ready to test who I am.

Today I say goodbye to my Keke family. They have been so sweet and provided a peaceful, healing place for me. I've learned much about the ceremonial beauty of Balinese Hindu life and I am grateful. We give big hugs and take pictures as they help me load my things in the taxi. The son cracks half a smile as he says, "Thank you."

As I leave, of course I am also thinking of all the things I didn't see or do here, but that was not the point of this leg of my trip. This was about me slowing down long enough to take a rest, and it has proved fruitful. It seems that much has come together for me here in Bali. I had time to reflect on the last year and see how far I've come. I contemplate the tumultuous roar of emotions I felt then, compared to the tranquil heart that beats in my chest now. I've stopped thinking with my head and started thinking with my heart again. I am finding and claiming the authentic me.

Part Six

Running Anew

Clarity is the fearless union of conflicting ideas.
—Jeffrey Shaw

Chapter Sixteen

In a few hours I will be landing in Vietnam, a place that existed in my youth as a central part of our history. My brother wore a black armband and wanted to register as a Conscientious Objector, but my dad wouldn't let him. Pa knew the army wouldn't take him anyway, because he had asthma. He tried to tell Donald that the choice of registering that way could follow him all his life. Donald was eighteen and trying to stand up for what he thought was right. It caused much anxiety in the family. I'm glad my brother did not have to go to Vietnam, or run away to Canada and hide out, as many young men did during that time. We watched the news as a family every night and heard all of the horror stories.

When I was in middle school, an organization began selling metal MIA (Missing In Action) bracelets, and the money went toward finding these soldiers who were unaccounted for. Engraved on my bracelet was the name and the number of a soldier who was missing in action. Each Sunday, the newspaper would list the numbers of the soldiers who'd been found. Faithfully I searched the paper Sunday after Sunday, and cried each time his number was not there. After the war was over, my mom finally convinced me to put the bracelet away because it was such an upsetting reminder.

To me it will be fascinating to see the visions I've held in my child's eyes from an adult perspective. I am excited to see the Cu Chi Tunnels, the Mekong Delta, and the thousands and thousands of bikes on the streets. I don't know how I will be received in Vietnam, as an American.

I will do my best to give them an experience of a friendly American and I'm hoping all is well between us now.

I take a taxi to the city and I'm surprised to see the bikes have been replaced with mopeds and motorcycles. I'm dropped at the Hanoi Backpackers Hostel and every once in a while I pay the extra few dollars for privacy. Sometimes I just need a little break from being constantly surrounded with people, and I consider it a treat to myself, so as I check into the hostel I say, "Private room, please."

I go out to roam about my surroundings, and decide I must attempt to cross the street. Hundreds of mopeds and scooters zoom by, with no road crossings or traffic lights. I've read you simply walk out and weave your way through the moving traffic. Simply? This is a death-defying feat! You walk slowly at an even pace, and whatever you do, don't stop, or you may get hit. As long as you are consistent they will weave around you. I dip my toe off the curb several times, but I'm hesitant as I'm waiting for the right moment, maybe a break in the traffic. But that doesn't happen. I see an elderly woman nearby. Aha, I walk over and stand right behind her. As she steps out, I follow and shadow her, in tandem, all the way across. The rush of adrenaline is like a wild ride at the fair. I successfully make my first trip across without being hit.

After a day of exploring the city, the tendency is for us backpackers to return to the hostel in the evening. In this Hanoi hostel there is a floor designated as a lounge with couches, tables and a television where a movie is featured each night. I'm curious to see who gathers here and I wander up to see what the flick is for tonight. I sit and chat with a young couple from Germany I'd met earlier that morning, Anneken and Omar. We share stories and experiences from our day.

Down the hall I hear a raised voice. It catches my attention and pricks my ear. I listen closely determining if it is true anger I detect, or just a couple being playful with each other. I hear the gruffness once again and my heart skips a beat. I turn my head to see what is going on, and my friends, not noticing, continue talking. I look down the hall just in time to see the owner of the gruff voice slam his girlfriend against the wall, pinning her to it with his hand against her throat.

In an instant my instincts kick in and I jump up because I know that if the violence is now public it has been going on for quite a while.

"Hey!" I yell as I race over to them. "You can't treat her that way!"

I grab his arm to try to take it from her throat.

In his anger his spit flies into my face. "This is none of your business!"

"It is now!" I seethe.

He smacks me in the face with the back of the hand that had been around her throat. "Get away or I'll hurt you too."

"I'm not afraid of you. And you." I look to his girlfriend who stands wide-eyed rubbing her throat and my voice softens, "You don't have to live this way anymore."

His fists clench and unclench as his veins pop out of his neck, "Mind your own business, bitch!"

The three of us notice now that the entire room has gone silent, the movie put on pause, and everyone in the room is staring at us.

I step in between them, protecting her and facing him saying, "Look, just go for a walk and cool off."

He reaches around me trying to grab her, as we see a guy jump up and come toward us. Uh oh, this could escalate. I get an inch from the attackers face. "Just go. Now!"

Watching the other man come closer he says, "Fine, but you better watch yourself."

I can't tell if he is pointing at her or me. He turns and storms out of the room, slamming the door. She collapses on the floor her hands covering her face.

"I'm so embarrassed," she admits through her tears. "I shouldn't have made him so mad."

I squat beside her. "You deserve to be treated with love and respect. This is not love."

She waves me away, "I can't talk about this right now. I'm going to my room."

"Okay. I'm here if you need me."

I help her up and let her go on her way. I turn around only to see that everyone is still watching. I head back toward the lounge and a guy jumps up and gives me a high five.

Another man slumps, his head in his hands, "I should have intervened, I feel like a coward"

A young woman says to me, "What you did was awesome! You're a hero!"

"No." I say loud enough for everyone to hear. "What I did was stupid. Someone could have gotten badly hurt here. And worse, he will probably take this out on her later. I got triggered because I was abused in my first marriage. The better thing to do would have been to find some authority to handle this."

I sit down beside my German friends as the movie cranks back up.

"I don't understand; why doesn't she just leave him?" Anneken asks as she hands me a bottle of water.

"It seems like it would be that easy, but it isn't. You see, most people think abuse is about anger but it's really about control. Anger is one way to get control but it's only one way. Abusers dominate using numerous tactics such as isolating you from friends and family, brutal intimidation or keeping control of all finances. He may threaten to kill her, her sister or her beloved dog if she leaves. He's probably told her that no one will ever love her like he does because she's worthless and she should be grateful to have him. He leaves nowhere for her to turn."

Omar shakes his head in disbelief, "How did she ever fall for him in the first place?"

"Oh, this is the best part." Now I shake my head because of the ridiculousness. "In the beginning they are so charming, romantic, loving, thoughtful and perfect. It's only after they have you isolated or locked down, signed on the dotted line, or fully brainwashed that they allow the real person inside to rage. Then they make you think it's your fault so you feel guilty, and you're too ashamed to tell anyone about what's going on."

Anneken's forehead wrinkles in a frown. "Are you saying she probably won't leave him even after this?"

"Maybe not, because he will apologize and tell her it won't ever happen again. Then they will go into the honeymoon phase of the cycle of control and he'll be good as gold again. That is until the tension begins to build, he starts to get agitated and finally explodes. Then it's back to good again. The absurd thing is this cycle could happen twice in a day or it could take months to run its course. After so much time you really believe they've changed for good, so you stay."

"At least this guy will have to be good for quite a while this time!" grins Omar.

"Crazy, right?!" I take a deep breath and let out a long sigh. "This has brought up quite a lot for me. I think I'll go back to my room and journal. Want to meet downstairs for breakfast?"

"Yes," Anneken nods. "7:00 a.m?"

"Perfect."

Omar hands me my small pack and says, "Thanks for what you did."

I nod a "you're welcome" and head out, thankful I had earlier claimed my own space. Memories of my own past flash through my mind, but I realize they don't hold the same power over me. I didn't get triggered by my own experience and sit back as a victim tonight, watching. This time I saw it as an observer, and was able to be an advocate. By my jumping in, maybe she has a new awareness that this is not right, just like when the police were called once on my marriage. It was glaring to me from the fact that people called the police and they showed up that this was not okay and this was not normal. I pray tonight she was given a moment of hope. Whoa, I realize I have released some dominion this had over my life. I drift off into an unexpectedly peaceful sleep.

* * *

In the morning at breakfast, there is discussion around the table of the night before. No one has seen the couple this morning. I'm pretty sure they checked out at the crack of dawn to avoid seeing anyone. I intend to hold her in my heart and prayers each day.

Anneken and Omar are leaving to go to Halong Bay for four days. I want to go, but don't have enough time here in Vietnam to make that happen. Instead I make friends with another traveler and we go north on a day trip. As we rent bikes, Sarah says we must rent bamboo hats as well. We ride all afternoon through the beautiful country full of rice paddies. Feeling very Vietnamese with our pointed straw hats, we understand they really are great for shading the sun and keeping us cool.

It's my last day in Hanoi and I go to the Women's Museum. It is a fabulous tribute to the strong, courageous, determined women of Vietnam. This pretty much sums up women everywhere, even though at times our self-confidence takes a hit, or our culture won't allow us to fully blossom. Yet inside every single woman there lies a supernatural strength, courage and determination. It is what we are made of, and as we become aware that it lives within us, we call on it more and more. Lookout, world. I'm just sayin'…

I catch a flight to Ho Chi Minh City, formerly Saigon, and check into the Duc Vuong Hotel. I find that South Vietnam is more relaxed and less stressed than the north. I speak with a Vietnamese man about this and he says, "In the north they have only known the hard life of war and communism. Here we are capitalist. More better."

I also found the people here to be warm, open and friendly. They don't seem to mind at all that I am American.

I ask him about this and he says, "That so long ago. We make peace now we forgive. And now we open commercial trade and love rich American to come here."

I laugh. "American, yes. Rich, no."

He introduces himself. "My American name Peter."

"Oh? What does that mean, American name?"

"My father was American soldier. He gets with mother and they have me. After war, he take her to the U.S. but I stay here because no one to take care of my grandmother. So I stay."

I admire the difficult life this man has chosen for the love of his family, knowing he could be living in comfort in the United States.

I stand in line for The War Remnants Museum and realize it is Memorial Day in America. Not a coincidence, I'm sure. A sense of sadness and awe washes over me for the impact on their country and ours. Studying the war from their side of the story is difficult and heartbreaking. Agent orange wreaked havoc and babies were born with all kinds of deformities, families were destroyed, and people's lives were forever altered. Halfway through the top level, I have to leave. I can't finish because I am so distraught.

I visit the Cu Chi Tunnels and I learn why this was such a crazy war. The VC, Viet Cong, lived in the south and acted like they were fighting for the south, but really they were fighting for the communist north. They posed as an ally during the day and turned on the Americans by night. Even the children were involved and posing as friendly. Everyone was killing everyone and no one knew who the enemy was, especially the Americans. I saw the killing and maiming booby traps and I can't imagine being on high alert for your life, every single step, movement, and breath you take around the clock. It all seems an impossible situation.

I take a boat up the Mekong Delta just like the soldiers did, many never coming back. All of the newsreels and movie scenes from my childhood come to life, and I have a moment of amazement once again for my life today. I develop a newfound respect for what our vets went through here. I also better understand PTSD because not only were they in danger on the battlefield, but in every moment of every day. I love, appreciate and feel immense empathy toward our soldiers on this Memorial Day.

Chapter Seventeen

I touch down in Cambodia at the Siem Reap airport. In my short time here, I have come mostly to visit Angkor Wat, the world's largest religious monument. It is constructed as a Hindu temple and it is a powerful symbol of Cambodia. I spend two full days touring the temples, which are unique and full of historical power. There are temples that are almost completely hidden by the overgrowth of tree roots. It's fascinating, and I feel myself changed somehow for the richness of the energy here.

One of the guides says he can take a picture of me going nose to nose with Buddha. As I sit for the photo op, thinking of my life, I ask Buddha, "What do you want me to do?"

His answer comes quickly to my heart. "The real question is who do you want to be?"

I also learn a lot about Khmer Rouge and his killing fields. He was a communist leader and more than a million people were killed and buried in mass graves under his rule in the late '70s. This seems to be a theme on my trip. Interestingly enough, I hear that in 2006 there was a Genocide Tribunal for these crimes. I am happy that we are making an attempt to no longer stand by and allow these atrocities to go on in any country. We must all band together and be advocates for every human being on this planet. We must be the voice for people who don't have their own.

The face of the Cambodians I have met here is one of sweetness. They seem pure of heart. They seem very happy to have tourists come to understand and witness their lives.

I make a friend at the hostel and we decide to go watch the sunset on a famous hill nearby. We get there early, scale an almost impossible climb to the top, and find a comfortable place to sit. There is quite a crowd gathered, which includes young Buddhist monks. I wonder what life is like for them day to day.

My new friend Holly lives in D.C. and has been sent here temporarily by some arm of the government. As we sit, we pray the clouds will part so we can actually see the legendary sunset.

Holly speaks, "Ah, it's nice to have a moment of peace without the kids."

"How many kids do you have?"

"Two. They're with my parents. I heard you raised six children."

"Yes, I did."

"What was that like?"

I laugh. "It was beautiful chaos every minute."

She tears up and I can't imagine why.

As she wipes her eyes she reveals, "I'm about to have a big family and I'm terrified. I have two children and my boyfriend has three. Their mother is out of the picture and he has them full time. We are talking about getting married and I just don't know if I can handle all those kids and being a stepmother."

I pull a tissue out of my bag and hand it to her. "Well it's certainly not easy, but it can be incredibly worthwhile."

"How did you handle the bedlam? I'm afraid I'll go out of my mind, and honestly I'm reconsidering even though I love this man and his children. I feel awful about it, but I am seriously frightened."

"One of the ways I survived was by creating systems for everything. If something was a continuous problem I created a structure or procedure that minimized the disorder."

"How so? What do you mean?"

"Well, when we married all of the kids were in elementary school, and getting everyone ready and out the door was quite a trick. I knew

I couldn't cook a full hot breakfast for eight, pack six lunches, answer questions, quell arguments, and help them find everything they needed for the day. So I had to figure it out. We had a cabinet in the kitchen that had four wire basket drawers inside. One I filled small packs of chips, pretzels, and crackers. Next were versions of canned or fresh fruits, third were juice boxes or drinks, and the fourth held desserts. All they had to do was make a sandwich, choose one item from each drawer, and lunch was packed. My only part was to monitor the dessert drawer, haha. Even Tessa, in kindergarten, packed her own lunch. Then, my husband went out and bought two huge baskets that stayed in the hallway. One housed all six backpacks, and the other all sporting equipment for after school. Lined up along the wall was a pair of everyone's current shoes. This meant that in the morning rush, everyone knew where their necessary items were and they could grab lunch, a backpack, shoes and go. It all made mornings a little more doable."

Holly breathes deeply. "Well, that helps, all of our children are really young too. How did you even keep groceries in the house for that many people? You must have gone to the store every other day."

"I would take the kids with me to get groceries, pair them up, and send them out to get certain items. I'd say you two go get the milk, you two get cereal and so on. They loved the thrill of the hunt and actually became bargain shoppers too, which was a surprise. The cart would be piled high and as we approached the register they'd all gather back like a flock of seagulls behind a ferryboat. It would start to get frenetic. Fortunately, the grocery store had a long bench at the front for people to wait as others checked out. So I would send them to the bench to play the 'Quiet Game.'"

"Oh my, what's the 'Quiet Game'?"

"One person is 'It' and the others can't make a sound. If the leader hears them, they are out. Often the leader will tempt them to make a sound, so there is a lot of grinning, but it's all silent."

"That's brilliant!"

"Yeah, I didn't make up the game, but all of the employees thought I was mom of the year because my kids would sit perfectly quiet on the bench until I finished checking out. They had no idea the kids were playing a game." I laugh. "Then we'd get home and everyone carried in bags."

Holly smiles. "That's awesome. More stories, please, because the clouds are making this sunset a lame one."

"Okay, my favorite system was born out of desperation. The kids were whining and crying that it was no fair that the oldest always had her own room and that the boys always got to live in the third floor. It became a source of consternation. I decided that each August, before school started back, we would change rooms for the year. It took us four full days to pack up, clean up, and move rooms. This meant that every year they were in a different room with a different version of sharing, and every three years they got a room by themselves. The awesome unexpected benefit was we found all the lost library books, shoes, and jewelry that disappeared during the year. The kids would go through their clothes, find out what still fit their rapidly growing bodies, and hand down the rest. Each school year began with a fresh start, and I only had to buy the oldest ones new clothes."

She gives me a high five. "I'm beginning to get the picture here."

"Yes, if something is a recurring problem, you create a system around it, and the problem disappears. It really helps keep the anxiety and panic down in the moment."

"Okay, one more question and I'll let you enjoy the sunset. How did you handle all the fighting?"

"We had a staircase that I called 'The Fair Stairs.' If the fighting between two kids got out of hand or couldn't be resolved, I would take them to the bottom of the Fair Stairs. We would gather closely while one child got to tell their part of the story, without the other interrupting, then the second would do the same. Each got time for rebuttal, and when no one else had anything left to add, I would interject my thoughts. Because each child had a chance to be heard and acknowledged, usually the anger would die down, and they could see the other's side of the story. It often ended with an apology, or on a really good day, a hug."

"Thank you so much. This gives me hope, and helps me feel a little less anxious."

I sigh. "I don't think we are going to see any sunset tonight, but maybe that's not what this was really all about anyway. I wish you the best in whatever decision you make. I was scared to death in the beginning too, and I honor the fact that you are not making this decision lightly."

"Thank you." Holly smiles. "Now, can you create a safe system for us climbing back down this wall?"

* * *

In the morning after breakfast I wander into the town of Siem Reap. There is an open market full of all kinds unrecognizable vegetables and creatures to eat. I can't seem to pass up a once-in-a-lifetime opportunity so I gather up my courage, strap on a pair, and try fried crickets and a tarantula. I gag for a second on the tarantula because it has a mushy center. Okay that's enough bravery.

I book a taxi to take me to see the river people. We drive for quite a while and I board a riverboat that tours through the river city. It really is a city on the river. The Cambodians live on one side and the Vietnamese on the other. There is a store, a restaurant, a church, and a school, all floating. I'm worried about small children or babies falling off the boats. I learn from the guide for their survival the children are taught early to swim. I try to imagine a life where your feet never touch solid ground.

I guess one could figuratively say that about me, but my feet are about to touch soil that I am afraid will lure me in with its magnetic tendencies. I am soon headed to America and I don't know if it is solid ground for me.

I spend a night back in Bangkok, in order to fly to Tokyo. From there I head to Hawaii. I'm settled in my seat after lifting off from Tokyo. I'm digging in my heels. I am so afraid that if I touch American soil, I'll never come back out again. I'm not ready to come home. I've been living in tomorrow, and I don't know what will happen if I stand in the reality of today. I don't even know what I'm going to do with the rest of my life! How can I not know by now? I've literally gone around the world in search of my next season and I still don't have the answer. And I'm headed into a guilt trip. I'm meeting Myriah in Hawaii because first and foremost, I love my daughter so dearly and I miss her, but it is also because I feel guilty for not slowing down long enough in Africa for them to visit me. I wasn't in a headspace for visitors then, and I have felt awful and selfish about it ever since.

Who in their right mind doesn't want to go to Hawaii? But my beliefs around materialism and luxury have changed. It's hard for me now, to go spend a gazillion dollars to stay in a nice hotel in Hawaii when I've been living on 25 dollars a day for a bed, food and transportation. This is causing me to bristle on so many levels. Yet I have made a commitment to her that I will meet her, and there is an underlying tone in our conversations that says she really, really needs to spend face-to-face time with me. I believe she may reveal things in her life that are troubling and she needs a mom to help sort it all out.

So you're going, Lucetta. You are on the plane already, taking your guilt trip. You need to get your head straight, switch your heart to the positive. Move yourself to gratitude.

Okay, what am I thankful for? Well, let's see. I am not afraid or intimidated by people anymore, anywhere in the world, any person. Be they a president, a king, an executive, a scary person in a deep dark corner of the city, a mentally ill person, no, I'm not afraid anymore. Traveling around the world has helped me grow to love people so much, everyone, everywhere. I have come to the place of seeing the human soul. I don't see the outer, or the prestige, or even the thugness; I don't see that anymore. What I see is their soul and their potential.

I have learned, as humans, no matter who we are, we all want three things: we want to be loved, we want to be acknowledged and we want our lives to mean something. So I am willing to go into many more experiences and situations than I ever was before. And this feels like freedom to me.

I now understand that this journey was for me to see my own soul, to learn to love me, all of me. Parts of me didn't want to know who I was without him, now I understand that I can be whole with me. And I don't see myself through the eyes of someone else anymore. I am not living for what others expect of me. I have run home to me. Now that I am firmly grounded in who I am, I have more of me to give to others. I've gotten my bold back, and my feisty, when it serves others. I've learned to love myself for all of my imperfections. And this feels like freedom to me.

I have also made peace with my past. I am okay with all of my poor decisions, mistakes, regrets, and life events as a result. For every moment of it brought me to where I am, and to who I am today. I have found a place of forgiveness and compassion for myself, understanding I made the best decision I could with the information I had at the time. It was all ultimately leading toward something; a more empowered me. I wish I could have gotten here sooner and with a little less tragedy, but here I am nonetheless and I am certain it took every single minute to get me here. When all is said and done, even those who harmed me were allies in the journey of bringing me to where I am. Truth be told, I would go through every moment of it all over again to be where I am today. And this feels like freedom to me.

It's all perfect. It really is. Everything that happens in our lives is for a purpose and it is all perfect even though perfect doesn't always feel good or look pretty or mean something right away. I was so wrapped up in my culturally correct, societally posh way of living that it took something as jarring as my marriage dissolving in a second to wake me up. To wake me up out of that slumber I was living in, so that I would then move forward, find myself and design a life that I love, full of purpose. The only place my tears live now are in gratitude. They don't come for self-pity or despair any more.

I breathe a sigh of relief. Ninety-eight percent of my fears were unfounded. Would I have missed this yearlong experience just because of that other two percent? Hell no. I didn't know when I ran away that I was running for my life, and where I was running to was back to me. Hell no, I wouldn't have missed this experience for anything in the world. I don't have the slightest idea what my future holds, but what I do know is that I am capable of figuring it out, and I'm okay being me while I do that. I have earned the right to trust myself. And this feels like freedom to me.

My plane touches down on American soil. Waves of emotions spill out of my eyes and onto my cheeks as I walk down the stairs of the plane onto the ground. A rollercoaster of emotions: gratitude, fear, familiarity, anxiety, safety, home/comfort, home/panic, flood my heart. This is so much more than just a visit with my daughter.

Remember you're okay. I'm okay. I'm okay. I'm okay. Gratitude. Deep breath.

I walk into the terminal and a small smile breaks out on my face as I realize all the signs are written in English. Ha, I'd forgotten how easy this is, and even my ears will get a break. I get in line for customs and pull out my passport. I rub its weathered edges in my palm. Thank you, my friend, for taking me around the planet and bringing me safely home. I wait and wait as everyone else gets their stamp and makes their way through the process. I enjoy watching the Americans. It feels very familiar and I had not realized how much I missed them until now.

It is my turn. I approach the desk and the officer, a woman, looks up. "May I have your passport, please?"

"Yes." I smile and hand it over.

She flips through the pages. Her head cocks to one side. She goes back to the beginning, slowly turning each page spending much time scanning the details. Her brow furrows. More time gathering information of the places I have been. I nervously shift my weight from one foot to the other.

Oh my gosh, did I miss something? Is there a rule about being outside the U.S. for a certain length of time, and then coming back? Did I go to places I wasn't supposed to go? You didn't do your research again, damn it. Is she not going to let me in? I twirl the strap on my backpack trying to rid myself of the anxious energy.

Finally, she looks up at me. "Lucetta. You have been gone a very, very long time."

"Yes, ma'am, I have."

She stands up and begins to walk around the desk. Is she coming to arrest me? My heart beats out of my chest.

She makes her way around the corner and reaches out, grabbing both of my arms. She pulls me forward, and embraces me in a full body hug. "Welcome home."

A sob breaks from my throat as she continues to hold me and speaks softly in my ear, "Welcome home."

If you like the pictures you have in your head
and you'd like to leave it there, that's cool.

If you'd like to see the real pictures of the journey visit:
www.lucettazaytoun.com/continuethejouney